WITHDRAWN

17.99 2018

RIVER OF STARS, NIGHTS OF JASMINE

KATRINA VALENZUELA

D1516640

NILEKAT
PRESS

This book is a memoir. The author has attempted to recreate events, locales and conversations from her memories of them. The opinions expressed within this book are solely her own and as she remembered them. The author does not assume and hereby disclaims any liability to any party for any loss, damage, or disruption caused by errors or omissions, whether such errors or omissions result from negligence, accident, or any other cause.

Copyright © 2018 Katrina Valenzuela
All rights reserved.

Cover Design and Layout: K.R. Conway

Copyright © 2018 by Katrina Valenzuela. All rights reserved. In accordance with U.S. Copyright Act of 1976, the scanning, uploading and electronic sharing of any part of this book without the permission of the publisher / author is unlawful piracy and theft of the author's intellectual property. If you would like to use material from this book (other than for review purposes), prior written permission must be obtained by contacting the publisher at katrinavalenzuela@gmail.com. Thank you for your support of the author's rights.

Library of Congress Cataloging-in-Publication Data

Valenzuela, Katrina / River of Stars, Nights of Jasmine, Pages: 340

Summary: A woman find herself spiritually and emotionally through her ties with Egypt.

Nilekat Press
231 Rte 6A, #711
Yarmouthport, MA 02675

ISBN: 978-1983939266
Published in the United States of America

DEDICATION

To my son, Justin, my greatest joy, and granddaughter, Isabella Rose. And to my 'Dream Lover' and husband, Ruben. With deepest appreciation to all the Egyptians who shared with me their wisdom and love.

AUTHOR'S NOTE

I've made every effort to relate my experiences accurately and to assure that I still have friends who will speak to me when the book is published. Names have been changed, and time collapsed, to allow for the story to move along. All of it, and a great deal more, happened over the span of twenty years between my time in the US and Egypt. The glossary includes only those Arabic words that may be unfamiliar to some readers.

ACKNOWLEDGMENTS

Thank you to my many writer friends who have believed in me; Anne, Suzie, Sharon, Nicola, Jamie, Kay, Kate. And to my weekly group, Writers in Common, Cape Cod Writer's Center and PEN Women.

PROLOGUE

CHILDHOOD - BOSTON, 1950

"We come spinning out of nothingness,
scattering stars like dust."
Rumi

From stories I'd heard growing up, Grandma Genevieve had once been a striking Celtic beauty with auburn hair, fair skin, and classic Irish features. She worked hard to keep her eleven children alive during times of war and famine. Her husband had taken to drink and offered little emotional or financial support, and so she worked harder and loved her children all the more to make up for his absence.

To me, her youngest grandchild, Grandma had always been old. Every day she wore a housedress and apron, her long white hair in a chignon on top of her head. She moved into my bedroom from her downstairs apartment when she could no longer take care of herself. Senile and arthritic, Grandma never spoke and mostly lay in bed sleeping.

At night, however, our shared room would be filled with spirits with whom she would hold court for hours. The nocturnal visits always began the same way. "Hello lovey, cup of tea?" she would greet each visitor as they arrived. "Come sit and talk to me."

At first, I was terrified and kept my eyes shut, but gradually, in a state of half-sleep, I began to see and hear the spirits as well. In time, this nightly dialogue with the 'other side', rather than being frightening, helped ease some of my fears. How weird could I really be if Grandma entertained the dead and served them tea?

When I mentioned it in confession, the priest scolded me about, "communing with the devil." Well, Gram was in on it and it was our secret, this time we both spent among the dead. The comings and goings of spirits occurred almost nightly, and I would arrive at school too tired to concentrate.

The stage had been set for a lifelong relationship with the unseen world of mists and shadows. I spent hours in self-imposed solitude inside the enormous lilac bush in back of the house. There I conversed with my imaginary friends, nature spirits, and my two lost little brothers whom I knew lived and grew up on the other side. I imagined I was hidden inside a fairy tree in the magical place called Ireland where my ancestors came from and where I longed to go.

My gift of 'seeing' was not at all comfortable most of the time. The dark phantoms that arrived with any sickness in the household were terrifying. After Grandma died, to my surprise, the gateway to the spirit realms remained open and I could still see and converse with the astral visitors as they would come and go.

I observed that each illness in the household had a particular entity attached to it. The worst by far was the entity of alcoholism that followed so many in my family. Sometimes at night, this demonic apparition flew right through the bedroom door at lightening speed, landing on my back and digging its talons into my flesh. I slept with my catechism and rosary beads under my pillow. Some mornings, I expected to find marks where the alcohol demon had dug into me as I trembled under the covers, but when I took Mother's mirror and looked at my back, there were no marks to be found. I knew there's a connection between the demonic attacks and the increasing amount of beer and whiskey in the house.

Uncle Frank, who lived with us, had taken to drinking heavily long ago upon returning from war to find his fiancée had married another. He kept to himself in his room downstairs, which was piled high with books and smelled of the turpentine he used in his paintings. His only task was to keep the furnace stoked with coal, the least logical assignment of household duties made by my father. Periodically, the basement would catch fire and all of us would take to the sidewalk with our cats, dogs, birds, turtles, and goldfish. My brother, sister, and I knew the drill and took it as a part of life, never realizing just how dangerous and dysfunctional the situation was.

At age 10 when I contracted scarlet fever and lay burning with fever for weeks, my spirit wandered far from my body and I watched as the doctor visited every day. There were conversations among the adults over whether I should be put in the hospital. It was decided I'd be better off where Mom could watch over me day and night. And she did, never leaving my side. I could feel her concern and love as she leaned over me, held cold cloths on my forehead and sang our favorite songs to me.

On the 13th day of scarlet fever, I awoke to see an amorphous grey figure being chased across my room by three blue jays. Instinctively, I knew the birds were saving my life by forcing the entity away from me and out the third floor window. At precisely the moment the monster leaped out, the fever broke. I had been freed from the grip of the scarlet fever entity and I was eager to tell my mother that it was not red at all, but a blurry grey darkness. Mom calmly accepted my story with relief and humor, hugging me and thanking God I was going to live. Yet, there was a look of trepidation in her eyes. I sensed that mother had become scared of me with my altered states and prophetic visions and she cautioned me to stop mentioning these things.

When Mother left, I got up and picked up the single blue feather from the floor and hid it in my jewelry box. I watched the ballerina spin around to the music of Clare de Lune and thanked the bird spirits for saving me.

At bedtime, Mom would recite poetry of Edgar Allan Poe, a Boston native with whom she shared a birthday. This story time marked our nightly ritual and set my imagination soaring. Mom's favorite was 'Wreck of the Hesperus,' while my favorite was 'A Dream Within a Dream,' which spoke directly to me of my own life. Mom would read with great drama, her tiny frame animated, her beautiful face expressive of every emotion. The oddity of Poe at bedtime never occurred to me until years later in college psychology class when I considered how ominous and dark Poe's writing was. In my childhood inno-cence, I was absorbing a sense of sad foreboding from Mother's impassioned readings. Poe's themes of disaster would frighten any child, but I pretended not to be affected by it. I wanted to keep mother sitting with me as long as possible, so intense was my love for her. All I knew or cared was that Mom was the most beautiful, enchanting human being on earth and our nightly readings were my special time to be alone with her.

When Mom returned thin and fragile after weeks in the hospital and without the baby brother I was waiting for, she stopped reading to me for months and locked herself in the bedroom and cried. I sat on the stairs outside my mother's door and rocked back and forth with my doll, mourning for the baby brother I had so longed to hold. His name had been Michael, that's all I ever learned. And, he had lived long enough to have been baptized in the church and given a proper Catholic burial.

Mom was never quite the same after that. When she gave birth to another baby a year later and it also died, she lost a part of herself and her brilliant light diminished. Not much was known about Rh negative blood type and Mom was only told that her body was rejecting her babies, adding to her guilt and remorse.

She explained away her bouts of sadness by saying we were Irish. In her thinking, this sufficiently accounted for the lineage of dreamers, artists, and mystics in our family, all of whom were gifted artistically, and self-destructive to varying degrees. I loved when she told me stories of how the people of Ireland still celebrated Pagan holidays under the open sky and they made it a crime to cut down a 'fairy tree.' I admired the Irish people and told Mother how I longed to become a Pagan and worship under the stars. She didn't seem happy about my pronouncement.

As much as I adored Mother, I determined early that her fear and sadness would not be mine to carry. She was a talented, powerful woman and yet she was often immobilized by fear and thwarted by the limited definition of what a woman could be. I always felt she could have been and done anything had she allowed herself permission and a fraction of the love and devotion she gave to everyone around her.

My mantra became 'acknowledge the fear and act anyway.' The frightened, timid child was securely placed out of harm's way while my young adult self rebelled and struggled to find her place in the world.

At age 15, I set out in search of those things I needed for my own survival. It was the late 60s in Harvard Square, Cambridge, the heart of the cultural revolution that was rocking our nation. I began spending more and more time with my Egyptian godfather with whom I had a powerful bond. He was completing his second doctoral degree and I knew he'd be called back to Egypt when his studies were complete. When that time came, I declined to go with him. I had become at home in the community of displaced wanderers of which I'd become a part. Besides, I had fallen in love with a boy, an entirely unsuitable boy, with whom I became married.

CHAPTER ONE

EGYPT

"One of the oldest human needs is having someone to wonder where you are when you don't come home at night."
Margaret Mead, anthropologist

To enter the land of Egypt is to move through a portal into another dimension, a golden world where all time and space meet and the miraculous become commonplace.

The seat belt signal awakens me as the plane descends toward Cairo airport. The 11-hour flight has allowed me to review the years that have led to my making this journey to Egypt alone. I gaze down at the shimmering Western Sahara as we make our final approach. Flipping the window shade all the way up, I lean forward and search for the misty forms of the pyramids but I cannot find them in the endless sprawl of dung-colored buildings. Just as well that I cannot see the pyramids, the aerial view of them has a strong nostalgic affect on me. Still, I am overcome with emotion and turn my face into the folds of my scarf to still the sobs that escape as I gaze out the window, wiping tears from my face.

The silver snake of the Nile curves and disappears as we veer across the stark divide between lush green farmland and barren desert. The ancient name of Khemit, black earth, can no longer be applied to present-day Egypt since the building of the High Dam put an end to the late summer flooding of the land. The trade-off for hydroelectricity has left only about seven miles of arable land on either side of the Nile.

The British gentleman beside me has napped, hands folded politely, for most of the flight. He taps my arm and offers me sour lemon candies from a tin. Mistaking my emotional state for fear, he reaches into his tweed jacket and hands me an embossed British Embassy card.

"You just call me, dear, if you have any trouble with these Egyptians," he reassures me in a paternal tone, "A little blonde girl like you should have someone looking after her. Egypt is no place for you to be traveling alone." He continues as if speaking to a child. "They'll try to trick you, but don't you believe anything they say. I've been dealing with them for many years now. Believe me, I know these Egyptians."

"Thank you for your concern," I say as I accept his card and put it in my jacket pocket. Upon descent, I close my eyes and press my back into my seat remembering the kindness of an Egyptian who took me in and saved my life when I was a lost girl in the cultural upheaval of the 60s. His caring nature and enthusiasm for life made it impossible for me to give up even on my darkest days as a teenager. I'm now in my late thirties and still have a powerful bond with the man I came to call my godfather. He was a close friend of my family and always available to me with non-judgmental listening and a few cheerful words of wisdom.

I have always been very good at leaving. Some women walk out of the house – I leave the country. Since I got my first passport, I've carried it in my purse. Heartbreaks and losses have led me to declare my freedom, not from men, but from long-term entanglement with them. Now it's I who determines whether or not things will go any further than a brief romance. When a relationship becomes confining, I bring it to a rapid close, leave town, and do whatever it takes to regain my balance.

I hadn't always been this way, but I'd lost the second of my husbands 5 years ago to a rare form of congenital heart disease. He lived to age 45 with a condition that takes most who are born with it by age 10. I was emotionally burned out and unwilling to jump into another relationship. John had been a loving and devoted father figure to my son and we were creative teammates. Our lives were filled with artistic adventures, and the happy chaos of raising a child, along with various animals who found their way into our household. As with those who are acutely aware of impending death, we lived more in a day than most people do in years together. A sense of gratitude permeated our lives and we never wasted time complaining about trivial things. He was the 11th person in the country to receive a heart/lung transplant and he lived just one year, hooked up to machines and never leaving the ICU at Stamford. On the way to the hospital following the surgery, my young son had asked, "Will John still love me even with someone else's heart?"

A WEALTHY PSYCHIATRIST I ONCE DATED HAD DIAGNOSED me "pathologically independent." I took it as a compliment. In his paranoia, two months into our relationship, he imagined I had a scheme to trap him into marriage and take his money. On the advice of his friends, he got a vasectomy as a precaution.

"I don't want to marry you, or anyone else. I have my own home, my own life," I told him once again as I drove him to the hospital two hours away, waited, then drove him back home again. After taking care of him for a few days, I left him a heartfelt letter in which I reiterated my thoughts on remaining single, and I wished him well.

As WE TAXI THE RUNWAY MY ATTENTION IS DRAWN TO A man on the tarmac in a blue jumpsuit, hardhat, and plastic flip-flops. He's hopping about and waving his arms to direct the plane to the gate. His broad smile welcomes us and he looks so happy. Can he really be this delighted with the arrival of another plane? This childlike exuberance is typical of Egyptians and always amuses and uplifts me.

The pilot announces in Arabic and then English that we have landed on Egyptian soil and I can barely contain my excitement. The catch in his voice reveals that he also is deeply moved to be coming home. There can be no doubt that Egyptians have a great love of their country, even with all its crushing poverty, crumbling infrastructure and overpopulation. What is it about Egypt that captures both natives and visitors unaware? It goes far beyond heart, mind, or reason. It's as if some of us carry a deep soul longing, a quest to return to a spiritual homeland. Once experienced, the ancient land becomes a part of them forever.

CHAPTER TWO

MIDAN EL TAHRIR - CAIRO

Bukra mishmish. Tomorrow there will be apricots.
Arab saying

My first stop in Cairo, over my years of visiting, is always *Midan el Tahrir*, Liberation Square, the heartbeat of Egypt. It's dusk and the 2-lane road has morphed into 5, with bumper-to-bumper traffic, horns blaring, yet the drivers appear calm and happy, reflecting the Egyptian attitude that everything is as it should be.

I've learned to walk like an Egyptian; head up, gaze forward, gliding with confidence, never slowing or breaking my pace as I dodge the careening cars and zigzag my way across the chaotic square. There's a timing to it, which, if lost for even a second, can lead to disaster. Drivers gauge their approach to within seconds of the lives of pedestrians. *Inshallah!* If it be the will of Allah, I will reach my destination unscathed. I hop up onto the high, zebra-striped curb just in time to avoid a car barreling toward me, grateful for my agility and the traction of my rubber-soled boots.

The security guard at the ministry checkpoint station glances at my passport as a matter of formality and then the enormous wrought iron gates part to let me in. Once inside, I race up the threadbare oriental-carpeted staircase and enter the formal great room. Typically filled with waiting officials and heads of state, the reception area is cool and peaceful now, although the stench of cigar smoke still hangs in the air. Grown boys sucking on pacifiers and posturing as powerful men, that's what they always remind me of.

I tap and then open the tall cedar and glass-paneled doors to the inner office where I find my godfather at work. We both have a sentimental attachment to the dilapidated former palace of Empress Eugenie. It was abandoned at the end of the French occupation in the late 1800's and has been used as a ministry since then. As always, he is poring over documents spread out on a long conference table as he intently prepares for the next day's meetings. My beloved godfather seldom leaves the old high-ceilinged building any longer, except to travel on government business, having fully married his work and his nation during the Sadat era many decades ago. His slight figure is dwarfed by the massive space. His shirtsleeves rolled up, he looks like a child who's been kept after school.

Finally breaking his concentration, he looks at me in mock surprise, "*Ahlen ya helwe,* hello honey. *Kull Sana w Inti Tayyiba!,* Happy Birthday!"

We kiss twice, as is customary, and then hug.

"So, you're still holding up in Eugenie's old palace even

13

though everyone else has moved?" I tease. "Good. We have the whole place to ourselves now."

"That's right. Those new government buildings in Heliopolis lack character, he states in his matter of fact way. I refuse to move from this place. Have you seen that new ministry? It's so ostentatious and modern. It has no soul." He's chosen to stay on alone, with only a few devoted and loving assistants. This is due to both his sentimentality and his stand against the current regime. The many Egyptians who love him refer to him as a martyr, although as he says with a laugh, "I cannot be a martyr. I'm not dead yet."

I know him too well to believe he takes it all so lightly. There's a sad resignation in his face at being so isolated since rising to the three top positions he now reluctantly holds. In rank, he's second only to the president. He's made it clear that he cannot abide by the decisions being taken by the current administration and so his isolation is a mutual agreement. He uses public transportation whenever he can and walks alone throughout the city just to feel connected to the common people he loves so much. I'm his touchstone to the carefree life he once lived while at Harvard University and he's free to relax and be himself around me.

"Just make yourself at home," he says as he collects a stack of papers. "I have to finish this shit for a summit in Geneva in the morning. The bastards booked me on a goddam 6AM flight! Do you know how early I have to get to the damned airport? No sense in going to sleep at all. *Ibn Kalb*, sons of dogs!"

"Lovely," I tell him. "Could you repeat that in the other six languages you know?"

Multi-lingual, creative profanity is my godfather's forte, his one diversion, and a trait for which he is infamous, although he keeps it in check unless with those closest to him. I smile, content just to sit and relax in the old-world atmosphere of the embassy, sip tea, and watch him at work. He's writing fast in Arabic, the graceful script forming hypnotic patterns from right to left across the pink legal-size paper. I always forget to ask him why it's pink paper. At last, he pauses and looks with tired eyes over his reading glasses, as if anticipating with a raised eyebrow that I'm up to some mischief. Our psychic connection never fails.

"*Amel ay ya 'otta*? What are you up to, my little cat? I can feel you're cooking up a scheme and your thoughts are distracting me."

"I came back to Egypt because, as I told you in my last letter, Adam has gone off to college and I feel lost. I just can't stand being without my son. Even though he's a full-grown man with his own life, he's still my best friend. I have to do something to release all this pain and sadness."

He nods as I kick off my shoes and sink into the old cut mohair couch, tucking my legs under me. In my son's absence, I am left without the star that has guided my life. The fulltime demands of motherhood have always given me purpose and a sense of belonging.

"Adam's the only man I want to be around for more than a few days. Although I drive north to see him every few weeks, living at home on Cape Cod just isn't the same without him."

In truth, my life had begun the day my son was born. My husband and I were both far too young and naïve to know anything of marriage. I'd been a child myself when I agreed to marry him. Two years later, our son was born. His father left while I was still in the hospital and so Adam and I grew up together. I came to consider the desertion a gift that allowed me to raise my child without his father's dark moods or the constant interference of his shrill mother. In spite of dire warnings from intrusive people that my child would become spoiled and rebellious from too much female attention, he could not have been a more delightful child; not just in my opinion but that of everyone who knew him.

I wanted Adam to grow up with an open mind and an appreciation of life. He may have been the child of a single parent, but he would never think of himself as deprived, or worse, as the product of a "broken home." There was nothing broken about us. Not only were we intact as a small family, we were honest and loving without fail and our household became a haven for other children in the neighborhood. Once my son started elementary school, I resumed my studies and completed two degrees while also working as a dance instructor and doing sewing alterations at home. We did our homework together each evening and I seldom went anywhere without my boy. There were theatre and dance rehearsals, meetings of the Theosophical Society, Sufi ceremonies, and Native American Pow-Wows. We would attend the Spiritualist Church, Catholic Mass, or visit a Hindu ashram. It was a well-rounded, if unconventional, life that encouraged a broad and tolerant outlook.

My godfather puts his papers down and sits on the couch beside me, waiting for the full explanation of my plan.

"I need to find a *Zar* ritual to help release my sadness." Noting the look of alarm on his face, I immediately regret having told him.

"Jesus Christ! The Zar has been forbidden since 1983. How do you even know about it?" His voice rises, "Do you want to be caught with all those *beledi* women in an illegal ritual?"

"Yes, I really do," I reply.

"You could be arrested for this and I won't be able to come and get you. I'm leaving for Geneva and I'll be out of the country for two weeks or more. You'll be on your own in prison."

"But the Zar is exactly what I need right now. The drums, the ecstatic movement, some real Egyptian sisterhood and support." I jump to my feet, pull the clip out of my hair and begin contracting and releasing my torso, flinging my long wild hair side to side to show him how freeing it is.

"You should try it for all the stress you have. Although it's a women's ritual, I'm sure they'd let you join in." I take his hands to get him up but he refuses and gives me a stern look.

Stepping back, I implore him, "Really, they wouldn't refuse you. Everyone in Egypt loves you for the work you do for women's rights."

He chuckles at my animated dance moves. "What you'll get is a sisterhood at Giza prison. There are laws against the Zar now. Nothing is the way it used to be, honey. Soon, any kind of fun at all will be forbidden and you'll have to leave Egypt if you need to dance. I stopped singing and dancing long ago." He says this jokingly but I can feel the regret and concern in his voice. He used to love to dance and play and we often would blast music and shake our hips and shoulders while cooking in his small Cambridge apartment.

I stand, hands on hips, and challenge him. "If we're going to discuss bad behavior and breaking the rules, how about your reference to dignified heads of state as "*ibn kalb*, sons of dogs?"

He gets up, shakes his shoulders a few times, and then hugs me, lifting me up off my feet. I'm always surprised at his strength for such a small person, only a few inches taller than I am.

"We're still rebel hippies aren't we? I guess that hasn't changed. Just remember, kid; this isn't a peace-in at Harvard Square in the Summer of Love, it's Cairo under an increasingly tough and restrictive regime. Just forget you ever told me about this Zar idea, right? At least keep the scandal away from your pharaoh godfather," he teases. "I get into enough trouble on my own. I can't be worrying about what you're up to."

I recall the death threats against him when he tried to turn an abandoned mosque into a women's clinic. I hold up my hand, *"Wallahi,* I swear I won't say a word about you. I'll even deny I know you if anyone asks."

"Don't worry, they already know all about you. Anyone near me has been checked out, especially this wild woman who's been with me since my college years."

"Oh, I'd love to see my file just for fun." I recall all the harmless shenanigans we've been involved in. "Do you think they have photos too?"

"Sure," he replies as he turns back to his writing. As I leave, he calls out, "I'll see you tonight. A car will come for you at seven. I'm taking you out for a birthday dinner."

"Sounds great. See you in a while."

I'm saddened to see that his freedom has been so curtailed by heavy responsibilities. It's well known that Egypt could not function without him. My godfather is one of the few leaders who dare resist the fundamentalist tide washing over the region. Although a thorn in the side of the current regime, he's brilliant and charismatic, and the only one able to negotiate with all factions and be heard and respected.

No matter how much time has passed, whenever I see my godfather it's as if we just picked up where we left off. No need to catch up or get into the flow of conversation. He's my guardian, my friend, my mentor, and has been since I was a young teenager. We share a psychic bond that links us no matter how far apart we are.

When he was knocked unconscious and left for dead during the assassination of his dear friend Sadat, I knew he had been injured even though I was 4,000 miles away. I called our mutual friends in the United States and they were dismissive of my intuition, "He hates those ceremonies. He wouldn't have been at a military parade." Still, I was certain he was in trouble. Two days later, he was found wandering the city with a head injury and was hospitalized. Although he stoically carried on, I knew he never fully recovered from the trauma of the massacre and the loss of his dear friend Anwar Sadat.

It's uncommon in Egypt for men and women to have such close friendships as ours, and so there are suspicions and snide remarks about our relationship. When I was 15, the age difference seemed enormous. Even our families and closest friends still can't figure it out and often refer to us as an "item" for lack of a better definition. We have always been of one mind, but never romantic, and often joke that we've known one another for hundreds of lifetimes. Our commitment to each other is born of soul love, and despite all rumors, we feel we are soul mates from many lifetimes.

I long ago fled my chaotic family and chose to live with my Egyptian godfather in a peaceful, alcohol-free Muslim house-hold. He'd been a graduate student studying international law and traveled often with Bobby Kennedy's campaign to observe the democratic process. His dream was to one day bring the high idealism of the Kennedys back to Egypt and help form a democracy for his beloved nation. He loved the Kennedy family and all they represented and he met with them at every opportunity.

In those years, I wandered in and out of his apartment, never needing to report my whereabouts to anyone. My family had fallen apart after a long series of crises, including the Vietnam War, which claimed the lives of many of my class-mates and neighbors. The war continued to wear the country down and the nightly body bag count on the six o'clock news was agonizing. It was an unprecedented time as our country shook to its core with protests, assassinations, and turmoil. Dark depression and anger lay over the country in those years and spilled into violence against the protestors of the senseless war.

I took refuge in my art and spiritual studies, walking miles each day alone. The door to my godfather's apartment was always unlocked for me and for the foreign graduate students who would stop by to visit and study. I had nothing to contribute to the academic conversations of the international students who visited, yet I listened with eagerness to the opin-ions about the world, politics, and religion. Although decades younger, I was always treated with respect and spoken to as an adult. I attended adult education classes at Harvard in the subjects I really enjoyed: art, philosophy and world religions, while ignoring my high school lessons.

Immersed in the charged, creative atmosphere of the times, I would go to love-ins, peace rallies, women's liberation and civil rights demonstrations - the revolution was happening right outside our door in Harvard Square and my mind burned with the idealism of those times.

One of the great pitfalls of the era was the proliferation of drugs, but I took no interest in that part of the revolution. My challenge as a sensitive, psychic child was to adjust to being on the physical plane. I instinctively knew that if I went on a drug-induced trip, I would likely never return. It's much harder to get the genie back in the bottle. Having been trapped outside my body on numerous occasions, I was vigilant about remaining grounded and drug-free. I was an uptight, hygienic hippy with flowers in my hair and much too shy and self-conscious to engage in any free love.

As a student of political science and international law, my godfather often traveled worldwide to lecture and would write me postcards from-far off places, places I could only dream about. I'd track his location on the old globe in his Cambridge apartment and imagine what those places were like. When he returned with fascinating stories, his wit and humor infused a magical glow to any gathering. I longed to travel and I set my mind to making it a reality someday although I had no idea how.

I close the doors to my godfather's office and dance down the stairs, giddy with joy at being in Cairo again. In the busy square, I stand outside in the cool air and drink in the sounds and scents of Cairo at night. The thick layer of dust that cloaks the ancient metropolis is hidden in darkness and a there's a rush of excitement as the city lights sparkle. To my ears, the mingling of traffic sounds, the call to prayer, and the lyrical cadence of Egyptian Arabic is sweet music. A breeze carries the scent of jasmine and orange blossoms and I flash back to scenes of past visits and happy times spent here with my son.

I RECALL MY LAST VISIT TO ADAM'S COLLEGE BEFORE I left again for Egypt. It was a cold, rainy day and we sat in the student cafeteria talking for hours over sandwiches and cups of tea.

"Look, I know we grew up together, Mom, and it was great. I had the best childhood ever." He ran his fingers through his black hair, his dark green eyes sparkling with mischief. Adam was born smiling and had inherited none of his father's dark personality.

"But I grew up, Mom. My friends' mothers go golfing and send them socks and tins of homemade cookies. You're off to Egypt again to take part in forbidden rituals. You trust every-one. I worry about you. Can't you just marry an American guy, settle down, and start living a normal life so I can stop worrying about you?"

I understood he was telling me this out of love and concern, but I had no solution to offer. I didn't have the slightest proclivity toward the Cape Cod pursuits of golf, baseball, or yachting. My fair skin burns easily and I'm a failure at all water activities in spite of being surrounded by miles of beaches. Sports don't hold my attention although I'm from Boston, home of the Red Sox and Boston Bruins.

American men find me odd and we share few common interests.

"I'm not sure what this 'normal' you talk about is, or if it's even something I want, sweetie." The tables were turned and my own son was speaking to me with a tone of fatherly concern. "Besides, aren't I supposed to be preaching such things to you? Do you forget that I'm the parent here?" This was a conversation we'd been having since he was a child.

Our only disagreement had been on how many hours he would be allowed work in a week. Adam had been so ambitious and eager to become a successful man that it seemed he never could stop taking on more work. He quickly rose to management level of every restaurant, hotel, or business where he worked, although younger than all his employees. I knew he was taking the opposite path of his father. There had never been a single child support payment or a birthday card and I worried that Adam pushed himself too hard to compensate for the lack of a male figure in our household.

"Right," he'd teased, "let's make a deal. Next lifetime, I get to be the parent and we'll see how that works out, okay? I'll make you eat miso soup with tofu and veggie burgers, and for dessert you'll get a handful of dried dates and some sesame halva candy."

I looked with awe at this beautiful, self-assured young man. I had forgotten just how many unusual things we had done together but he, on the other hand, didn't forget a thing.

"We'll go to weird spiritual gatherings with people with names like Dancing Bear, Star Child, and Indigo, where we'll channel dolphins and make those sounds like the California channels made." He was having such fun recounting his childhood as he began making sounds like a dolphin, exactly as the channels had done at my friend's home in Los Angeles.

"Stop," I cried, laughing and holding up my hand. My eyes were watering and I struggled to breathe.

"Wait," he continued, "I didn't channel the Boston cod yet. Remember my idea for how we'd make a fortune? Who wouldn't love to hear from the cod after all the centuries they've been swimming around Boston Harbor?"

I thought he would stop with the stories, but he continued, "When you get into high school I'll pick you up in the middle of third period to fly to Egypt and visit friends on a farm in Fayyoum Oasis. We'll ride in a Mercedes with a guy named Mohammed across the desert for three hours, blasting Arabic music."

He stood up and danced like an Egyptian man while singing the first verse of a popular Arabic song he recalled.

"From Fayyoum we'll explore tombs in the scorching desert and drink hot tea and smoke shisha while we sit on a blanket with Bedouins."

Other people in the cafeteria were staring. We wiped tears from our faces and gasped for air through our giggles.

"You must admit it was an education you'd never have gotten in school. Which of your friends has ever experienced Sinai Bedouin life?"

"Right, and that trip helped me so much with my final exams when I got home. It's a good thing my teachers liked me and allowed me to repeat all my exams a month later. "

"You were supposed to do your school work along the way. That's why we lugged that backpack full of books up and down the Nile." I knew I was to blame for failing to enforce stricter homework rules.

"It's okay, Mom. You did a great job."

"You were so cute and funny, it was impossible to be strict with you."

I've always felt blessed to have such a great relationship with my son. We were kindred souls from the moment he arrived. Adam had never given me one moment of trouble, only the usual parental worries, most of which I created myself from my own active imagination.

A BEEPING TAXI PULLS UP AND CALLS MY ATTENTION INTO the moment. I hop in and head to Giza to visit my uncles, Zacharia and Mohammed. Retired officers from the Nasser regime, they're now the owners of a tiny jewelry shop on the second level of the famed Mena House Hotel. The history of the hotel, with its gilded coffered ceilings and pink Italian marble floors, is so rich and fascinating that a book has been written about it and placed in each guest room. An entire chapter is dedicated to the illustrious Khettab brothers.

The former extravagant hunting lodge of the 1800s, it had become a guesthouse during the building of the Suez Canal. Later purchased by an English couple, the wife set out to collect the finest crafted décor in the world as she created an oasis of opulence and old-world beauty for her visitors.

The handsome, distinguished brothers provide an element of the original charm of the Mena House. They are the perfect balance to one another; Zacharia is the heart, always ready to share in the stories of passing spiritual pilgrims, while

Mohammed is the mind, businesslike and reserved in nature. Of course, it is to the sympathetic ear of Zacharia that I pose my question of the Zar while his brother is busy closing a major transaction with an elegant matriarch from Sweden.

"Allow me to help you, my dear," Mohammed says as he ceremoniously places the gold-winged Isis necklace on the woman's parchment throat, leaning in to fasten the clasp, his breathe on her neck. He then stands before her, kisses her trembling hand, and bows deeply.

"Ah, now you shine like the beautiful goddess Isis herself."

"Oh, but where shall I go in such a fine necklace, Mr. Mohammed?" she asks in a quivering voice. "Perhaps you would accompany me to the Cairo Opera House one night?"

"It would be my honor, my queen," he responds with a sparkle in his dark eyes as he kisses her hand again.

They both know it is just legendary Egyptian flirtation, but for a brief moment she is an irresistible young woman again and he, perhaps, a sheikh or a long-departed husband. I am reminded that Mohammed does have a sentimental side, especially when a very good sale is in the offing.

Zacharia walks around from behind the display case, a velvet jewelry box in his hand, and takes my arm.

"Now, let's go for a coffee and you can tell me what you've been doing this past few months and you can open your birthday present. What are your plans this time in Egypt? And I want to hear all about our dear Sybil and your family back in the States."

An innocent crush has developed between Zacharia and my beloved secretary Sybil who joined me on a trip the year before. I often joke with Sybil that she's so filled with love that she needs a body large enough to contain her expansive heart. They've been exchanging long letters for a year and sharing such happiness with only written words between continents.

My uncle and I stroll at a slow pace down the hallway to the Khan el Khalili Café. I notice that although his body is beginning to fail and he now walks with a cane, Uncle Zacharia's mind and sense of humor are as sharp as ever.

We take our usual booth in the far corner, where we can talk freely without being overheard, our conversations some-times meandering into matters of the occult. Zacharia orders his Turkish coffee and my pot of black tea, and a tray of desserts, a ritual we follow each time I visit. He insists I have a piece of *basboosa*, the honey, and semolina dessert I love but which expands my behind at an alarming rate of speed.

"It's your birthday. Anyway you can afford to add a few kilos to that tiny frame of yours." I've frequently heard this kilo coaching from Egyptians, but never once from an American. In fact, I often wonder if the American men I've dated seek a woman at all, or just someone resembling an adolescent boy.

Zachariah's gift to me is a gold *ankh* on a fine chain. "Thank you so much, I love it," I say as I fasten it around my neck. He then listens as I outline my plan for taking part in a Zar ceremony now that my son has gone off to college. My uncle's expression is intent and patient. He looks down at his folded hands and thinks for a moment.

"I'm sorry I can't help you. I never hear of such ceremonies any longer, although when I was a boy they were common among the women. But I am sure if they still exist, you shall find them. If anyone can, it will be you, my determined girl.

I've never known you to give up on anything once you've set that mind of yours."

Together we gaze out the expanse of floor-to-ceiling windows with long strands of turned brass and amber beads as the sun disappears over the plateau. The pyramids, illuminated by sunset gold and orange, turn to pink and then deep crimson. The call to prayer echoes across the plateau and all is right with the world for this moment.

We sit silently for a long while, Zachariah's dear face in a wistful smile as if recalling the past. I know he misses his wife and has never stopped grieving her death even after so many years. His large, liquid gray eyes become far away and dreamy as tears roll down his face. I watch him, marveling at how this sweet man with the soul of a poet could have served most of his life in Nasser's army and risen to a high rank. He's much more a Sufi mystic than a military man. Our talk is interspersed by long silences as we both drift in a comfortable companionship. We agree it's a sign of a deep bond when two people can fall into silent reverie and feel no need to speak.

The sky is almost dark, the lights around the pyramids go on, and the cafe is empty. I stand and gently kiss Zacharia's cheek. "I promise to come back soon and report what I find in Upper Egypt. I'm meeting my godfather for dinner this evening, so I have to go now. Thank you for the beautiful gift. I will treasure it always."

Zacharia abruptly returns to the moment and grasps my arms with both his hands. *"Khali balek ya habibti*! Take care!" His tone is startling. "Don't draw the jinn to yourself. Remember, the jinn of Upper Egypt are not just lost souls; they are the dark sentinels of the pharaoh's tomb. As you know, they aren't the 'genies' from American movies. They can attach themselves to people and cause great harm. You must be careful."

"Don't worry," I try to assure him. "I'll use the words of protection and wear the ankh you just gave me. Besides, I could never pass through customs on my way back home with ancient pharaonic jinn in tow. Someone would surely notice."

He laughs deeply, his teeth stained with black grounds from his Turkish coffee. He coughs a deep, rasping cough and then shakes his head and gives me his blessing. "*Maasallamah ya helwe*, May Allah go with you."

CHAPTER THREE
JASMINE NIGHT - CAIRO

"Set your life on fire. Seek those who fan your flames."
Rumi

I was born at midnight, the new moon, or 'black moon' of the autumnal equinox. "If we were in Ireland," an astrologer had told me in my teen years, "you would have been left at the crossroads for the fairies to raise you. You have all the signs in your chart of the witch and the sorcerer." She was half-joking, but I always remembered it and wondered if this accounted for the oddity of my life and the visions I've always had.

This year my birthday happens to fall on a full moon when the sky is bright, rather than the darkness of the new moon, and I'm out with my godfather to celebrate. The dinner cruise boat is a replica of a royal pharaonic barge and I feel I'm floating in another world. Bare-chested, handsome young men in white kilts line the gangway, holding golden bowls of pink rose petals, which they strew at the feet of the guests. It's a rare occasion to be alone with him and without interruptions from his colleagues. I think how unusual this is and then I spot a tall, nicely dressed man lingering off to the side alone, and I give my godfather a look.

"Sorry, *habibti,* I couldn't lose them this time. One creep has to tag along."

I'd watched his most recent speech on TV about modernizing Egypt and was aware it had stirred retaliation from the conservatives who complained the nation was being westernized. Although he appears calm and jovial, he lives with the constant threat of assassination.

During dinner, a six-piece Arabic band plays classical Egyptian music and an entrancing dancer emerges in clouds of white and silver veils, her thick black hair reaching to her waist. I watch in awe and long to someday dance as well as she does, although my fair complexion could never match her gorgeous dark coloring.

Returning to the hotel early after my birthday dinner, I stop in the lobby to say hello to Amira, the guest relations' manager. She's the real source of the calm and efficient atmosphere of the hotel. An attractive man walks past and waves goodnight to her, turning and smiling at me in passing.

Amira looks at me. "Handsome, isn't he?" I nod and she sees the look of interest on my face. "He just came from celebrating the birthday of his nephew in the restaurant upstairs. He's a fine man, widowed a few years ago, with two small children," she continues in a whisper. "I don't think he's dating anyone although there's great interest from all the single women in Cairo. He's from a very good family too." She motions to him to join us and he walks over. "This is my friend Kara from the States. Today is her birthday as well."

Amira has smoothly paved the way in giving us something to talk about. The man smiles and his eyes crinkle with warmth. He's balding, as so many Egyptian men are by midlife. To me his baldness only accentuates his strong masculinity.

"Hello, my name is Naim," He steps toward me and offers a broad, smooth hand.

I note that his hand is nicely developed and balanced, his nails manicured. I've made a lifelong study of hands and can tell a great deal about a person through this one observation. Everything about this man makes me feel safe and relaxed. I ponder that with his muscular physique, he must have his clothes custom tailored, as my son Adam does. He doesn't strut or preen like a body builder, but he moves with assurance and comfort in his body. Naim finds a way to continue the conversation, "May I buy you a birthday drink? It's early yet and it's a beautiful full moon night. Won't you join me?"

I know from experience that when an Egyptian says it's early, this only means it's not sunrise yet. In Egypt, no one has a set bedtime, not even children, and sleeping is a nebulous and changeable concept. The requirement of ablutions and prayer five times a day, signaled by the loud call of the muezzin, has the effect of suspending deep REM sleep and yet people have an endless supply of energy and cheer. And, an extra benefit is they're clean and glowing due to the repeated bathing every few hours.

I had intended to go to sleep early so I'd be fresh for a

morning excursion inside the Red Pyramid of Dahshur. "Thank you," I hesitate as I weigh the situation. I come to the conclusion that since the Red Pyramid has been around for thousands of years, it can wait until another day. It isn't often I meet a man who intrigues me so and makes me forget both the ancient past of Egypt and my own dismal past with men.

Naim waits patiently as he looks at me with an expectant expression.

"Yes, that would be nice," I hear myself respond and we walk towards the exit. From the corner of my eye, I see Amira smiling. I wave over my shoulder at her as we leave.

Naim and I sit at a café table near the pool talking for a long while, as if we're old friends with so much to catch up on. His attentiveness and gentle smile disarm me. "What does a holistic health counselor do? I have never heard of this before."

I begin to explain how I work with vibrations and energy and then I stop. I feel he already gets who I am as we sit and absorb one another's energy. "It's not so important that you understand, let's just enjoy this time together."

"You're right, let's just feel each other's 'vibration' as you call it." He takes and kisses my hand. "I am intoxicated by this energy between us, whatever it is."

As he pays the check, I watch him tip the waiter and shake his hand with appreciation, looking directly into the other man's eyes. There is a natural elegance and charisma about him that appears to be totally without pretense. He returns and holds out his arm to me. "Shall we go for a walk around the gardens?" We walk along a path lined with aromatic roses and jasmine and then stand close together to gaze at the full moon over the pyramid. The Milky Way is visible on this clear night, like a path through the heavens.

Turning, he holds both my hands in his and then presses our hands to his heart in what strikes me as an old fashioned gesture. "If I never see you again, I'll be happy just knowing that you exist." He hesitates and lowers his eyes. "Although I did love my wife, we were cousins and childhood friends and we grew up together. It's an old custom for parents to arrange the marriage and it was decided when we were both young children."

I wonder what it must be like to marry someone who's a blood relative and childhood friend. He reads my mind. "It wasn't a romantic marriage, but we grew to care for each other. She was a good wife and mother." He moves closer to me. "I have dreamed of you for so many years; all my life, in fact. You are all my heart has ever known."

Had I been in the United States, hearing this from an American man, I would have laughed aloud. However, the deep sincerity in his voice and his searching gaze reach into the core of my being. I feel a delicious heat and passion radiating from him and I resist the urge to pull back and shut him out. Instead, I lean toward him, mainly to keep from passing out, allowing myself to be gently held in his muscular arms.

The night is balmy as the heat of the day rises from the ground beneath us. A cool breeze wafts in from the desert and shimmers the branches of the eucalyptus trees that line the pathway. As we walk back to the hotel entrance, a vendor passes by with a pushcart full of fragrant jasmine. Naim purchases a necklace of seven rows of the hand-strung delicate white flowers. As he lifts my hair to place it around my neck, shivers run down my back. I'm enveloped in the intoxicating sweetness of the aroma and the awareness that this moment will be etched in my memory forever.

I turn toward him and he looks into my eyes, "May I see you again this week?"

"I already have plans for the next few days before I leave for home, I reply. I'm visiting a friend in Athens. From there I'll head back to Boston. There's no time for us to meet again."

"I will follow you," he replies, not missing a beat. "I have some work to complete here in Cairo and then I will come to Athens. It's just a short plane ride from here." He leans towards me and whispers, "I won't let you get away." He then reaches into his jacket for a pen and business card. "Please, write the phone number of where you will be staying in Athens and I will come to you as soon as I arrange myself."

I stifle a giggle at his quaint use of English, noting that he is being sincere and doing his best to express himself. I give him my travel information and wonder if he'll really fly to Athens on such short notice. He's a business owner after all, and must have many responsibilities, including the care of two small children.

"Who will mind your children?' I ask, both out of curiosity and my innate nosiness, especially concerning the welfare of children.

"All of my family lives in the same building. My parents are in the flat downstairs and my sister upstairs, so the children will be well cared for. In fact, they will have a great time being spoiled while I'm away. Here's my card with my mobile number."

I lean toward the light to read his name. 'Naim el Masri.'

Loosely translated it means 'Dream of Egypt' or 'Egyptian Dream.' Either way, I'm convinced. I place his business card in my silk evening purse; I click it closed and look up into his dark eyes. I try to speak, but nothing comes out.

"It was so nice meeting you." is all I can say at last.

Searching each other's eyes for a few moments longer, we say goodnight and then part. Careful not to look back, I can feel his gaze follow me as I float across the wide entrance of the hotel, through the polished marble lobby and up the red-carpeted stairs.

I pause at the entrance of the piano bar where my friend Bassem, a young virtuoso, is playing soulful music with eyes closed. His ectomorphic form leans into his violin as if it is his lover. Rimsky-Korsakov's Scheherazade always sends waves of emotion through me. On many nights, Bassem and I sit and talk after he's done playing, but I have a full day ahead tomorrow in preparation for my flight to Athens. Upon seeing me, his eyes light up and he urges me to sit and listen. I shake my head, wave goodbye, and continue upstairs to my secluded room in the palace section of the hotel.

As I light a candle and some myrrh incense, I fill the claw-foot tub with steaming hot water. The walls and even the ceiling are tiled in the deep lapis blue I love and I feel I'm embraced in the arms of the sky goddess Nut who created the universe. I immerse myself and it's as soothing as a sarcophagus.

With a sigh I reflect on the night's events. Can there be a more intoxicating place than Cairo on a full moon night in late September? I think I may have fallen in love. Or, does every interaction resonate with deeper meaning in this place, as if we move outside reality in some numinous realm beyond normal time? No matter, it was magical and innocent. We never even left the hotel courtyard as we gazed at the full moon framed by the silhouette of the pyramids. The moonlight and the encounter with the charming Egyptian have made it difficult to sleep. I get up and sit on the balcony and gaze at the clear sky. I hear the deep vibration that comes from the pyramids, a sound only some are able to hear.

The Milky Way, the legendary river of stars, spans across the clear night sky over the Giza Plateau. It brings to mind the mythology of the ancients who believed it to be a gateway to other dimensions and the Giza Plateau a precise reflection of the stars and planets at the time the pyramids were built. I gaze in wonder for an hour or so, then lie down and succumb to enchanted dreams.

The new day dawns and I make my rounds to say goodbye to family and friends, then dash to the marketplace to complete last minute shopping for family in The States. I recall an old Egyptian saying: 'Once you have drunk from the Nile, you must always return.' While I would never be so foolish as to drink from the Nile, I am certain I will always return. A part of my self lives in Egypt and always will.

CHAPTER FOUR

ATHENS

*"One does not discover new lands without consenting to
lose sight of the shore for a very long time."*
Andre Gide

A walk through the National Gardens in Athens clears my mind and helps me adjust to the starkly different energy of my new location. In the ex-pat section of Athens, I'm guest of a family friend, the wife of an Egyptian. Although her expansive flat is impressive, my hostess has isolated herself out of fear of strange people and places. It amazes me that she hasn't felt drawn to explore the grandeur and history of this ancient country in her nearly two years living here.

"The Greeks are so bohemian," Soheir informs me with a gesture of disdain, flicking her manicured fingers.

I laugh at her expression. "Well, then it would seem there's lots of fun and excitement to be found in being bohemian. From what I see, the Greeks have a gift for joyful abandon. Maybe you could make some friends among the locals and not just with other Egyptians in your social circle. You might find the bohemian life exciting." Soheir shakes her head, holds up her hand, and will hear no more. She rises and dotes on her row of citrus trees in large urns on the balcony.

GREECE IS SO VERY DIFFERENT IN FEELING FROM EGYPT. I observe that each country I visit has an entirely unique vibration, and the inhabitants are so distinctly different from one place to the next. On my walks in new places I observe people closely for features, expression, tone of voice, mannerisms, ways of dressing, but most of all I observe their energy. I make sketches for some future date when I have time to get back to painting. After my walk, I return to Soheir's apartment exhilarated by the change of environment and with a map of historic sites to explore right in Athens.

"You had a call while you were out." she greets me as I enter, her resigned expression animated for the first time since my arrival. "An Egyptian man with a nice voice. He said he just checked into the Meridien Hotel in Syntagma Square and he'll call back in an hour."

I put my drawing pad down and smile to myself. My hostess is bursting with curiosity. "I wonder how he managed to get from the airport with all the confusion of the taxi and car rental strike going on. There are always demonstrations in Athens, it's one of the many reasons I don't like living here, but this strike is particularly bad.

This man of yours must be a very determined one," she calls out as I head to my room to wash up.

"Yes, he has a quiet determination about him. I'm surprised he followed through on his word. I really didn't expect he would."

"Come on out to the balcony. I need to hear all about how you met him." Soheir says as she goes to the kitchen and returns with a tray of iced tea and cookies. "I don't have such exciting times as this in my life. Let me live vicariously through you for a little while."

The afternoon humidity intensifies the fumes from the heavy traffic as I walk the few blocks to Syntagma Square. Naim, looking elegant and calm, sits at the outdoor cafe in front of the Hotel. He's even more handsome than I remember him to be as he rises to his feet to greet me. We order ouzo, a taste that makes my nose crinkle and my chest burn. I give mine to him after one sip and order lemonade. He catches me staring at him and says, "What is it?"

"I'm thinking I've never met an Egyptian who so promptly followed through on his word. I didn't believe you'd really come."

"This you must know about me," he leans toward me, "When I say I will do a thing, I will do it. I try always to keep my word."

I have my doubts, having wasted endless hours of my life waiting for Egyptians. It's not that they're inconsiderate; it's more that they don't share the sense of time or urgency that consumes many westerners. Living in a timeless, overcrowded land changes one's perspective of linear time.

We enjoy appetizers of spanakopita and stuffed grapevine

leaves, and then stroll through the bazaar and uphill through the Plaka region. At the ancient Roman Agora, we view the mysterious Tower of the Winds, delighting in our mutual love of history and beauty. The following day we explore the ruins and monuments of Athens, and at nightfall we explore each other.

Our few days together fly past and we regret saying goodbye and returning to reality. We stand atop a rocky hill at the Temple of Zeus at Sounion and the fiery sunset marks the close of our time together. The colors change in the sky before us and then he holds my hand as we walk back down the hill. The entire ride back to Syntagma, he continues holding my hand as if I am a small child who might be stolen. I almost envy his children at having such a gentle soul as their father. That evening we part and vow to meet again as soon as possible. I'm not sure when it happens, but at some point I realize this is not a man with whom to have a light fling. He has touched my very core, my soul, and it will be impossible to forget him. I realize I may have met my match.

CHAPTER FIVE

RETURN TO CAPE COD, MASSACHUSETTS

"Remember that wherever your heart is, there you will find your greatest treasure."
Paulo Coelho

R eturning from Logan Airport to Cape Cod, the sight of the Sagamore Bridge that leads onto the Cape is comforting to me. Anyone who has emigrated knows the constant feeling of homesickness for two places and two families. Since moving here to the Cape from Boston ten years ago to be near my parents, I have grown to love the quiet beauty of the place. I'm a city girl with a passion for the deep history of New England and I cannot imagine living in any place without history. Cape Cod and Egypt are now both my homes and I am constantly missing loved ones in one place or the other.

I've arrive home during what New Englanders refer to as

'Indian Summer' and the trees shimmer with red, orange, and yellow foliage as I drive along the historic Old King's Highway towards my holistic center on Barnstable Harbor. A light wind swirls the leaves on the ground as the humidity rises, signaling a storm is on its way. I pull into the parking lot to find the waves are already building in the bay and the misty air smells of salt and brine. As I approach the entrance, I glance down through the slats of the wooden pier to see the beach below; a familiar place where I often take a walk when the tide is out. I have a list of 25 clients waiting for callbacks and I don't feel ready to see anyone. I always arrive home in stages, a part of myself still drifting above the Atlantic.

After lighting incense and candles, I look out over the harbor. A whale watch boat passes the window and I recall what a thrill it is for visitors to come to this unique spot, a place I so often take for granted. I can hear the captain announcing on the loud speaker to passengers to take Dramamine and be sure they have their sea bands on. I wonder if they'll be safely back to shore before the ocean becomes choppy.

My first client will arrive in a half hour so I put on my Egyptian prayer shawl and sit cross-legged on my old oversized antique chair with green velvet upholstery and I prepare to meditate. Within moments of invoking my higher self and my spirit guides to join me, I feel that I am surrounded by their loving presence.

In two decades of teaching and counseling, I've formed a strong community of spiritual seekers on Cape Cod. Most are professional contacts, but some have become close friends with whom I share the spiritual path. My weekly students have bonded and become an extensive loving family. There's always a great comfort in sitting in circle with my students, exchanging thoughts and supporting one another, especially on days when the wind howls, the building shakes on it's pilings, and the draft from the ocean-facing windows makes the candles flicker. Sometimes on clear full moon nights, we huddle wrapped in blankets on the beach just outside the center, looking at the moon and stars and listening to the ocean tides as we perform a ceremony for world peace. Then, indoors, comfortable and cozy, we share our dreams and make intentions for our lives. It's good to be part of a spiritual community, to feel a sense of belonging.

Over many years and much study, I've become a minor celebrity in my hometown as a metaphysical teacher, clairvoyant, artist and dancer. It appears to others that I'm a courageous and even trailblazing woman. I'm invited as a guest on television shows and at healing conferences, which are growing in popularity with the dawn of the New Age spiritual movement. All of these public roles I accept with a degree of reluctance. Then, following each appearance, I go into isolation and solitude to recover. I'm an introvert and it has never been my nature to be in the limelight as a leader, but the role is given me at every turn. As a big fish in a small pond, I've been interviewed many times by local media and gained a reputation as both a curiosity and a pioneer.

In a TV interview I feel like a circus freak when the female host asks the inevitable question, "When did you realize you had "psychic powers?"

Immediately I feel I've been separated from humanity and

am being presented as an oddity. I'm ready for the inevitable question and unwilling to fall into the trap.

"There is only one 'power' and that power is equally accessible to all of us."

"But not everyone can see things and relay messages from the dead as you do," she prods.

"With sufficient dedication and training, most people can." The TV host looks disappointed to find I won't jump at the ego enticement.

I continue, "It's just not common knowledge in this society where there's so much fear of the unknown and life after death."

She ignores me and carries on with the sensationalism that makes for better TV. Her goal is to present me as an anomaly, a weird and foreign element, a misfit. I've lived with this all my life and it still feels alienating and lonely.

She shifts her questioning to my other profession as a teacher of Egyptian dance. Most Americans refer to it by the misnomer "belly dance" and it's perceived as risqué in New England. Provincial attitudes are that the ancient feminine dance is just a step above stripping. Those independent-thinking women who attend my classes rave about the effects of being present and empowered in their bodies. The new mothers feel rejuvenated and healed after giving birth, one of the many reasons the dance survives through generations of woman over thousands of years. I love to see my students come to life as they shimmy, whirl and spin, their silk veils flowing with tears of joy and laughter. The dance is not new to the U.S., but the spiritual and health benefits have been featured far less than the sexy, seduce-your-man approach to this ancient women's ritual. My expanding dance practice leads me to create my own local access TV show, which features my students. I present the dance in an empowering and artistic way, thereby helping women and girls to feel good about their bodies and their passion for life and for the dance.

AT MY OFFICE, I STAND IN THE FADING LIGHT AND WATCH the fog roll in off the ocean. The storm has passed quickly and left an eerie silence in its wake. Clouds open to reveal thousands of glittering stars and I wonder if Naim is looking at this same sky, an ocean and two continents away. It's comforting to know that we stand beneath the same sky, even though it will likely be months before we meet again.

In spite of all our plans and attempts, the months turn to years and the failing health of my father delays my return to Cairo. My parents insist upon remaining in their own home and won't allow anyone but us kids in the door, not even the 'meals on wheels' delivery. They are fiercely loyal to one another and will not be parted. I wonder at the bond they share and doubt I will ever experience a lifelong committed partnership in my own life.

CHAPTER SIX

MARRAKECH

"Somewhere beyond right and wrong . . . there is a garden.
I will meet you there."
Rumi

It's deep into the dark month of February, the coldest and bleakest month for those of us who live in New England. An unexpected late night call from Naim brings a thrill of excitement and I leap out of bed. We've agreed not to speak until the pain of our forced separation has faded and so far we're not doing so well in keeping to that agreement. We have to admit that we're deeply in love.

His voice sounds sad and yet hopeful. "We must find a way to meet if only for a while. It's been too long since I've seen you."

My mind begins searching. "What country is equidistant between us? Do you have a map in your office?"

"Yes, of course." I hear him moving things as he searches and returns to the phone. "Exactly halfway will put us in Morocco."

I ponder the idea. I have no money in my savings account and badly need to generate more income. What I do have in abundance are enough frequent flyer miles to get me to Casablanca. The last thing I should be doing is taking off on a trip to Morocco or anywhere else. "Shall we meet in Casablanca?"

Without hesitation he says "I will order our tickets now. You save your frequent flyer miles and your money. I insist you don't pay anything at all. *Ana Bahebik*, I love you, and can't wait to see you."

Two years have passed since our last meeting and these years have been filled with anxiety and stress over the failing health of both my parents. The weeks leading to our Moroccan rendezvous pass slowly and at last I fly toward my love. Looking forward to the warmth of Moroccan sunshine, I arrive in Casablanca seven hours later to a cold, torrential rain. Naim stands smiling at the gate, elated to have purchased his first umbrella, which he holds up to show me with childlike excitement. We embrace for a long time and it feels as if the sun is shining.

"How I've missed you." Naim stands back and looks at me. That odd feeling of deja-vu washes over me. It's as if we have done this before, in countless places and times, meeting as lovers, one hour of every century. That this has been the pattern between us forever, to meet and part and never spend more than these fleeting times together. I push this feeling aside as we leave the airport and take a taxi to the city where we check into our hotel.

WE AWAKEN TO A BRILLIANT DAY AND LEAVE CASABLANCA on our trip south; Rabat, Meknes, Fez, the colorful cities of legend are all more beautiful than we could have imagined.

A small hotel in Marrakech becomes our fairytale home for the week. It's decorated in the rich hues of ochre and red, accented by peacock blue vases of lemon trees in bloom The air is rich with the scent of orange blossoms and the long white curtains sway in the breeze at night like dancing spirits. We live inside a dream, a dream that ends as I board the Royal Air Maroc flight for Boston and the cold reality of winter without the man I have grown to love.

In the United States, as is the usual case when I travel to Arabic-speaking countries, I'm pulled aside, questioned, and my luggage opened and torn apart. The immigration official finds the box of chocolates I bought for my son and pokes his finger into each one as he watches me with a sinister grin, handing them back to me when each chocolate is ruined. I glare at him and throw them in the trash, gather my belongings, which have been strewn over the area, and struggle to repack my suitcase. A woman in hijab, also arriving, helps me repack and lift the case onto the trolley.

The noise and bright lights of the airport blast me into reality. I feel dismayed by American culture, the careless speech patterns, and sloppy dress. I rush to the bus in time and drag my belongings up the steps and find one remaining seat, next to a saggy-panted young man listening to offensive rap on his headphones. The culture shock makes me cringe.

THERE HAVE BEEN TWO COLOSSAL SNOWSTORMS SINCE I left. My car is buried at the parking lot, and my hands are frozen as I clear it off and shovel enough space to back out, a daunting task after traveling for 24 hours.

At home, five-foot high snowdrifts cover the walkway to my front door. When I at last get to the door, it's frozen shut. I recall the fascination Egyptians have with the idea of snow. The reality is another thing. I bang the door with my hip, kick hard, and at last it opens. When Adam lived with me, he took care of shoveling, priding himself on being a responsible man even when he was only a teenager. I think of how blessed I am to have him and wish he still lived close to me, but he's at college three hours north.

The next day, stacks of bills sit unopened on my desk as I resolve to return to some kind of normal life. I ground myself by walking in the cold but beautiful dunes and marshes of Cape Cod, meeting with women friends at the local coffee-house, and sitting by the fireplace with my mom at night talking and watching old movies. We watch Dr. Zhivago, one of our favorites.

"So did you see Omar Sharif over there this time?" she asks.

"No, Mom. I was in Morocco. Maybe next time I'm in Egypt I'll find him for you and get a photo." She asks me this every time I go away, and sadly, I have yet to see the famous Egyptian actor.

"I watched Lawrence of Arabia again while you were gone.

That Omar is such a dream. No wonder you keep going back there if they're all as gorgeous as that."

My dad ignores our banter, leaves the room, and takes the opportunity to sneak a bowl of chocolate chip ice cream. Since becoming diabetic, he's an expert at covert operations. I pretend I didn't see him tiptoe past us. My parents are happy to have me back, although it's difficult for them to understand my life or to keep track of the exotic places to which I travel. They can more easily remember the day-to-day, moment-to-moment events of my sister and her three children who live nearby. I don't blame them; I have difficulty keeping up with my own schedule and sometimes forget where I'm headed next.

I often marvel at the love my parents have shared since the day they met in high school. Their devotion endures even now that they've become old and forgetful. They bicker almost constantly, always ending in laughter. The concept of divorce, or even separating for one day, is never an option to the Great Generation. They committed for life and they never waver.

In contrast, as a child of the 60s, I vehemently opposed the idea of becoming a wife, anyone's wife. I observed the limiting choices presented in the media to girls and wondered at the banality of such a life. The very thought of it makes me feel suffocated. I'm by nature undomesticated, and determined to express myself freely as an artist, dancer, writer, and mystical seeker. I have long observed that some women strive for a wedding, a day to be the center of attention; they seem to want a wedding much more than they want a soul partner. I want a partnership with some of the elements of my parent's marriage, but with a great deal more excitement and freedom. I have yet to find a couple that fully models the kind of ideal partnership I seek.

The only person in my family who takes the slightest interest in my travels, besides my son, is my older brother who once dreamed of world travel before he married. I've stopped searching for gifts when abroad for everyone and now bring back a few small trinkets and many photos. And stories that no one in the family cares to hear.

My metaphysics students, who have an appreciation of the spiritual significance of Egypt, beg me to bring them on my next trip so they can experience the magic of the pyramids and temples firsthand.

My family suggests I go back to being an intake worker for social services, a job that nearly killed me with boredom and toxicity. A creative life is not a straight path and there's much uncertainty, but I know I must follow what brings me joy and makes my heart sing. Many of my decisions in life are fueled by enthusiasm and an unwarranted sense of optimism, and so it's no surprise to my parents when I begin planning an Egypt tour and Nile Cruise. I make the impulsive decision to form my own tour company and specialize in Egypt, not considering all that could go wrong and how little practical knowledge I have of the tour industry.

My first group is comprised of 25 of my friends and students. It's a two-week tour including a Nile cruise and an excursion across The Sinai to the Red Sea. I underprice, over-promise, and make many mistakes. The all-inclusive tour is priced lower than the listed round-trip airfare alone. Who could resist such a bargain? I've never been good with figures or analysis of the bottom line and ultimately give away my profits no matter what business I'm in. Added to my resistance of math, I have a stubborn habit of always seeing the best in everyone and believing they will reach their highest potential. Once my tours become popular, offers of help pour in with the stipulation that they "help me" by taking fifty percent or more of the profits for my hard work. I at least have the good sense not to fall for that.

My close friend, Anne, tells me that being the goose that lays the golden eggs is a good deal for everyone but the goose, and apparently, I am that goose. She's right, and yet the idea of a tour has gained a momentum of its own and we are off to Cairo. When I appear unannounced at the ministry, my godfather is astonished and amused that I've begun a tour business specializing in Egypt without ever asking his opinion. He wants no part of my latest venture and stays clear of any involvement as it would be unfitting for a government official to be in the tour business.

The next three years are filled with teaching of workshops, classes, lecturing, and leading tours. There are brief flirtations with men I meet in transit - exotic men with dark eyes and continental ways. I push Naim out of my mind between our brief meetings, yet always he is there as the standard I hold for a great love. If only we didn't live on differing continents.

CHAPTER SEVEN

SERAPIS REVEALED - LUXOR, 1989

"You will do foolish things; but do them with enthusiasm."
Collette

I 've always had an invisible presence guiding me, one I've come to think of as my spirit colleague, a sort of silent business partner who shares every step of my venture. I call him Serapis as he asked me to do early on in my meditations. Neither he nor I are great at the financial side of life and spirit guides aren't shaken by anything. The name 'Transformations' came to me years ago when I first set up my holistic center on Cape Cod, and it has become the umbrella under which I lead my tours as well.

Each of my sacred site programs has it's own theme, magic, and synchronicities. My company grows through word of mouth and requests for specialty tours begin to arrive. The groups are made up of New Age seekers, scholars, healers and educators, researchers and wanderers. However, shepherding the flocks throughout a developing country is exhausting. Each time upon returning to the States and declaring that's the last tour, a newly opened temple, an excavation in the Valley of the Kings, a documentary on the History or Discovery Channels prompt me to begin again. I sense that this is all a part of my soul contract, something I agreed to give back to Egypt, and I will somehow know when the terms of my soul contract with Egypt are complete.

As an artist, it's my nature to work by instinct and intuition and I'm accustomed to living out on a limb. Yet I long to know more about the guides and helpers who work silently by my side. I sense a particular presence whenever I walk in lonely and dangerous places. It's as if a cloak of invisibility allows me to move unnoticed. In meditation, I ask to see or hear my guide Serapis with my physical senses, or at least to gain a clearer understanding of who he is. Sometimes I can almost make out his features, but the eyes are so intense with light that I'm unable to focus on them for long. I'm sure he is a being of stern demeanor, yet benevolent and kind. Given my uncertain finances and lack of business training, it seems he believes in me far more than I have ever believed in myself.

I whisper to him in my meditations, "Please go ahead of me, Serapis, and arrange all necessary meetings, clear the path for connections, flights, and most of all, the safety of my passengers and myself."

There's a steady increase of hijackings and terrorism worldwide and I reason that if I am ever to see more of the world, it's best to do so while it's relatively intact. Not everyone sees it this way and registrations come and go according to the most recent sensational news. Each time a group forms to make the pilgrimage to Egypt with me, I ask my guides for a dream to determine the number that will sign up and whether those registering would follow through or drop out before departure date. Unconscious fears often surface in people as they sense the profound changes that await them in going to Egypt. Their anxiety is magnified by the dire admonitions from friends, family, and the media. One best-selling spiritual writer declares to her group that an earthquake will cause the Great Pyramid to collapse while we are all inside, and this causes all her followers to pull out at the last moment. I'm left explaining this to my land agents in Egypt, who are convinced that Americans are all insane. I'm able to get the deposits back for the writer and her group based upon this flimsy excuse for cancelling.

ANCIENT EGYPT HAS ALWAYS FASCINATED ME AND I HAVE my favorite Pharaohs spanning the 7,000 years and 30 dynasties of Egypt's documented history. The late 18th dynasty is of most interest to me as it is filled with magic and intrigue. However, I begin to notice that at the mention of one called Serapis, there's a rush of energy in the back of my neck along with a deep feeling of nostalgia. It's as if I'm hearing the name of someone I once knew and loved from long ago. While wandering the temples of Egypt, I am often overwhelmed with emotion upon entering a section of a temple complex and always it turns out to have been dedicated to Serapis. Who was he? There was no pharaoh of this name, only grand temple complexes exalting his name in hieroglyphs.

This question led to my research into the early cult of Serapis, which at its height had extended through Egypt, Greece, and the Mediterranean. Over centuries, successive occupiers of Egypt tried to eradicate the worship of the old deities and impose their own religions. This suppression of the mystery teachings only resulted in a rise in popularity of the occult or hidden teachings. Temple inscriptions describe the glory of Serapis, yet there's no mention of an individual of that name who had once lived and died. It seems he existed as an archetype, but not as a living person. However, the spirit who guided me was most definitely an individualized presence, one I seemed to be deeply connected to from a shared past.

A valuable clue appears one rainy day in downtown Boston when I wander into an old used bookstore. An out-of-print book with a mysterious looking cover catches my attention and I climb the ladder to reach it. It opens it to a page that mentions Serapis Bey- an entire chapter devoted to the incarnations and accomplishments of that great soul. His good works were legendary even in ancient times, and he was bestowed the Turkish title of 'Bey' or highly esteemed one. As I read with fascination about each of Serapis' supposed incarnations,

I'm drawn to a lifetime in which he was supposedly Amenhhotep III of the early 18th dynasty. Pharaoh Amenhhotep III was, according to the author, the reincarnation of the legendary Serapis of the pre-dynastic era. His devotion to Egypt and the Ancient Mystery School apparently had called his soul back to Egypt repeatedly over millennia. It was far-fetched, even for a mystic like me, yet it rang with truth somehow.

Months later upon my return to Egypt, I set out on a search for statues and temples dedicated to Pharaoh Amenhhotep III. There are few monuments dedicated to him in comparison with other more notorious pharaohs such as Ramses. His nephew, the boy-king Tutankhamun, gained world attention in the 1920s when Howard Carter discovered his tomb.

While visiting the temple of Luxor, I turn to my Egyptologist friend, one of the most learned in his field, and ask him to tell me all he knows about Serapis.

"Serapis?" My colleague leans on his cane and looks at me with curiosity. "The cult of Serapis was too far back in time to know much about it. What does he have to do with Pharaoh Amenhhotep of the 18th Dynasty? Why are you so interested in all this?"

I don't want to reveal too much of the unorthodox theory and make him doubt my credibility or sanity. "It's an obsession I have; the intrigue of the 18th dynasty. Murdered siblings, missing mummies of the royal families, corrupt Amun priests with dark powers who plotted against the pharaohs. You must admit it's a most interesting time in Egypt's history."

"I suppose so," he replies, "Yet Amenhhotep wasn't even a powerful warrior, never waged any major wars, or seized any lands." My colleague picks up his valise and begins walking toward the entrance of the temple. "You know, a peace-loving leader is never great or famous. Look at what happened with our dear Pharaoh Hatchepsut. Twenty-five years of peace and prosperity and the people around her rebelled and killed her, chiseling her every name and image from her own temple as well as all the many majestic obelisks that she and her architect/lover Senmut created."

I'm reminded of the price women have paid throughout history for being too powerful. Hatshepsut was one whose place in history was almost entirely erased from all records. We walk across the expanse of the hypostyle hall together and through the smaller anterooms as we round up our group.

My guide is a sympathetic and kind man. "I know, the murder of Hatchepsut was tragic and a terrible loss to history, a story that's been repeated throughout time whenever the high priests felt threatened. Still, no one understands who this Serapis really was, or even if he was a living man."

My mind drifts back to the old text I found in Boston and a reference in that book to the temples of Atlantis. There was a description of the final hour when that advanced civilization was about to perish. It was the one called Serapis who took the teachings and the ascension flame to Egypt where he established the mystery teachings at the great Temple of Luxor. The description of those final days of a highly advanced culture called Atlantis touches me so deeply and I long to learn more. This sacred site of Luxor that we stand upon was designated so long ago as the center of learning. Pharaohs of successive dynasties upheld the tradition of building their own temples upon an existing revered site, creating layer upon layer of temple complexes. The powerful mystical reason for doing so was lost and it became more a custom than a spiritual edict. Each temple and site we walk upon contains thousands of years of former sacred sites beneath our feet and this brings a great thrill to my imagination.

LATER THAT WEEK WHEN I RETURN TO LUXOR TEMPLE with my group, I ask my land manager, Rafiq, about Serapis, mentioning my strange feeling of déjà vu when in the temple complex associated with the legendary figure.

Rafiq's reply is dismissive. "You're such a dreamer, Kara. These things are not real, just romantic stories to give hope to people like you. Hope that we live again, that there are great spirits watching over us, that they care enough to speak to us in dreams. New Age fairy tales, that's all it is."

As with most Egyptians, Rafiq is Muslim and these topics are in opposition to his religious upbringing. He pauses a moment and seems to be considering the Atlantis theory, then reverts to his original stance.

"This kind of thinking is against the Koran. If any of it were true, Mohammed would have mentioned it."

I don't want to offend him and I suggest with caution. "There must be many things Mohammed didn't mention, but we cannot dismiss everything outside of the Koran, can we?"

Rafiq narrows his eyes at me and doesn't reply. I decide it best to drop the subject and I ponder the issue silently and keep my heretical thoughts to myself. Still, if Plato's account of Atlantis was allegorical, why do I have such a sense of rightness within my being upon hearing the Atlantis legend? I learned long ago not to ignore a feeling of truth, even if no one else shares it.

CHAPTER EIGHT

OF FATE AND DESTINY

"Important encounters are planned by the souls long before the bodies see each other."
Paulo Coelho

It's well known in the travel industry that there are two groups of Americans who continue to travel in areas of unrest. They are journalists, who must travel of necessity, and New Age spiritual groups who believe they have a special indulgence of protection from higher realms. In spite of recent horrific incidents of terrorism, intrepid women, one after another, call to say they've decided it's time to go to Egypt.

In the weeks prior to our departure, I'm shown in meditation that there will be 7 participants, plus myself, in this group. With such small numbers, this will be another financial loss for me and I will even have to pay my own way. And so, as any savvy business owner would do, I put down the financial ledger and consult my spirit guides. The reply from my guides is a resounding "Go!"

After confirming all the reservations, I make a transfer of the full balance to my land agent in Cairo who will book the hotel and cruise reservations ahead of our arrival. As I drive home from the bank, I tell Serapis he'd better help me pay my bills somehow in case I get in worse financial trouble. The expenses of running my household are barely covered by my combined counseling and tour work. Always there are unforeseen costs to any trip and each time I return more broke than before.

At JFK airport, we meet at the gate and I find the women to be congenial and unpretentious. I like them right away and there are no grandiose egos among them. We bond and create a sense of sisterhood before we even board our flight and I immediately know taking this group was the right decision.

This entire trip is touched with magic that allows us to have private time at every temple along the Nile. The Jolie Ville Hotel on Crocodile Island, a peaceful resort just across a small bridge outside the town of Luxor, is our base for 3 nights. There's camaraderie, laughter, and celebration at the end of each long touring day and we become like a little family.

The women linger over dessert, sharing stories of the day's adventures. I walk outside to meet with the taxi drivers and secure our departure for the following mornings excursion. The women are still telling stories when I return and go over to their table.

"Sorry to break up the party, but wake-up call is at 3:30AM. Everything is set for our sunrise ceremony at Luxor

Temple." The ladies gather their things and leave the table to get a few hours of sleep.

I call out, "Three taxis will roll in at 4 in the morning, with engines and headlights off so we don't wake the other hotel guests. We'll move quietly from the lobby." Each one has a look of excitement at doing something clandestine. "The temple guard has been properly bribed with a stack of bills the equivalent of 25 USD to allow us entrance before opening time." There are a few concerned faces. "Don't worry, bribery is a common practice. We won't get in any trouble," I assure them. "This is how we get into the sites every day for our private time, in case you wondered. It's by careful distribution of baksheesh."

With a joyous sense of conspiracy, all go off to their rooms, although they could stay and chat for hours longer. I've explained to them about my spirit guide Serapis and asked them to pray for an experience of confirmation tomorrow at his temple at Luxor. I remind them of the special item on their packing list---a white garment for ceremonies, and to be sure they wear all white in the morning and bring any items to place on the altar.

CHAPTER NINE

THRILLER NIGHT IN LUXOR

*"When you reach the end of what you should know, you
will be at the beginning of what you should sense."*
Kahlil Gibran

A crescent moon shimmers in a deep indigo sky and the clear night is charged with energy and anticipation. Even the taxi drivers are excited to be part of this escapade as they sweep into the driveway of the Jolie Ville Hotel, their headlights off. Each young driver has acquired a cassette of Michael Jackson's hit song, "Thriller," which they play on full volume. I run and motion for them to turn the music down but it's too late. The hotel security officers rush to the door to see what's going on. So much for being clandestine and moving unseen.

We emerge from the lobby dressed in white, carrying flowers and velvet pouches of stones and incense. The young drivers shimmy and undulate their slim torsos and display their best imitations of Michael's moonwalk as they open the car doors and help us climb in. The sight of foreign women dressed as virgin brides is not lost on them and they cry out "Marry me, marry me!"

The moment we turn onto the corniche along the Nile, the music goes back up, our meditative mood shifts into thriller madness again, and our noisy entourage makes its way through the empty streets. The drivers settle down and turn the music off as we pull up to the main temple gate. Two night guards crouch over a brazier preparing their thick Turkish coffee in a small brass pot. The smell of kerosene from the stove is sharp on the cool night air. I look around, but there's no sign of the guard I'd met and bribed the day before. My careful planning of our illicit entrance and the small roll of baksheesh seems to have ensured nothing. One of the young guards jumps up and greets us.

"We know who you are, Miss Kara, our friend told us to expect you and to let you in. But there is a problem. The temple keys are with the Rais, the captain, and he has gone home to sleep."

The stouter of the men shakes the locked gate to make his point. "You see we cannot let anyone inside without the key. He puts his hands out in front of him in a gesture of defeat. "Nothing to be done now, *malesh*, never mind."

In my ever-optimistic and determined thinking, for every problem there is always at least one solution. I ponder a moment. So, Serapis is presenting me with a riddle to solve, another initiation. Judging from the look on their faces, the guards are clearly terrified of their boss. They're afraid to risk losing their jobs and I cannot blame them. I am not about to coerce them and get them into trouble. The only solution is for me to go to the *Rais*, wake him, and implore him to give me the key. I share my plan with the two guards.

"You are joking," The first guard shakes his head, incredulous, and wide-eyed. Then he becomes pensive as he considers my plan. His face lights up with amusement. The idea of my personally visiting his boss, the Rais, in his bedroom and waking him for the key to the temple is an outrageous scheme and one they find amusing. "I like this plan, this is very funny," he says.

"You will really do that?" his friend chimes in, "You will go into his room, alone? I am telling you he is *afrit, magnoon*, crazy, not a good man! You must be *magnoon* too!" The shorter of the two guards, who seems to be the leader, shakes his head in disbelief and mutters prayers under his breath as I follow him along winding dirt roads for about a quarter mile. We arrive at a small, flat-roofed house and he pushes the door open and motions for me to enter. When I turn, he's gone, and I'm alone in the dark with a mammoth, snoring hulk of a man.

The Rais' long limbs and round belly spill over the edges of the single-sized mattress that sags to the floor under the weight of him. For a moment I stand still and adjust to the darkness. As my eyes come into focus I see a neatly rolled prayer rug against the corner of the sparse room. Next to it, a Koran rests on a carved wooden stand. It's clear that the man is a meticulous and pious Muslim who enjoys order. The small space is likely his sanctuary from his public position at the busy temple. I admire the cleanliness of the room and speculate that maybe he's just a lonely and obsessive old man.

Perhaps, I ponder, he's misunderstood and not a bad person at all.

Now that I stand before the sleeping Rais, I don't know how to begin. I breathe deeply and struggle to recall my most formal and respectful Arabic phrases in an effort to impress him with my sincerity. Summoning my courage, I speak Arabic in a gentle, low voice.

"*Low samaht*, Excuse me. Please awaken sir, we must enter the great temple and pray." He doesn't stir and so I wait a moment and then repeat the same formal phrase. The Rais opens his eyes but shows no response. I move closer and say the words again in a more urgent tone. I think perhaps he cannot see me in the dark and so I step into the narrow shaft of moonlight streaming from the small window, hoping to be more visible. He stares at me with bulging eyes and struggles for words, but none come out.

I raise my arms, my glittering white shawl dropping open and draping down my body. "Soon the sun shall rise and we must stand before the holy of holies. It is time."

The old man begins to tremble and call out to Allah, praying and wailing in terror. He seems far more frightened of me than I am of him and I wonder why. He then falls into a violent fit of coughing and trembling. I fear he might expire, but I don't dare move closer to assist. I wait and watch him with concern. The coughing subsides for a moment and I bow slightly in greeting. Using my most soothing hypnosis voice, I reassure him that there is nothing to fear. His moaning starts again and becomes louder as he covers his eyes in terror.

Outside, a rooster starts to crow, a dog barks, and the howls of the Rais merge with the distant echo of the call to prayer. I fear that soon the entire village will awaken and rush to his aid, causing a scandal that will travel far and wide. My godfather will hear of this in Cairo. I can already see him sitting at his desk, his tired eyes looking over his reading glasses as I struggle to explain the odd circumstances leading to my arrest and internment in Luxor prison. It's not uncommon for me to do illegal mystical things that my godfather frowns upon, but this could push his patience with me to the limit. But, far worse, it would bring scandal to his sterling reputation.

I've never considered myself to be a threatening figure at just five feet tall. But now, as I stand in the narrow shaft of light, clothed in a long white robe, my hair flowing, it occurs to me I may look to the old man like the angel of death. I imagine how I must appear from his perspective. Were I a religious person, I'd be taken aback by the image I present, looming over him as he lay trembling in his bed.

I try again to make myself understood and plead, "*Maftouh! Maftouh*! The key! The key!"

The Rais rises in one frantic move, gasping and wheezing as he reaches under the bed. Does he have a weapon? Oh God, of course he does, he's a high-ranking guard! Why didn't I think of this? I freeze, trembling with fear, trying not to collapse into a faint or wet my pants. He lurches and flings a heavy key ring across the floor. He then falls back onto the pillow, moaning, as he clutches his chest. The keys make a sharp scraping noise on the stone floor and I dive in the direction of the sound, snatching them and rushing toward the door.

Cast in the pre-dawn light, the neighborhood looks entirely different from when I arrived in full darkness, and I have become disoriented. I run left and right, searching for some familiar sign. Then the far-off whistle of the worker's ferry crossing the Nile offers a clue and I head toward the sound, hoping this will lead me to the front gate of the temple. I don't dare look back in case someone is pursuing me. With a few heart-pounding twists and turns, my long garments held high and the key ring clutched to my chest, I make my way back to the main gate.

In unison, the women and the temple guards cheer my arrival. Within minutes, the large metal gate creaks and drags across the pavement and we're on the other side of it. My victory, however, is tempered with regret for causing the old man such a fright. What if I've killed him? His age, along with that hacking smoker's cough, would have put him at risk for a heart attack or stroke. I feel terrible to think I may have caused harm to any human being.

"Tell us again what you said, please," the guards cry out. "No one has spoken this classical Arabic since the days of the Prophet Mohammed, Peace be upon Him!" They appear to be enjoying this moment far too much and beg me not to leave. "Where did you learn Classical Arabic and how is it you speak it so well?" They listen, tears of laughter rolling down their faces, their arms around each other to keep from falling over.

"I had no idea my speech was so amusing," I say as I recount all that happened, the phrases I used, and how the old man had relented and thrown the keys at me. Since I seldom have living people with whom to converse in Arabic back home, I can only surmise how I sound. My cat Rashid is fluent and understands all Arabic dialects with ease. He's never once corrected me or laughed at my archaic use of the language the way these men are doing.

For decades, I've been devouring every Arabic audio program I can find and I practice almost constantly while driving. I repeat the formal Arabic phrases again to the two men. I'm getting tired of the situation and have to get going before the sun has risen. "It's not actually that funny," I tell them, "I may have killed the poor old Rais." This causes the guards to double over, choking and dropping their heads as they sit on the edge of the stone wall.

"Don't worry, you didn't kill him, he's too mean to die. *Inshallah*, God willing, your visit did him some good and he will return today a better man. Maybe he won't beat us with his cane today."

Leaving them to talk between themselves about their abusive boss, we compose ourselves and move on to our first stop, the small temple dedicated to the lion-headed goddess Sekhmet. The hidden temple is off the main path and seldom visited by tourists who tend to look for more grandiose locations. Sekhmet's temple continues to be frequented by local women who implore her to right the wrongs done to them and to protect their children from harm. We enter the small, dark room and stand before the black basalt statue of the dark goddess of fierce compassion. Someone has left a bunch of wild flowers at her feet.

Sekhmet stands alone in the small room, regal and powerful, ready to lead her children through initiation by fire. One by one we step forward and touch our foreheads to her feet. The dim moonlight from the opening above casts a shimmer on the ankh in her hand. The statue begins to heat up as Sekhmet responds to our presence and appears to come to life. I feel a searing rush to my solar plexus as the chakra of inner power is activated. Tears flow freely, as always, in the presence of the protector of women and children. We thank her for allowing us to commune with her, say farewell, and file out silently into the soft light of predawn. The skeptical, no-nonsense CEO in our group is sobbing and her shoulders shake with the release of whatever pain she carries beneath her hardened exterior.

At the far end of the immense Luxor Temple, we continue to the innermost chamber of Amunhhotep. The furthest vestibule of any Egyptian temple is the "holy of holies," the place of ceremony and worship. The sacredness of the place is palpable and I can easily imagine a time when offerings were made to the gods and goddesses. The hieroglyphs on the wall describe these rituals in great detail. Each of us places a white votive candle, flowers, amulets, and crystals upon the smooth black granite altar. We light our candles and gather around the altar in a circle, hands and bodies pressed against the cool stone as we begin chanting. My throat burns with a fire that rises up from my heart and I have a strange sensation, and feel compelled to speak.

Never a fan of direct voice channeling, I much prefer to stay present while accessing other realms, trusting that my own higher self is sufficiently connected to the source. I take a deep breath and an unintelligible chanting begins rising from my vocal cords in a language vaguely familiar yet unknown to my conscious mind. On a deep subconscious level, I know it's an ancient Egyptian prayer and I understand the meaning of what I'm saying. I can hear my voice intoning sounds and incantations from the distant past. They are words and names my ears have not heard in this lifetime.

The group joins me in chanting the strange sounds and time is suspended. Our bodies sway with the spiraling energy moving through us and none are willing to break the circle as we stand absorbing the intoxicating vibration of the holy place. It feels as if we're suspended in a timeless state of bliss for hours, but in fact only an hour or so has passed. We collect our things and close our sacred circle in silence.

The spell is broken by the first dim rays of light entering the chamber and the sound of voices from somewhere within the temple, voices of men shouting ever more loudly. The shouting gives way to a sharp cracking of pick axes and stones being moved. I wonder who would be digging in the center of the temple, especially at this early hour.

Curious, we emerge into the main courtyard where our eyes meet with an incredible sight, that of dozens of workers lifting a magnificent statue out of the ground. They place it on the stone floor with care and then continue to dig. One after another, beautiful statues are being birthed from right beneath the slabs of stone, the stone upon which thousands of tourists walk every day. We stand in awe at the sight of the most exquisite images, carved from basalt and granite so smoothly, as if by laser. Transfixed, we watch as the men lift four statues of a pharaoh, followed by female statues of what appears to be a royal family - eight statues in all. Each precious find is hurriedly packed with wet clay to protect it from cracking in the dry, chilly air.

Our group of eight lines up opposite the eight statues, the excavation pit between us, as the sun rises and illuminates the scene. The team leader kneels down, clicks his flashlight on, and rubs his sleeve against the royal cartouche inscription. His voice shakes with excitement. "It's Amenhhotep III!"

This refrain carries through the crowd, which has now expanded to include a reporter and Nile TV camera crew with an assortment of sleepy-eyed Luxor government officials. Everyone stands still, speechless. The silence is broken when the chief archeologist turns and sees us for the first time. He stares with an expression of disbelief, which immediately turns to fury.

"Who are all you women and how did you get here?" he yells, throwing his arms up in fury, "This is a restricted area! You cannot be in here, go!" He turns, red-faced with rage, and berates the police officers. "Who let these women inside the temple?"

No one responds and our appearance cannot be explained by anyone present. I am not about to betray my friends at the gate who've so kindly let us in. Not to mention the chance of this incident leading to another unsolved mystery---that of my unintentional act of murder of the old Rais. With no further questioning by the outraged authorities, we leave as silently as we entered, filled with gratitude for the blessing we have received. Before passing through the final gate, I turn and look back. I steeple my fingers, bow my head, and thank Serapis for orchestrating this miracle, this confirmation of his presence. And I vow never again to doubt my inner guidance.

FEBRUARY IN UPPER EGYPT IS EXQUISITE, MUCH LIKE THE most perfect fall day in New England. However, today is going to be uncharacteristically hot. The remainder of the day is free of commitments and I have so much to process from the long morning.

Alone at the outdoor café of the hotel, I sit under the shade of a date palm and order a continental breakfast and a pot of tea. The excitement of the morning has my mind in overdrive and I have to be sure to recall everything in proper sequence. Groups are headed out to start their temple tours; coaches line the curb, engines and A/C going. I open my journal to record the improbable events that have occurred since dawn. Just then I hear my name being called.

Rafiq, my land manager, approaches, and leans to kiss my cheek in greeting as he envelopes me in the suffocating scent of his cologne. Self-confident and high-strung, he has a tendency to overdo everything. As I pull back and sneeze, Rafiq folds his arms and eyes me with impatience, tapping his Gucci leather shoe on the ground.

"So, why are you still here drinking tea? The crowds will be at the temple before us and you won't get your private meditation time today. I can't help you Kara if you don't stay close to me. You know that." Rafiq revels in his role as the dashing, in-charge tour manager and he's earned the reputation of being the best in the business. I hire him as my on-site manager for every one of my tours and we have a good, if sometimes contentious, working relationship.

I survey his immaculate attire. "You'll suffer in that suit out there. It would be forgivable to dress more casually today considering the heat."

Rafiq grew up in Alexandria where people pride themselves on being sophisticated and a cut above the rest of their countrymen. His expensive European suits fit his tall, lean frame perfectly and his dazzling smile and chiseled features always thrill the ladies. Young and virile, he has an inexhaustible amount of testosterone and stamina to please them all. Without fail, mid-way through every tour, there will be a catfight as it becomes clear he's providing 'room service' to all of them. Yet, foreign women, married or single, continue to fall at his feet. His scandalous behavior and the gullibility of female tourists annoy me, but I've learned from experience that human nature is not to be regulated or changed.

Rafiq adjusts his crotch in a peculiar and distracting nervous tic he's had since I've known him. Each time he does this, I'm confused as to where to put my eyes as we speak. I force myself to maintain eye contact, unblinking.

"Why aren't you and your group joining us? This is a big day on the tour and I know you love this temple. What's wrong with you, Kara?"

I look up at him and carefully weigh my response, knowing he will be slighted at my having taken my group on a dawn trip to Luxor Temple without consulting him. I purposely withhold that information, as there's no reason to tell him. He could never stand still for an hour of meditation and chanting even if I had invited him.

"All of us are staying back today to write and meditate. You go ahead, and then we can check back in later at dinner time." He eyes me with suspicion and waits for me to explain, his foot still tapping.

" I'll gather my group later and we'll go inside the temple tonight when it's nice and cool. I'll ask them later if they want to do that." It then occurs to me I can send him on a bit of reconnaissance while at Luxor Temple. "Oh, Rafiq, wait.

Would you please do me a big favor when you get there?" He stops in his tracks. "Find out if the Rais is still alive. You know him, the large man who always wears a dark blue *gallabeya* and a white turban. He's the one with the single gold tooth and he carries a big bamboo stick. He looks mean and he coughs and spits a lot."

"Alive? Why should he not be alive? Did you have another one of your dreams?" he mocks. My colleague Rafiq doesn't put any stock in dreams, or reflection of any sort, preferring to pounce like a lion at whatever crosses his path, as long as the prey is female.

"Yes, that's it. I dreamed of him. Just find out and call me as soon as you see him, Okay? It's really important."

Rafiq's eyes narrow. "You and your dreams and visions, Kara. I wish you would forget all this spirit stuff once in a while and just relax and have some fun. Come on, we can sit together on the bus and I'll tell you all about the party I had in my room last night." He lifts his eyebrows and rolls his fringed, bedroom eyes. "You should have stopped by. I needed more harem."

"Your kind of fun doesn't interest me, besides, there are enough women in your harem already."

He moves closer, tilts his head, and peers down at me. "You know, sitting there in that white dress with the sunlight on your golden curls and with your blue eyes, you look just like an angel. Everyone thinks you're an angel, but sometimes I wonder if you really are a devil." He leans in with a probing, seductive stare, resting his hands on either side of my chair, as he licks a drop of perspiration off of his upper lip with a flick of his sharp tongue. "So, which is it, devil or angel?"

Clearly, he believes he's having a powerful effect on me. Although he's handsome and a lively, fun character, I despise the way he uses his looks and charm to relentlessly seduce women. As the one who brings new women every few months, I feel as if he's turned me into an international madam. The problem is, no matter how I try to change this dynamic, Rafiq's charm works with most of his prey, and no one calls him on his behavior except for me. In fact, the women become angry with me if I try to put the brakes on his rampant sexual activities.

I pull back from his intensity and cloying cologne and look up at him with a blank stare, "We'll find out by the end of the day if I am devil or angel. You shall know soon enough." My stomach tightens with fear at what may be found out.

Rafiq turns to leave, then turns around again, looking disappointed and perplexed. "You dream of him? What about me? Don't you ever dream of me?"

"You forget, Rafiq, I'm part Egyptian. I'm immune to you." I wave him away. "Go. Your harem is waiting, they're already getting on the bus."

"Right, soon they will be horning me."

"Beeping, Rafiq. We call it beeping."

He stops, concentrates, and repeats the word twice.

"That's a funny word, I like that. You teach me so many good words. I like this American slang. When I get back from the temple we can shoot the shit. Your son Adam taught me that one."

"Well, actually, in this case 'horning' is a more accurate term now that I think of it. Just remember, look for the Rais and don't forget to call me as soon as you see him, okay? If you can't reach me in my room, leave a message at the front desk."

He turns again and takes a few steps towards me. "That old, ugly man with one tooth? You have dreams about him and not me? *Afritah Magnoona*! Crazy she-devil!" He shakes his head and laughs as he walks away in long, confident strides. His harem calls out to him to hurry as he leaps onto the coach in one bound. I hope the women will at least give some attention to the scholarly Egyptologist assigned them for the temple visit and not spend yet another day vying for the attention of the Egyptian Casanova like foolish schoolgirls.

So he thinks I'm a crazy she-devil. This is the second time I've been called that today, and it's not even 9 am. While I'm a far cry from being an angel, I pray I've not become a murderess. I return to my journaling and the luxury of having the café to myself for a few hours.

At noon I pass through the lobby and the desk clerk calls out to me, "Miss Kara, you have a message!" My heart jumps. At the reception counter, I take the folded note and turn away from the clerk to open it, fearing the worst. It reads "The Rais Lives."

CHAPTER TEN

DREAM LOVER - CAPE COD

"Ever has it been that love knows not its own depth until the hour of separation."
Khalil Gibran

Dream: *I'm traveling by rail. The crowded train comes to a stop and everyone exits except for a man who is standing at the opposite end of the car. He is the composite of all the dark, exotic, and mysterious foreign men I'd ever known or longed for. He looks directly at me, nods in recognition then smiles, deep dimples showing on his cheeks. It's as if we know each other and I'm touched by his gentle expression, which softens the intensity of his features. His black hair is pulled back in a ponytail; such as a Native American man might wear, yet he's dressed in a casually elegant Bostonian manner. Breathless and stunned by the feelings I experience, my heart, my entire being, rushes toward him, as I stand transfixed in one spot. Although embarrassed and disconcerted by his knowing gaze, I'm unable to look away. The train starts again and then brakes squeal as we reach the final stop. The spell is broken and we look away from each other, exit through opposite doors, and go our separate ways.*

I AWAKEN SAD AND DISAPPOINTED TO REALIZE IT WAS ONLY a dream and that the tenderness of the experience was not reality. Anonymous in foreign countries, walking alone for hours, the occasional flirtation, this has become my idea of romance. I'm addicted to the unceasing emotional intensity of romance and longing. For days following the dream, I feel unsettled and disturbed. It's become apparent to me how unprepared I am for the day-to-day intimacy of a real relationship with a living, breathing man.

Could I really stand to be looked at so intensely as the dream lover had done, to be so exposed and vulnerable? What kind of man would be accepting of my bizarre affairs with spirit and my two-way conversations with the dead? He would probably go running like my first husband did once he found out who I really was. Or worse, die on me like the second one had. Even my first love, a 6th grade classmate named David, had died within weeks of our first meeting. No, I have to accept that romantic partnerships are just not my lucky area of life and it's time I resign myself to that. I have a life of adventure that's the envy of my married friends and I enjoy my travels and brief affairs. Still, I wonder what it would be like to come home to a partner at the end of my travels.

For weeks following the vivid dream of the intriguing man on the train, I am unable get him out of my mind. I look forward to sleep each night in hopes of another glimpse at him and some clue as to where he may be. I search for him in my waking travels to no avail.

Months pass, the cold starkness of winter moves in and sleep becomes silent, deep, and dreamless. I dismiss the dream as just a fantasy born of a long New England winter and too long a time without a romantic interlude in a far-off place. There are far more urgent and practical matters to think about than the handsome dream lover. Dad's worsening illness requires I cancel all upcoming travel assignments as my siblings and I struggle through the many agonizing decisions about his care. Dad has stoically endured lingering illnesses for many years, but it seems he has exhausted all strength to pull through this time. Many weeks of intensive care and dialysis in Boston make our frequent visits difficult. In his drugged state, Dad insists he's still on his beloved Cape Cod and will hear nothing to the contrary. Mom is wracked with guilt at not visiting him daily, and both of them are failing from the ordeal. Twice he becomes comatose and is given last rites. Each time, however, with the first step Mother takes across the threshold of his hospital room, Dad awakens and calls her name, his Irish eyes smiling.

"Here's my little bride," he announces with pride to everyone present, lapsing back into coma the moment she leaves the room. The spiritual bond between them is remarkable and I wonder if they can ever survive apart. Except for wartime, they've been together since high school. The long months ahead are without joy and I forget about dreaming as Dad slips away.

True to his Irish heritage, he leaves the physical plane for a great party in heaven on New Year's Eve where, no doubt, his friends are waiting for him. I imagine him looking handsome in his Aran Isles sweater and his tweed Donegal cap, absent-mindedly singing Irish songs as he often did. He will regale his friends with stories until all hours, his eyes sparkling with wit as his buddies roar with laughter and toast his arrival with another pint of Guinness.

Only after all the stories are told and the crowd has thinned will Dad notice his little bride is not there with him and tears will fill his eyes. He'll turn back to search for her, only to find her sitting alone, unreachable, in the little house they built together on Cape Cod. After fifty-five years of marriage, each is without their best friend and life partner.

The sound of taps echoes on the cold air of the national cemetery. A uniformed officer hands the folded flag to Mom. She accepts it and her head drops in sorrow, her shoulders shaking. We climb into the back seat of the black limousine and sit close as I place my arm around her. As the limo drives away, Mom holds the folded flag to her chest and silently weeps. As we reach the cemetery gates, she turns her head, looks through the car window one last time, and waves like a small child. I hear her whisper, "Goodbye, my darling. I'll always love you."

CHAPTER ELEVEN

DR. MANSOUR AND THE BOTANICAL
GARDENS, KITCHENER ISLAND ASWAN EGYPT

*"You have enemies? Good. That means you've stood up for
something, sometime in your life."*
Winston Churchill

Dr. Ibrahim Mansour, esteemed professor of biology, horticulture, and ornithology, has agreed to accompany us and act as our study guide in Kitchener Island. The island is named after the British Lord, who created a Botanical Island to resemble his homeland of England. As lush gardens are not abundant in an arid climate, locals come to this green oasis to escape the heat. For travelers, it's a break from trekking the desert and a relaxing pause in the program.

There are a number of gardeners in our group and it's a special treat for them to have a horticulture guide. The professor arrives at the dock in Aswan in his pristine white felucca sailboat, navigated by a Nubian captain in a crisp blue gallabeya and white sailor hat. The felucca sparkles in the sun and is in a different class than the other more utilitarian fishing boats on the Nile. They're an impressive duo among the rough laborers and fishermen on the dock. Dr. Mansour wears a neatly pressed tan safari-style shirt, a felt hat, dress pants, and his ebony walking stick bears a handle with the carved head of a bird. A charming old-fashioned academic of the pedantic teaching style, he speaks flawless classical Arabic, French, German, and English. Meticulous and quietly enthusiastic in sharing his vast knowledge, the doctor holds his audience in close attention and taps his cane if we grow restless. He's a caricature, but to me he's a lovable one.

We climb on board the vessel. "Please take a seat, you are most welcome," Dr. Mansour says with a bow and a proud sweep of his cane. Fit and slim, he appears to be in his early eighties, but I know he is nearing ninety.

"I only ask that you take care not to place anything on the cushions that might soil them. My wife bought this fabric in Cairo and she worked hard to make these for my boat. I just put them on this morning."

It's immediately apparent that the little man is set in his ways as he adjusts the Egyptian flag on the mast and brushes a speck of sand from the prow. He folds his handkerchief neatly and places it back in his pocket in a slow ritual while we wait. Satisfied that everyone is seated and attentive, he announces in a soft but certain tone of voice,

"Please, I expect all of you to keep up with me and to pay close attention. There is much to be learned today about the rare exotic flora of *Geziret an-Nabatat,* the island of plants." He makes a sweeping gesture toward the water. "We are at the first cataract of the Nile and in view of the West Bank of Aswan, Upper Egypt. You will have time to wander when the lessons are completed. Or, if you like, you may stay with me after my talk and ask me any further questions."

A few people roll their eyes at being addressed in this way and the swarthy Sicilian Strega sisters whisper as if placing a curse on the old man. They remind me of the evil witches of Grimm's' fairytales, warts and all.

I feel compelled to put in a few words of support for our esteemed guest. "Since his retirement from Ain Shams University, Dr. Mansour leads only occasional tours of Kitchener Island.

Although we're not in university, we're lucky to be his students for the day. I assure you we will all learn a great deal."

He helps each of us climb on shore, and we follow the little man along the manicured paths where a canopy of green trees provides a shady refuge from the sun. Dr. Mansour stops and breaks off small bits of leaves and rubs them between his thumb and forefinger so that we can smell the aromas of medicinal plants as he explains their uses in great detail.

Small children on field trips pass by, call out, and wave hello. Dr. Mansour frowns at the interruption. When he isn't looking, I wave and take a few quick photos of the children's smiling faces. The avid gardeners and medical professionals in the group hang on every word of the commentary and some even take notes. All is going well until we hear an unsettling loud splat. We turn to see one of the group members, a dedicated crystal collector, lying face down in wet mud. She's spotted a shiny stone in the wet soil among the freshly watered plants and has to have it. I've been keeping an eye on Dorothy, since only yesterday she caused a commotion when she lit her foot on fire. Her cult leader, the wild-haired Stella Strega, had staged a clandestine channeling session inside a tomb in the Valley of the Kings. In spite of 120° Fahrenheit temperature and numerous warnings about the dangers of heatstroke, they had a picnic and a ceremony inside a tomb. Stella had gone around to every cabin late at night and slid notes telling certain members of the group of her special morning channeling session in the tomb of Pharaoh Thutmoses III. I didn't receive word of it until too late and they had gained access to the tomb and begun the ceremony in a circle seated on the stone floor.

The previous day, my friend Mostapha reported to me that two swarthy sisters visited his shop and inquired about certain stones that could increase their power to control others, stones that he did not keep in his shop. He overheard my name being mentioned and so he warned me to be wary. He sensed I was in danger.

Dorothy, being an obedient devotee of her guru, had kept her eyes tightly closed as commanded. In an attempt to ease the discomfort of sitting her large derriere on a stone floor for two hours, she stretched out her legs without breaking the circle. Dorothy's foot had rested next to the large candle in the center of the circle and in time it caught on fire. She was compelled not to disturb her leader's channeling of an ascended master who had promised to reveal the 'true story' of the 18th Dynasty, clearing up for the Egyptians any unsolved mysteries.

The self-proclaimed omniscient guru had repeatedly appalled all of us in the group, except for her devout followers, with her loud declarations that the Egyptologist's facts were erroneous. Now, at last, in her devotees' minds and her own, she would be proven correct. Stella Strega had issued a stern edict that if anyone broke the circle by letting go of another's hand, she would be trapped outside of her body, her astral form would shatter, and she would suffer an agonizing and certain death. The obedient Dorothy stayed still as the rubber sole of her tennis shoe burned right through her shoe and sock, singeing her big toe.

At the smell of burning rubber and flesh, someone began screaming. Panic ensued, bottles of mineral water were retrieved from backpacks, and the smoldering foot was doused. It was at that moment, hearing the screams, that the Egyptologist and I ran in and observed the commotion. The cultists scrambled toward the entrance, pushing and cursing in a most unenlightened manner. Stella jumped up and pushed ahead of them and was the first one out, no harm done to her astral body as far as anyone could discern.

In a voluminous flowered sundress and straw hat, the naïve Dorothy edged her way toward the shiny object, one foot a smooth, wet paving stone. She lost her balance and twisted sideways to recover. Undaunted, she righted herself and lurched toward the sparkle and then fell facedown into the wet soil with a loud squish. We rush to help and hoist her to a standing position. She's fuming with anger and covered head to toe in the rich black mud of Egypt. The stone in her hand is common jasper and it had appeared, as all stones do, to sparkle in the water.

Dr. Mansour grimaces and shakes his head in dismay. We try not to laugh, although the antics of the previous day with the flaming tennis shoe had diminished our empathy. Dorothy rummages through her enormous kite-shaped straw tote, pulls out a wad of tissues, and attempts to rub the dark soil from her face, working it into her skin until it appears she's wearing an African ceremonial mask. Her cotton dress is soaked through, far beyond fixing with tissues, and clings to her body.

She clutches the stone as if it's a pharaoh's jewel, rubs it clean, and opens her bulging velvet stone pouch which is growing heavier by the day. She drops her latest treasure into her purse with a victorious grin.

A few moments later, Dr. Mansour appears before us in the middle of the path, holding a long garden hose streaming with clear water. His face has an expression of determination. I freeze in my tracks to think what he has in mind.

"Miss Dorothy, come and stand here and I will give you a douche," The professor implores as he reaches out for her.

"Don't you come near me!" shouts Dorothy as she backs away.

The guru rushes to her devotee's aid and begins shouting and swearing at the little professor, calling him a perverted old bastard. Her language is losing its lofty spiritual tenor.

"Come, the water is pleasant, not too cold," the professor continues calmly. "A nice cool douche will be refreshing."

The defiant Dorothy holds her arms across her chest as Dr. Mansour inches his way closer. "I cannot allow you to get on my felucca like that, he says in a steady voice as if talking to a toddler in the midst of a tantrum. You'll soil my new cushions." He continues to pursue her with the hose, holding it in front of his trousers in an absurd manner.

His target lumbers further from him, clutching her straw

tote against her body. It's a contest as to which of the two is more comical as we us stand spellbound and watch them.

Dorothy, who apparently had never heard the innocuous French term douche in reference to a shower, is outraged. The linguistic gaff is causing offence to some, and hysterical laughter to others. We try to reassure her that the dear professor has not gone mad, but is just trying to be gallant while at the same time protecting his new cushion covers. The scene escalates to absurdity as each is determined not to give in and the Strega sisters screech at the poor man. Passersby by stop to watch with quizzical expressions as the large American woman rants and the little professor chases after her while begging her to submit to a refreshing douche.

The crisis is resolved when the park manager emerges from his office with a large beach towel and wraps it around Dorothy's shoulders. Cocooned safely, she fumes and climbs aboard the felucca. Dr. Mansour follows with a watchful eye and a hurt sense of pride at being treated so poorly and scolded so harshly for his attempts at helpfulness.

Before we leave the dock, I overhear the park manager explaining to Dr. Mansour the double meaning of the word 'douche.' Dr. Mansour blushes deeply and hangs his head in embarrassment.

As each group departs Kitchener Island, local Nubian craftsmen climb on board, arms laden with beaded necklaces and carved jewelry for sale. Dr. Mansour purchases three necklaces of tiny shells and beads, walks over to Dorothy, and presents them to her as a peace offering. I overhear their conversation.

"I apologize for upsetting you, I didn't know why this word

was so disturbing to you." He leans toward her, his offering in his outstretched hand, "I hope you will accept these necklaces as a token of my sincere apology."

All of us wait in silence as a tense moment passes, then Dorothy reaches out, accepts the gift, and offers Mansour a hesitant smile. She motions for him to join her and Dr. Mansour sits down beside her while she opens her pouch of stones and explains to him in which part of Egypt she found each one.

By the time we arrive at the dock on the other side of the Nile in Aswan, the two are engrossed in conversation about the variety of minerals to be found in Egypt. They continue the conversation as they walk back, arm in arm, toward our hotel. The Strega sisters cross the street and go their way as they scowl and cackle. I wonder what kind of scolding they'll give Dorothy when they get her alone later. This American group is one the genteel professor won't soon forget.

"This woman Stella, she is what you would call the female Jim Jones, yes?" the dear little man asks me later over tea. I laugh and agree.

Two days later, I bid goodbye to the cult members at Cairo Airport and I'm happy to see the back of them. The Strega sisters, stand off to the side and level the evil eye at me as the rest of the group hugs goodbye. I've experienced imposters and egomaniacs on my trips, some who delighted in tearing others apart, but never had I encountered such venomous "spiritual leaders."

I'm heading home to Cape Cod for a two-week rest before my next tour. I pray it will be an easier assignment.

CHAPTER TWELEVE
THE NILE SMILE

"Travel brings power and love back into your life."
Rumi

The winter of 1992 is brutally cold and snowy and the harbor alongside my center is frozen into large, drifting chunks of blue ice. The pilings that support the building groan as the ice floes stack themselves against the dock with each rising tide. The wind howls as I lean into the wind and hurry from my office to my car, throw my bag onto the seat, turn the ignition, and blast the defroster. As I scrape ice off the windows, my hands become numb with cold. I pull out of Barnstable Harbor and drive east on route 6A, past fallen trees, stalled cars and mounds of snow, my thoughts wandering to warm winters in Egypt. At home, my driveway froze over and is now a rock-solid sheet of ice. The mailbox has disappeared, plowed under a ten-foot bank of snow. Taking light steps so as not to sink, I walk on top of the snow to where the front stairs are disguised as a white ramp. Hat and wet coat thrown on a chair, I turn the heat on and curse the winter.

Upstairs in my studio, I find a message from a former Boston Museum School colleague I've not seen or heard from since our college years, but smile as I recall how wild and adventurous she had been then and how much fun we'd always had together. Once warm and settled, I call her back and we pick up our easy rapport as old friends do. She's now a professor of art history in Boston. She tells me with sadness that her husband died four years ago. She's still in a slump and needs to get away. Andrea and her colleagues formed a study group focused on the art and architecture of ancient Egypt and they want me to arrange a tour for them. My old classmate jokes that they've heard of how handsome Egyptian men are and they especially want some excitement and romance. I detect the theme of men and romance is of far greater interest than history, and I know it will be a lively and fun-loving group.

"Don't get me wrong. We're interested in the history and the mystical aspects as well, we just want to experience all that Egypt has to offer, past and present-day."

As her friends call in to register, my intuition tells me there may be some emotional instability in a few of the women I speak with, but I know from experience that groups tend to self-regulate after a few days together. Most often, the difficult personalities will fall in line as the rest of the group monitors them. They're in a hurry to get moving on their plan and within one month we 're gathered at Logan for an overnight departure on Egypt Air.

It's peak season and the only cruise boat I'm able to book us on in such short notice is one with the amusing name of 'The Nile Smile,' which seems appropriate for this fun-seeking group of women. This time, the cruise would occur before the land portion of the trip due to scheduling of cruise departures, so we have two nights in Cairo to rest up after our international flight and get a quick view of the great city. We fly to Luxor, embark the small cruise boat by midday and take our cabins, unpack and then go to the top deck for teatime. The schedule is to sail through the night and arrive in the town of Aswan at daybreak for our first temple visit.

There's always something mysterious and thrilling about an early morning excursion in Egypt. The haze over the pink cliffs of the West Bank, the low voices of the felucca men as they repair sails on the swaying vessels while singing songs of love and loss. The sweet smoke of sugar cane fills the air, as the fields are set afire in preparation for another planting. Egypt's fellaheen, farming people, first sing of heartache, followed by clapping and energetic songs to lighten their work.

The 4:00AM wake-up call is unavoidable if we're to have a private visit to the temple of Isis on the island of Philae. Our felucca waits to take us south to the first cataract of the Nile, where the temple rises like a white diamond upon the water. After the sunrise visit, the plan is to take a short flight to the grand temples of Ramses at Abu Simbel. In the afternoon, following teatime, we'll set sail to Kom Ombu and the dual temples of the gods Sobek and Horus.

One by one we wander to the dining room for a quick breakfast of coffee, juice, and pastries before disembarking for our day of adventure. There's no one else around and we have the breakfast room to ourselves. The waiter, a baby-faced Nubian adolescent, has been given the unmercifully early shift as the newest hire. In spite of the hour, he's pleasant and accommodating.

"Our waiter is so happy considering how early he had to get here to serve us. Isn't he adorable? He reminds me of my son," I say, with a pang of heartache at missing my own son so much. He's much too grown up now to be persuaded to join me on another overseas adventure.

"I need coffee right away," commands Margaret with a snap of her fingers as she sweeps in like a storm, letting the door slam behind her. She then, in her characteristically ungraceful manner, drops herself into a chair. The table shakes as everyone holds onto their coffee cups and braces for what may come next. Margaret is the owner of a famous five star restaurant in Copley Square and she expects to be treated royally wherever she goes.

She commands the attention of the group. "My roommate Andrea won't be joining us today. She was up on deck all night screwing that Italian tour guide. She had the nerve to yell at me for waking her this morning and refused to let me to turn on the light to get ready. This, after all the noise she made coming in at two-thirty last night. Can you believe that? I swear she would drop her drawers for anyone, even him," motioning to our young waiter. "She'll probably call him for room service as soon as we leave."

I'm losing patience and feeling protective of both Andrea and the innocent waiter. "It's a bit more than you think with Andrea and Mario. They're both art history teachers on break and they've been talking since we boarded this boat, even exchanged numbers and made a plan to meet during summer break." I lock gazes with Margaret. "Now, let's stop this slander. This is supposed to be a spiritual group and we're on our way to a ceremony dedicated to the Goddess Isis. Let's have some display of sisterhood. Andrea isn't here to defend herself, and what she does in her free time is not anyone's business. And leave our darling waiter."

Margaret interrupts, "I had to dress in total darkness and forgot half the things I was supposed to bring for today. Now she's double-bolted the door to our cabin so I can't get back in." The diatribe goes on and on to details of bathroom use, wet laundry, lost keys. When she pauses for a breath and no one responds, she turns her wrath on me with a maniacal glare.

"I thought you said you'd find me a suitable roommate? She has ruined my entire trip so far. I want a cabin of my own and she can pay the difference for being such a bad roommate."

"As I told you already, the cruise is fully booked. There are no other cabins to be had."

"What about yours?" she demands. "Can't you move in with your old college friend Andrea and give me your cabin?"

All of us are all short on sympathy, having been subject to this tirade since day one at the Cairo Marriott hotel, when Margaret had declared in a loud voice that her diet doesn't allow a single thing on the buffet table and would I to "talk to the chef right away?" She wanted stir-fry with tofu. Chinese food in Egypt.

Francine, the eldest and most soft-spoken of our group, levels her soft, blue-eyed gaze in a most motherly way, placing her hand on Margaret's.

"Andrea has had a rough time since her husband died.

Maybe she just needs to have a little fun and get over her grieving."

"Well, she's doing that alright!" Margaret retorts. "All of us are healing from something. Does that mean we should all be up there going at it on deck every night?"

"My, that would certainly cause some listing of this old boat, wouldn't it, dear?" Francine turns and gives me a conspiratorial wink, then turns to Margaret. "Count me out, I'm in bed by eight and I need sleep at my age, not sex."

How I was growing to love that wise old woman!

Sex on deck at any hour, even at 2AM, is not within the rules of the Nile Smile Cruise ship, or of Muslim society. Still, having watched the Italian tour manager, Mario, strip down, and swim each afternoon upon his return to the boat, each of us smiles at Andrea's good fortune. Daily afternoon tea on deck is made so much more uplifting by the sight of the young Italian stallions, brash and loud, as if determined to live up to the reputation of their countrymen as they prance about in their neon Speedos. Mario has given up on trying to manage his rowdy students and instead just does what he can to corral them and minimize the damage. The young men are amusing to watch, but the day the well-oiled Mario tired of swimming, turned, and floated on his back, many a teacup was spilled.

We glance around the table as Margaret fumes, each of us secretly proud that one of our own has taken the prize. Yes, Andrea did it for the American team and we're proud. Not the sniping German women who watch everyone from behind their dark glasses and seldom break a smile. Not the petulant French girls who look so chic, even after the dust storm yesterday, but one of our home team has won the trophy. No doubt, we will get a juicy blow-by-blow account when our heroine resurfaces at the dinner table at the end of the day.

We're succeeding in maintaining our composure when the outspoken Janet stands and leans across the table with narrowed eyes. She slides her glasses down her nose, peers over them, and then replaces them again, squinting at Margaret.

"Am I imagining it, or is that a pair of panties on your shoulder?"

All of us turn to look. A large pair of mint green polyester panties drapes diagonally over Margaret's right shoulder with a jaunty *je ne qua pas*. They could only belong to her; Andrea has always been more of a black lace thong type of girl. Margaret whips the hang-gliders off her shoulder and shoves them into her purse, her eyes wild with anger.

"It's her fault!" Margaret's face is flaming. "Everything is such a mess in our cabin because of that scatterbrain. I can't find a thing and it was so dark I couldn't even see in the mirror while I got dressed."

It's not often that karma is so swift, or so entirely satisfying.

THE BABY-FACED WAITER RETURNS WITH THE CHECK AND our bottles of mineral water just as we break into laughter. He glances down the table to where Margaret sits, and his expression registers relief that the panties are gone. The crazy American women aren't trying to start a new trend. Flushed and struggling to maintain composure, the shy young Nubian rushes back into the kitchen as we head out into the pre-dawn light.

"Enjoy your day, ladies," calls Mounir, the dining room

manager, from the top deck as we disembark and begin our ascent along the gangplank to the waiting feluccas.

"Oh, Mounir, would you please send a pot of tea and a light breakfast to 209 at around eleven? Andrea isn't coming on tour with us today. And tell housekeeping not to disturb her."

"She's not going on tour? Is she sick? Shall I send some Entocid? Does she need a doctor?" He's concerned that one of his passengers has fallen ill, especially one of his favorites.

"No, she ate something last night. She should be just fine with a few hours sleep."

THE BOATMEN ARE LINED UP IN A ROW, SINEWY ARMS ready to assist us along the uncertain cobblestone surface of the dock. The day promises to be charged with high spirits as the women claim their places on the flowered seats of the felucca and we head out into the gentle current. A wind rises and Margaret's fashionable new raffia sunhat flies off and almost hits the water. The captain deftly catches it in his net and returns it with a deep bow and an appreciative glance at Margaret's overflowing cleavage.

"American women, you are my favorite, you really know how to enjoy life." he makes the typical Nubian gesture of joy, one hand to his heart and one to the sky. His smile is wide and enthusiastic as he looks into her face. Margaret blushes at the boatman's gallantry and obvious interest as she smiles up at him and bats her lashes.

"Miss Margaret," he says, his eyes feasting on her bosom, "You make my eyes so happy. Come sit up here beside me and help me steer the boat." He reaches out his enormous calloused brown hand to her. "Please, I need your help, my sweet lady."

To our delight, and with a bit of steadying, Margaret climbs over the wooden seat and joins him. Within moments, we hear her giggling like a schoolgirl as she tells him of her life-long love of water and her "30-foot wooden boat" back home at Rowe's Wharf in Boston. Ah, the power of a little romance in softening even the most hardened and stubborn heart.

CHAPTER THIRTEEN

TO FLY AWAY

*"My soul wants to fly away when your presence calls it so sweetly.
My soul wants to take flight, when you whisper arise."*
Rumi

Years of organizing, promoting, and leading tours to Egypt by myself have left me beyond exhaustion and ready to quit. Some members of the New Age "spiritual" community prove to be incorrigible and less than spiritual when taken out of their habitat into a place as foreign as Egypt. They try to hijack the tour and waylay group members to join them on side trips across the Sinai, having no knowledge of the potential dangers they are leading people into. They insult the locals and 'talk down' to them, contradict the archaeologists, and generally behave like the proverbial ugly Americans.

Not all are like that, of course, and most of my passengers

are polite and respectful of other cultures. Yet there are a few spiritual snobs in every group who cause endless disturbance and will ruin the tour if I don't keep a close watch on them. I'm losing patience with the bad behavior. The last straw comes when one person files a lawsuit against me because she returns home harboring an array of parasites. In defiance of my admonition that sushi in a developing country is guaranteed to be unclean, she and her friends search out the only sushi restaurant in the entire country, owned by recent immigrants from Asia who apparently didn't do much research into the condition of Egyptian water.

Back home, out of faith and funds, I spot an ad for a tour management certification course offered in Boston. The once-yearly training would begin next month. I'd had enough of barely breaking even on my tours and being so burned out by the work. I register the same day and soon begin the four-hour commute, devouring every moment of the training where I learn of all the things I've been doing wrong. A pushover in business, I give people too many chances and seldom even look at the bottom line when figuring the expenses involved in running a tour. My instructors, who know too well the life and pitfalls of a tour director, tell me how to keep better control of my business and to add a percentage to the price as my own compensation.

Once graduated, major tour companies begin hiring me on the spot upon hearing of my daring and foolhardy adventures with my own tour company specializing in Egypt. I immediately qualify to be overworked, underpaid, and solely responsible for the lives of unknowing, innocent elderly people in far-off countries around the world. It could be called a lateral move, going from counselor to full-time director of 'senior' tours. I'm still taking care of people, only in different locations with no support system or emergency back up.

My life has been dictated by the needs and dramas of others for as long as I can recall and I delight in my new freedom. Off the radar now, I can live the life I choose. Family has my itinerary, but they will think twice before calling overseas to draw me into family dramas. So what if I'm on call day and night to large groups of strangers in varying stages of decline? Most of them are delightful and I get to visit parts of the world I would never have seen in my life otherwise.

Things often go wrong, but always there are miracles to offset the catastrophes, and I remain determined to plan more international tours on my own. Leading a tour in a developing country presents far greater challenges than in a well-run 'first world' location, yet I find I'm more at home in places where people are authentic and unpretentious.

Assignments keep me booked, and in between the mainstream tours I still lead my own Mystical Egypt tours. The dawn-to-dusk workdays on the road scarcely pay my rent back home - no insurance, no benefits, no retirement, or even a paid sick day. Yet, at the end of each tour I can say goodbye to my group and send them off on a plane to wherever they came from, and then revel in a few extra days to wander the streets in whatever city the tour program ended. It's a high price for a quick visit to in an interesting new place, but I'm hooked on adventure. The anonymity and even the demanding pace of it all is addictive and there's always another country I've not yet seen. I've led groups throughout Europe, the Caribbean, the Near East and Africa, Central and South America.

Months pass before I return home to spend time with family, pay bills, rest and catch up with friends. It's early summer and Cape Cod is in full bloom and the miles of beaches beckon. I'm tempted to stay home and enjoy the glorious summer and all that tourists return here for each year, catch up with friends I seldom see any longer. After a month of playing at being a tourist, wanderlust returns and I find myself browsing the latest catalogue of the senior tour company.

I need something entirely different, an easier destination where I won't have to run after the bus in my pumps, play nurse, or try and guess what locals are saying. Most of Canada speaks English, it looks clean and safe, and so Canada becomes my next assignment of choice. I choose a two-week tour of the Canadian Rockies, with lots of outdoor adventure; including a helicopter ride through mountain passes and a jeep ride across glaciers.

CHAPTER FOURTEEN

ROCKY MOUNTAIN DETOUR, CANADIAN ROCKIES

"Whom the gods would make bigots,
they first deprive of humor."
Hanlon's Razor

How I came to be in the bathtub of a burly Canadian truck driver, a glass of merlot in my hand, will forever remain a mystery, even to myself. The tour of the Canadian Rockies is confusing to me on many levels. It sounded so relaxing when I chose it from the options of assignments in the new catalogue of the tour company 'Mountain Magic, Western Canadian Rockies.' I need a break from being in charge of my own "Mystical Egypt" tours and to go someplace far away from my Egyptian ex-fiancé Naim, and all that reminds me of him. Although we've ended it, the love between us is still alive and draws us to each other from any distance.

The Canadian coach tour would commence in Alberta and travel through a vast and pristine wilderness surrounded by beautiful scenery. There would not likely be a single tempting Egyptian man in sight. In my haste to take the assignment, I never considered the avid hunting mentality of rural Canadians or the lack of proper heating in many places we went. It's early fall but the temperature is biting winter cold as I arrive in Alberta. Winter sports have never appealed to me since becoming an adult, although I do have fond memories of sledding and ice-skating as a child in those days when I had better tolerance for cold. In my adulthood, however, I might go for a brisk walk on a frigid winter day, and then return home and curl up with a good book and a nice glass of wine or cup of anything steamy.

Day one is a shock to the senses for this vegetarian city girl. The sight of beautiful dead animals strapped to vehicles, their soulful eyes staring, is deeply disturbing to me.

"On the right!" the bus driver calls out, "Look at the size of the rack on that buck." He gives the hunter thumbs up and sounds his horn as he allows the hunter to pass out of deference to his achievement. I hold back nausea and close my eyes. A few moments later he shouts, "Look, here's another one, right in front of us. Did you see it Kara?" He turns for my approval.

I lift my head and look at him. "No, I didn't see it. My eyes were closed. I was still praying for the last one."

He gives me a strange look. "You eat meat don't you? Where do you think it comes from?"

"No, in fact I do not eat meat."

"Hunting's a sport, that's all, nothing to get so worked up about." He shakes his head and makes the face I've so often seen on men when they don't get what a woman's saying.

"How can it be a sport if one team doesn't know they're playing?"

The driver moans and stops talking to me. This senseless killing of magnificent animals is all too much for me, and I put my headphones on and pretend to be sleeping for the rest of the drive. We weave through darkening steep roads toward our hotel and it takes far longer than the estimated two hours on the itinerary.

Just the week before, I was working in sunny Portugal, buying a light cotton blouse in the charming hill town of Sintra. And before that, I was rambling the Sinai on my favorite camel, my head wrapped against the blowing sand.

My group this time had flown in from England in anticipation of observing the flora and fauna of the great open spaces of Canada. Studious and gentle Brits in sturdy shoes, each one comes equipped with binoculars and a dog-eared Baedeker guidebook describing the natural beauty of Canada. They've memorized every detail of every bird, tree, and animal in their Baedekers. In my tour directing experience, I find the Brits more knowledgeable on such matters than any nationality I've worked with. They shake their heads in dismay at both Americans and Canadians who can't identify the plants of their own homeland, or even the flowering trees on their front lawn. They even take to gently scolding the proprietors for their carelessness in not knowing the trees on their property at every opportunity.

Western Canada is astoundingly gorgeous, even more so than the photos in the tour catalogue. Still, I can't relate to the culture of rugged outdoorsmen and women. On the other hand, the subculture of entitled international skiers leaves me clueless as well, with their pricey designer gear and absurd enthusiasm for sliding about on the ice in bitter cold.

I grew up in Boston where we co-exist nicely with animals and stay home by the fire with a good book on frigid, wintery days whenever possible. I've never ventured out in snow to hunt anything except a sale at Filene's Basement in Downtown Crossing. To me, there wasn't ample reason to drive three hours north with a car full of equipment in order to scale frozen mountains, no matter how attractive the man who invited me might be.

It's a damp afternoon and we stop at a small diner for lunch. Minestrone soup sounds good and might warm me up, I think, as I join the queue to order a large bowl. I'm a nerd, I confess. In my obsessive need to read everything that crosses my vision, I peer at a handwritten sign right next to the soup tureen. It reads "live bait." I shiver and feel a wave of revulsion. What if the bait has crawled into the soup tureen? Didn't they even consider this possibility? There's no way I can eat now, or even watch other people eat. I sit alone, my back to the room, with a cup of tea and wait for everyone to finish.

I've been shivering with cold since arriving in Canada and now it had become an uncontrollable core trembling. My teeth are chattering and I can think of nothing but getting to the hotel and a hot bath. When almost to the hotel, the driver suggests a show of hands as to a stop at a liquor store. The group comes to life with a rousing response and all march off the coach in single file to their joyful mission. I join them and purchase a small bottle of red wine to warm me later at the hotel, being certain first that it has a twist-off cap since I don't travel with a corkscrew.

It's still summer according to my body clock and I'm not adapting well to the drastic change of climate of the Canadian Rockies. My elderly Brits are never so jolly or lovable as when they climb back on the bus, their purchases clutched tightly.

"Thank you so much, Kara, you made our day with this stop," Mr. Chauncy taps me on the back, "This was the best visit so far on this trip, young lady. Let's try and do this every day."

We arrive at our hotel and file into the small lobby as I present the passenger list to the manager and apologize for our late arrival. Each couple double-checks that they've been given two beds and not a double, or what's called a 'conjugal bed' in other parts of the world. Conjugal relations are not on their agenda, just a good night's sleep.

In my years as a tour director, I've learned a great deal about marriage from my passengers. Only the newlyweds want to sleep in the same bed and couples delight in leaving their spouses behind in foreign locations. They even encourage the driver to leave when the partner isn't back to the bus on time. As tour manager, I can't allow this dumping of spouses along the road and have to be a spoilsport and retrieve the discarded spouses.

Check-in finished, keys distributed, the group goes off to their rooms clutching their purchases of whiskey and gin. I take my own room key, maneuver my roll-a-board suitcase onto the lift, go up one level, and enter room 133. Irritable and chilled to the bone, I'm becoming snarly. I step into the room and see a small black suitcase in the middle of the floor. Annoyed, I grab it and throw it out into the hallway, giving it a good kick to get it far from my door. I then flip the 'Do Not Disturb' sign onto the doorknob; double-bolt the door and begin undressing. I run the hot bathwater on full blast, squeeze two complimentary tubes of 'Canadian Pine' bath gel into the steaming water and ponder the fate of the animals that live in peril in those fragrant Canadian pine forests. I'm unable to shake the image of the poor, lifeless deer and wonder what will become of its baby does.

The phone rings and it's my son calling to check up on me. "How're you doing up there in the Canadian Rockies? Haven't heard from you and just wanted to see if you're okay."

"I'm fine. It's been a rough day, cold and drizzly, but the worst of it is seeing all the gentle deer tied to the backs of vehicles. I just cannot stand it and it makes me feel sick."

"You wanted a to get far from Egypt, remember? You're in the real world of hunters, Mom. At least they're not shooting all the unicorns in that big forest. That would really upset you." My son loves to tease me about my beliefs and my tendency to be a romantic.

"Very funny. You always find a way to make me laugh. Seems the unicorns are laying low up here. It is beautiful country though, and the people are friendly and polite in spite of their hunting problem."

"Only a few more days and you'll be back on beautiful Cape Cod. I'll meet you at the gate at Logan and we'll go to he

North End for a nice Italian dinner. We can celebrate my good news.

"What's that?" I ask.

"I got into the Florence study abroad program and I'll leave for Italy next month. I'll major in Tuscan cooking and Italian language."

"That's fabulous! I'm so proud of you. Love you, Sweetie."

" I love you too, Mom."

I feel so much better having talked with my son and my mood has lifted. A candle and some incense clear the smell of cigarettes left by the last occupant. I savor the delicious warmth, quiet, and privacy as I claim the space as my own. With one foot immersed in the steamy bath, I remember my purchase of red wine and go to get it from my carry-on. I unwrap the plastic hotel cup from its paper cover and pour the contents of the small bottle. It glows a soothing garnet red.

As I settle into the scalding water with my cup of merlot, I feel some modest triumph over the challenges of the day in the Canadian Rockies. I know I'll never be a mountaineer, a brave pioneer woman, but at least I've almost completed my assignment in this cold place and soon I can go home. This hot bath is as close to heaven as I'll get for a while. There are still two more days of the tour and I determine I won't break down now. I close my eyes and breathe a sigh of relief as I immerse my head underwater and imagined floating in the Red Sea on a warm day in Sharm el Sheikh.

A persistent knock on the door disturbs my reverie and I call out to housekeeping, "I don't need anything right now, thank you." They could come back later and finish tidying the room. It did look as if they were not quite done, but it was of no concern to me. I put the matter aside, but calls keep coming in from the front desk manager.

"Who are you?" the male voice inquires, "and what tour group are you with?" Each time the phone rings I climb out of the tub and answer the same inane questions.

I repeat again for the third time, "I'm the American tour manager from Boston. I was just down there thirty minutes ago checking in my British group. I think it was you who handled our check-in. I'm sure you have all our information."

My good manners are becoming compromised and I'm close to behaving in a rude manner, an indulgence I seldom allow myself, and one certainly not allowed in the hospitality industry. "Please stop calling me now, it's been a long, cold day and I'm taking a bath." I hang up and return to the tub. When the manager calls a fourth time, I hear a commotion in the background.

A booming male voice shouts, "If that feisty little strawberry blonde is in my tub, let her stay there. I haven't been with a woman in six months. Tell her I'll be right up!"

The manager's voice shouts, "Settle down Charlie, this is all a mistake."

"Like hell it is," yells the Charlie voice. "This is fate, my lucky night, and don't you ruin it for me, John."

The phone drops with a clunk and it sounds as if they're wrestling. Then the manager takes the phone again, breathless, and clears his throat. His voice is stern. "This is John Rowan, manager of this hotel. You've caused a lot of commotion here at the front desk, young lady, I'll be up there right away and you'll have to move to another room." Minutes later, he arrives and I'm escorted up to room 233, directly above room 133.

I wear a modest arrangement of large white towels, one wrapped as a tall turban on my head. This ensemble is set off by my chic fur-trimmed black boots, which I'd purchased while on assignment in Florence. I lift my rib cage, hold my head high, and carry my glass of merlot in one hand, my purse in the other. I glide with nonchalance, imagining I'm Cleopatra entering Rome after vanquishing Julius Caesar with a yearlong Nile cruise on her golden barge. The manager trudges ahead of me, accompanied by a bellboy who carries my suitcases and books while stealing glances at me with a lecherous smirk.

Mr. Chauncey, my 90-year-old British passenger, stands speechless at the ice machine; bucket in hand, as we march past. The bellboy turns and gives me a leering grin. Nothing to grin about, I think to myself. Just keep walking, you deer-killing country boy.

I smile and wave to Mr. Chauncey in my most gracious manner. He looks confused, and then, recognizing me, breaks into a hearty laugh, one hand clutching his belly, the other steadying himself against the ice machine.

No one in management is able to explain how my key had worked in the wrong door.

"I tell you, it was a sign, our destiny to spend the night together." Charlie, the lonely truck driver is sticking with his story the next morning. "All of you ruined it for me. Who knows now what it might have come to had we let destiny take its course."

I feel certain I have no destiny with the portly bus driver named Charlie although I enjoy his sense of humor. He and I joke about the mishap at breakfast while my passengers eavesdrop with delight, eager to take part in another chapter in their zany tour manager's life.

"That Charlie the Trans-Canada bus driver seems like a nice enough fellow. He's just looking for some companionship after so many weeks of driving with busloads of old people," Agatha Chauncey says, "We've all decided you should join him for dinner tonight. You can meet him right here in the hotel dining room where we can all keep an eye on you."

Dismissing her comments, I must regain my authority and so I climb onto a chair with my clipboard, call attention, and read the schedule for the day aloud to the group. The itinerary includes a ride through a mountain pass to the highest outlook, followed by an outdoor barbeque, no doubt consisting of an assorted selection of native mammals, all to be consumed while standing in the freezing air. There are the usual questions of what to bring, how cold the day might be and if there would be any bathrooms in the mountains. At the buffet table, I take out my Ziploc bag and stock up on bread, cheese, and fruit. It will be another long day in the Canadian wilderness and this time I would be prepared. We file out to the waiting bus and as I climb aboard, the driver gives me a smirk.

"Did you get those deer all the way to heaven last night with your prayers?"

"Yes, in fact, I believe I did," I put down my purse and clipboard on the passenger seat and then stand to take a head count, "And there's no need to point out any deer today, alive or dead."

On the ride, I think of how many bizarre things have happened in my recent tours. Since my hormones were hijacked by menopause, strange occurrences follow me. It's as if my energy field creates a disturbance in the very atmosphere around me. Try as I may to be organized and professional, something always goes awry. After last night's misadventure, I feel my professionalism has fallen to a new low.

"Flaky as a piece of baklava, she is, but we love her," I overhear Mr. Chauncey say to his friend. "We haven't had a dull moment since she collected us at the airport in Vancouver, have we?"

His buddy Mr. Bottomsley hits him on the back. "That's for sure. The best laugh was when she went out with you on that Capilano suspension bridge the first day of the tour.

"Indeed, my 90th birthday, and it was the best one in memory," says Chauncey.

"The way you both fell over and rolled around trying to right yourselves while all of us cheered and took photos. I'll admit now I was the one who started the bridge shaking from where I stood on the ground."

Mr. Chauncey turns and shoots a look at his friend. "You could have thrown me and our little Kara to our deaths, you jealous rascal. You just wish she had taken a liking to you instead of me."

"No, I think you and our little tour manager make great mates. You're both more than a bit daft."

Mr. Chauncey has a wistful look in his eye as he looks over at me with mischievous, rheumy eyes. "If only I'd met a girl like her when I was young. Life would have been a long series of adventures."

"Well, from what she's been telling us, she believes in reincarnation. Maybe you two could set a plan before we head back to England, meet up next time around and get married." Mr. Bottomsley teases.

"Why that's brilliant, my friend," Cyril lights up with glee. "I'll see what my wife Agatha thinks. She might welcome a lifetime or two away from me."

At day's end we file into the dining room. Charlie the driver sits alone at a two-top and waves me to join him, rising to his feet. The group nudges me toward his table and I relent and join him.

He helps me to my seat and I note that he looks tidy and smells of Old Spice aftershave.

"First, I want to apologize again that I got so worked up about your being in my bathtub last night. My line of work gets lonely and I seldom have the company of a woman, especially a woman like yourself," He stammers, "My head spun around when you walked into that lobby. I mean you're not a mountain woman by any means, with your manicured nails and soft, feminine look. It was like seeing an angel or a goddess emerge from the woods. My first thought though was, that little girl isn't dressed warm enough for this cold."

I'm taken by his open nature. "Thanks, and I apologize for breaking into your room and throwing your belongings out the door."

He laughs. "Yeah, and throw them you did, all over the hallway. You remind me of a woman I once knew, she was a little, feisty woman like you, cute and nice as could be, but boy she did that woman have a temper when it finally came out."

"Yes, I do have a limit to my patience when I'm tired and cold. My Irish comes to the surface."

"God, I miss having someone cuss me out like that. The

way you commanded the manager to stop calling because you were taking a bath, it was great and I was getting such a kick out of it."

His eyes water, "You know, it seems we never know what we have until we lose it."

"That's for sure," I think of the years I had with my partner who died and how quickly my life changed when he began to fail.

He looks serious, "You have somebody waiting for you back home?"

I shake my head. "No, I have no time for a relationship. I'm all over the world leading tours. Someday, maybe I'll try again. It's just not my lucky area."

"Well, don't wait too long to get off the road and find someone. I wish I'd stopped my wandering and made a commitment to my girl instead of leaving her alone all the time. She got tired of waiting for me and married someone else while I was away. Can't say I blame her."

I hear the pain in his voice as he continues. "You get too used to the freedom and excitement in this business and start to thinking it's all you need. But then suddenly you're old and you find you're at a dead end with nowhere to go. I'm sixty-eight now and I can't change direction at this point, no one wants to hire someone my age."

I thought of all the places I had been in the past year, all the people I had worked with and connected with, all the time I spent on the road. It would have been unfair to leave a partner waiting for me, yet I sometimes wished there were someone to go home to, someone who missed me and wondered about me. I know my son misses me, but he's also having the time of his life and soon will be living abroad in Italy.

I feel myself getting emotional, "I seldom think of the future, it's something I've always avoided doing. I'm not fond of talking about the past either, just try to live in this moment."

"Sorry," Charlie says, "I don't mean to depress you, but the future comes whether we think about it or not. I'm just sharing the bit of insight that comes with age. Here in the wilderness you have lots of time to think."

"Right, I've been doing a lot of reflecting since being here myself. There's not much else to do, no distractions like in the big, exciting cities where I'm usually sent on assignment.

Charlie nods in agreement, "Right. You're driving around with a bunch of old people who are ready to die, and you start wondering if you've really lived the life you were meant to live, or if you're just running away from life, avoiding commitment to anyone or anything."

The waitress returns with our food and two glasses of wine. Charlie smiles and raises his glass.

"Now let's make a toast and enjoy our dinner for this one enchanted evening."

We talk for a while longer, sharing stories about people and the challenges and responsibilities of being in charge of groups. As we talk, I am thinking to myself it's as if this nice man named Charlie has been sent to deliver a message to me, a message to think about my own future and not just about the well-being of others. Charlie may have been right in insisting yesterday that ours was a 'fated' meeting. He's much wiser than

I first thought and I appreciate having been reminded of what I need to do for myself.

Back in my room, I lay awake thinking of where in the world I would settle. if I ever did. Someday I would have to "take myself off the road" as the wise man Charlie said. Maybe that day was coming soon.

CHAPTER FIFTEEN

CAIRO RHYTHM

"Home is not where you live but where
they understand you."
Christion Morgenstern

Strange, I think, how scent can evoke so many memories and emotions. As I step into the blinding sunlight at Cairo airport, I'm intoxicated by the scent of Cairo - jasmine with camel dung and cumin, accented by a spritz of diesel and a note of Drakkar Noir cologne. Sometimes, on a winter's day in New England, I've been known to open my empty suitcase just to savor the lingering scent of Egypt. If only perfume oil could be blended from this, it could make the long absences from my beloved Egypt tolerable.

Work has taken me to so many other parts of the world and all the while my heart longs to sail in a felucca on the Nile.

Tour programs, both my own and for other companies, take me to destinations as far flung as Alaska, Peru, Europe and Bermuda; so many places, I can scarcely recall. Then, the opportunity to go back to Egypt appears when I'm contacted by a group of geologists who are studying erosion on the Sphinx. I'm giddy with excitement at having some free time on my own in Cairo following the study tour and I plan to stay in Cairo for three months until April when the magnolia trees bloom in the Back Bay of Boston.

Past the crush of taxi drivers, all shouting, and frantically gesturing for attention, I spot my regular driver, Hossam. I learned long ago that having a taxi driver of one's own is the easiest way to manage in the traffic nightmare that is Cairo. Hossam has become an essential part of my life in Egypt over the years. The old black and white taxi gleams in the sunlight and my young driver stands apart in his best clothes, his wide eyes searching the crowd.

"*Ahlen we Sahlen*," hello and welcome. Hossam places my bags in the car and we take off in a cloud of dust toward the city, the latest song from superstar Amr Diab blaring, the taxi bumping and shimmying to the beat on what seem to be no shock absorbers at all.

"You need new shocks, Hossam," I call out above the music.

"Socks? You need socks? No problem, we stop on the way."

I recall the last time he tried to be helpful and shop for me. I had asked him to pick up a dozen boxes of Entocid to allay mummy tummy in my next group of women who were arriving soon. He had emerged, red-faced, from the pharmacy; arms piled high with large boxes of spermicide. Relief washed over his expression when I sent him back in with more specific instructions for the tiny boxes of antibiotic.

I don't try to explain about the shocks, but instead inquire about his family, noting a new photo on the dashboard, that of a smiling face of a tiny girl with a large pink bow on her dark curls.

"My new daughter, Hadiyya." Hossam beams with pride as he hands me the photo.

I sigh and look closely at the child's remarkable dark eyes. "*Masha'Allah,* she is "*hadiyya*" for sure, truly a gift."

Hossam turns fully around in the driver's seat to chat with me about his new baby, laughing and offering a Cleopatra cigarette as the car steers on it's own. He knows I don't smoke, but he must offer out of custom. I motion to the road ahead and he turns back to his driving with a laugh.

Along Sharia el Haram, Pyramids Road, the heavily loaded camels vie for space alongside shiny black Mercedes and tour buses, as pedestrians dart nonchalantly through the confusion. I can just make out the hazy outline of the pyramids in the distance, nearly obscured by the smog of the encroaching city. We veer slightly and they disappear, peeking out now and then from rooftops like a mirage.

We careen toward an oncoming donkey cart piled high with garlic cloves; a small boy of no more than 5 years old perches high atop the cargo and waves at the cars below. "You are welcome in Egypt!" he calls out. The child's father waves too, a *miswak*, a makeshift sugar cane toothbrush between his teeth. My heart jumps to my throat as we narrowly miss the cart.

"Relax, sit back, Miss Kara," Hossam reassures me. "You

are safe now, you're home in Egypt. *Mafeesh mushkelat,* no problems here."

Honking his horn in concert with hundreds of other drivers, all of them making this racket for no particular reason, we navigate the traffic. Red lights are merely a gentle suggestion and drivers ignore them.

"Does a stop light mean anything at all here in Cairo?" I ask.

"Yes, Hossam says, "It means try to stop if you are able, but we are never able."

Negotiating traffic in Cairo is an intuitive process and the effect is surreal. Hossam spies an opening in the gridlock and gestures with his right hand from his forehead, focuses his gaze and points his index finger directly ahead, moving through the parting rows of cars. This gesture is for the benefit of other drivers, who acquiesce without a hint of annoyance. Deftly grabbing the wheel with his right hand, his left arm reaches out the window as he opens and closes his hand in an absurd grabbing manner to create a flashing signal. I've come to understand that there's an intricate language of gestures all drivers in Cairo know and they manage with remarkably few accidents.

"Is that supposed to be your directional? Very creative!"

Hossam laughs in response as he continues to weave around donkeys, camels, and trucks. A family of five passes us, helmet-less, piled circus-style on a moped and loaded down with black plastic grocery bags.

We break free of the traffic and I resume breathing, recalling the old proverb, "Trust in Allah, but tether your camel." All camels tethered as best as possible, there's no choice now but to surrender and trust. The late afternoon call to prayer begins to drone as I relax against the threadbare back-rest, a wave of jet lag washing over me, and I fall asleep for the rest of the ride.

CHAPTER SIXTEEN

ZEMALEK

*The adhan, like the ringing of church bells, calls us to
gratitude, appreciation and attentiveness. That's why the
adhan can be good for everyone -- even for those who
aren't Muslim, and even for those who don't believe
in God.*

The four-story building that is to be my home in
Cairo for three months is in a heavily populated
section of Zemalek. I enter the cool marble foyer
and ponder my next move with my heavy cargo. There's no
light bulb in the staircase lamp, as is usual in apartment buildings in Cairo, so I wait for my eyes to adjust to the darkness
before I open the gate to the ancient cage lift. I slide the suitcases and then myself through the accordion-style wrought
iron door, shift my hip to keep the door from closing, maneuvering the awkward case inside the lift. I press the third floor

button and the contraption awakens with a start as though no one has asked anything of it in a long while. It shakes and rattles its way to the top floor and bumps to a stop. Leaning against the wall to catch my breath, I determine to give away half of the clothes I brought and learn to travel light.

Upon entering my spacious new flat, I congratulate myself on this great find in 'Cairo Life' magazine for just three hundred U.S. dollars per month, no security deposit. This outrageously low rent includes all utilities, my favorite exotic style of low, rich-hued Arabic furniture, oriental rugs, and mosaic tile. There's a fully equipped sunny kitchen, daily maid service, and a massive rotary dial phone that, with coaxing, does on occasion connect a call. If I'm efficient with my words, I can get a message through before the line dies.

I luxuriate in the bath as the travel weariness begins to dissolve away. Thirty minutes later, still disoriented and dizzy with exhaustion, I slip between the deliciously soft cotton sheets and fall into a travel sleep, the kind that starts with a sudden feeling of stopping short, and then falling into a well.

The blaring sound of the *adhan* awakens me before dawn, my heart pounding. How could it be so impossibly loud, as if the imam is right here in the room with me? Dazed, I stumble to the bedroom window and lean out into the cool air. Not ten feet away, squeezed between the two apartment buildings, is one of the legendary 1000 minarets of Cairo. There's a mosque on every street in the city and I have unknowingly chosen a building directly across the alleyway from one of them.

The sound permeates even the hidden catacombs with its haunting, mesmerizing cry. *Allahu Akhbar, Bismah Allah el Rahman el Rahim*, God is great, kind, and merciful. I've always loved the sound of the muezzin call as it echoes from the east, before the first rays of sunlight touch the forehead of the Sphinx, as it has for millennia. I like to envision the sound moving in a serpentine pattern across the vast city, the haunting cry weaving and dancing its way into the villages. Five times a day the world is reminded to pause, be silent, and turn its attention to God. I love this tradition and am certain it contributes to the calm good nature of Egyptians. However, I cannot fall back to sleep after being shaken by the volume of the call.

There's no choice now but to begin the day as dawn breaks; this certainly is not the leisurely sleep-in I had planned. I've now missed the prime sleeping period, that one brief lull in traffic that occurs just before dawn. Soon the traffic noise will start up again and it will be impossible to get any rest. Even the earplugs that I travel with are not much use once the street noise begins.

Still shaken and foggy from lack of sleep, I begin to get settled into the flat, walking aimlessly in circles, and at the end not knowing what I've done with my most essential items. The housekeeper arrives and sets out to mop the already spotless floor on hands and knees, proceeding to hand-wash my travel clothes, furtively grabbing them from my hands in a quick, almost rude, gesture. The woman doesn't respond to Arabic or English, only bows her head, and avoids all eye contact. This subservience annoys me and I begin to suspect there's some hidden reason behind her obsessive behavior. I've never encountered an Egyptian so unfriendly and reticent to speak, especially a female. Egyptians have a minimal sense of boundaries and are the chattiest and most friendly people I know. At last it occurs to me that the landlord is trying to appease me with this obsequious and unnecessary maid service, now that the real reason for the low rent is apparent. He doesn't want me to leave. After all, only a Muslim fanatic or a person with no hearing whatsoever could endure the five deafening calls each day.

CHAPTER SEVENTEEN
THE LUXOR GRAPEVINE

"You can tell whether a man is clever by his answers. You can tell whether a man is wise by his questions."
Naguib Mahfouz, writer, Nobel laureate

There's an excellent opportunity to practice my Arabic as I do my errands in the neighborhood, but everyone wants to practice their English. Back in my flat at Zemalek, I put away groceries and then haul the heavy black rotary phone onto my lap. I hit the button repeatedly to get a dial tone, and then coax it to connect me with my old friend, Mostapha, in Luxor. After many attempts, I'm about to give up when the call goes through.

"*Marhaba*, welcome home! When are you coming to see us?" Handsome and intense, with piercing dark eyes, a quick intuition, and an even quicker temper, Mostapha is one of my slightly dangerous male friends; one I choose to keep as a friend in spite of my better judgment. I trust him in the way one trusts a wild animal that has been tamed and become devoted to its human, always with a bit of caution and distance. I keep in mind that my friend's nature is essentially feral.

Each time I'm in Luxor, I visit him to swap stories in his narrow shop, surrounded by glass cases overflowing with brilliant-colored unset gemstones. Sometimes we work together doing energy healing on clients in exchange for whatever donation they wish to give.

He's delighted, as always, to see that I have arrived with a stack of new books on healing and metaphysics. Today is a quiet day in the shop and we sit and talk as Mostapha shows me his newest shipment of brilliant, flawless lapis stones, the smaller of which he will turn into pendants and earrings to sell. Most of the raw stones will go to foreign merchants who turn them into expensive jewelry to be sold in the best shops throughout the world. Mustapha periodically gets up and paces like a caged lion, his energy and presence far too large for the confined area of the small space. He looks out the window at his stooped and aged father who sits playing tawla with his friends.

"When Abu is gone, I will leave here forever. I never want to see Luxor again once my father dies."

For as long as anyone can recall Mustapha's father, has been the village counselor. He can be found each day sitting at his round mosaic table on the sidewalk in front of the shop, wearing a loose fitting grey gallabeya, his dark blue wool scarf wrapped around his neck, a white turban intricately wrapped around his head in the traditional style of men's dress.

Today, as every day, Abu is smoking apple-cured tobacco from an ornate glass shisha pipe that rests on the sidewalk and he's oblivious to the bustle of tourists passing as he absorbs himself in an endless game with his old friends. No one in the town seems to know for certain which one of the small group of men is the eldest. Abu leans forward, one gnarled hand on his chin, and peers at the backgammon board through thick glasses, deeply engaged in the next move. A dog walks toward him and breaks his concentration and he strikes out at it with his cane. I observe that Abu has a determination and quickness with his bamboo cane that would be frightening to a child. I wonder what kind of father he was to his sons, all of whom have moved abroad except for the youngest, my friend Mostapha, who is left to care for the old man. There seems not to be a shred of joy or father/son warmth between them.

The nondescript, smoky shop is the center of local gossip and the hangout of foreign archeologists from the Chicago House Oriental Research Center nearby. Scientists and academics arrive regularly in hopes of hearing some insider information, gossip of antiquities unearthed beneath the homes of the locals. The wary villagers, always one step ahead of them, carefully guard these secrets in order not to lose their homes to an excavation. I've visited homes where a tunnel under the living room leads to underground chambers, long ago emptied of treasures sold on the black market.

"I hear there's going to be a *moulid,* a celebration, in honor of a Sufi saint today," my least favorite self-important scientist named Jacob announces. "Shouldn't you be over there checking it out, Kara? You love that voodoo spiritual stuff, don't you? I don't know how an educated person like yourself can believe in all that nonsense."

I ignore him, feeling no need to defend my beliefs, and I slide off the tall chair and put my backpack on my shoulder. "I'll come back later, after the Sufi ceremony," I tell Mostapha.

I've heard so much about the popular *moulid of El Haggag* celebrated annually in Luxor and I'm excited at an opportunity to attend. Mostapha is a secret Sufi and I practiced Sufism when I lived in Boston and we know firsthand how entrancing and beautiful a ceremony can be.

"The ceremony won't be allowed for long," growls Mostapha. "Sufism is against the law now, along with everything else that people love. The ugly face of extremism is everywhere."

We had been heartbroken to learn that following Sadat's assassination, Sufism was declared by Islamic clerics to be contrary to Islam and so the peaceful religion was abolished in Muslim countries.

My friend Mostapha is angry and on a tangent. "The only difference in the rhetoric of all these new fanatical groups all over the world now is the name of their God, and of the prophet who dictated "The Truth" as they call it. I'm so sick of their lies and how they keep making up new laws and calling it all the word of God. If everyone in the world could graduate from religion to spirituality, we might have a chance at peace."

"I wouldn't share that with anyone else if I were you, son. It's dangerous to have thoughts like that!" shouts Abu as he enters the shop, whacking his cane against the glass case with a sharp rap. I jump, startled by the sudden outburst from the old man, who is normally silent.

"You'll bring trouble to all of us with your crazy talk." He turns to me with an angry stare, "You young people have no respect for tradition. Always wanting to change things. It's time we went back to the old ways."

Mostapha motions to the young boy who waits for a chance to earn a few piasters by running errands. "Kara, take Mounir with you. Here's money to buy him some food, whatever he wants." He hands me a 50-pound note, more than enough for snacks.

I don't wish to be present for another argument over politics, family values, and religion. I take the hand of the thin child and we leave for the park. Black-uniformed police have already arrived with their batons and a crowd has formed in anticipation of the celebration.

The tiny boy and I walk over to the food stand and I buy a falafel sandwich and a Fanta for him and he runs off to a patch of grass to sit and eat.

Three musicians are playing soothing, hypnotic Sufi music, the scent of frankincense floats on the air and bystanders sway with eyes closed. A few men in robes and ornately wrapped turbans are turning in place, arms at first crossed over their chests and then raised heavenward in blissful expression of worship The atmosphere is reminiscent to me of a love-in on Cambridge Common, in the 1970s, and I revisit those idealistic times in my mind. Already I'm becoming high with the energy, the frankincense, and the trance-inducing music. In just these few moments amidst such joy, my mood has brightened considerably from when I left Mustapha's shop. The lush aroma of Turkish coffee wafts past, and feel I'm back in Cafe Algiers on Brattle Street during my years as a transient among the regulars, a collection of foreigners and misfits who didn't really belong anywhere.

A sweet-faced young officer steps into the center of the crowd; head down as if apologizing for the interruption. "This singing and whirling about is a disturbance of the peace," the officer says in a timid voice, pretending to overlook the fact that half the town is in attendance and thoroughly enjoying the break in the workday. The shade of the trees is cool and refreshing and a vendor is circulating with a large brass samovar of sweet tea. There is no sign of any disturbance, only a happy gathering of local people.

"Everyone must leave now," the officer declares as he lifts his chest and looks around at his neighbors, the same people who made up his extended family all the years he grew up on the streets of Luxor. They observe him and nod in agreement, but remain where they are.

The officer is standing beside me and I ask him, "Do you really believe that?" He shifts his rifle to the other shoulder, leans toward me, and replies in a low voice, "You know it doesn't matter what I believe, we all just have to do our job. I am sorry if I ruined your day."

"I understand you don't have any say in this crazy rule," I reply. "It's just a shame people cannot be allowed to enjoy such a simple pleasure. Look at how much fun they're having."

The young man nods in agreement. I notice beads of perspiration on his face as he looks around at the crowd with a worried expression. He is obviously reluctant to use force to move the people out of the area. I want to hug him and reassure him that no one holds him responsible for the narrow-mindedness of the officials. Hugging a police officer in public is out of the question in most places in the world and so I suppress my sympathetic maternal instinct and instead convey my feelings with a smile as I touch his arm and say goodbye. Taking a quick photo of the gathering, I leave, along with the rest of the crowd.

Mostapha waits to hear my report about the ceremony. There's no one in the shop and so we can speak freely now. He's scowling deeply and there's rage in his voice.

"There were questions today from the neighbors about you being here," he says, "The other shopkeepers are curious about our relationship and are searching for a reason to start problems. They want to know why you sit alone with me and other men when it's haram."

He knows I'm aware of the strict Muslim rule, especially here in Upper Egypt, which forbids women to be alone with men they are not related or married to. I look out the window at the locals all around us and feel annoyed that they have nothing better to do. We need to be especially careful in our inquiries about the Zar, we agree, since the active Luxor grapevine could stir up too much attention.

"I've noticed too," I tell Mostapha, "things are changing not only here in Luxor, but all over Egypt. The people are becoming cautious and suspicious of one another."

"Especially women like you, who travel alone. After you left, Abu accused you of being a *schura*, a sorceress, and says you've put a curse on me to influence my thoughts."

I laugh. "It would take some powerful magic to influence a man as stubborn as yourself."

Mostapha smiles and nods in agreement, "I just don't want you to get hurt. At least cover your hair when you come to

Luxor so you don't draw so much attention to yourself. You know it's much more conservative here in Upper Egypt than in Cairo."

"No, I refuse to cover my hair in this heat. I only wear hijab when I'm in the desert to keep the sand and sun off my head. I'll wear black shrouds as soon as I see you and Abu and the rest of the men wearing them. Let them suspect me, I have nothing to hide."

We say goodbye and I hail a *caleche* on the dusty Temple Road. Placing my belongings on the seat, I climb into the colorfully decorated horse-drawn carriage for the five-minute ride back to the small hotel where I'm staying for a few nights. I could have easily walked back to the hotel, but I enjoy the happy clip-clop of the horse's hooves on the pavement as the carriage moves along the corniche, the embankment road that follows the Nile. Bells jingle and the yellow fringe of the bonnet sways as we move along through the late afternoon traffic and my mind is distracted from the upsetting conversations about hijabs and Sufis and Shuras.

The sun is returning to Amenti, the West Bank, where the Valley of the Kings can be glimpsed; the ancient limestone hills aglow with a final wash of apricot and lavender. The effect of the backdrop is surreal. Feluccas drift on the deep blue water as the ferry returns packed with weary workers and faded tour groups who walk in small groups up the embankment. They disperse to the luxury of their waiting cruise boats, their boarding passes and black plastic shopping bags in hand, excitedly chatting about their purchases.

I overhear two American couples with deep Southern accents. "That vendor offered my husband 500 camels for me.

My Stanley counter-offered with 800. At least I know my husband cares."

"That fella's flattery worked," her tough-talking friend, replies. "Look how much money you spent in his shop. That guy knew exactly what he was doing. You went in for one scarf and bought fifteen, plus a wall hanging that you didn't even like when we first went in there."

Her husband puts his arm around his shop-a-holic wife and teases, "Oh, it's okay sweetheart, It's all a game, and you fell for it. Not to say you aren't worth 500 camels." She slaps his arm in pretend anger and everyone laughs.

"Now, if he'd gone up to 1000, you'd be sleeping in a tent out in the desert tonight with a guy named Mohamed."

"And you'd be the owner of a thousand smelly camels," she retorts.

"I don't know how I'd get them onto the plane, but I'd sure have a story to tell our friends in South Carolina."

I'm glad to see people enjoying Egypt and contributing to the economy. The foreign atmosphere and strange customs are such a contrast for Westerners and the interaction can create an opening for tolerance and acceptance, or at least I like to think it does.

My wizened old driver calls out to another caleche driver who has pulled up close to us, our wheels almost touching. The two old men appear to be sparring partners as they shout back and forth with bravado. Within minutes we're moving and they're in fierce competition, calling out commands to their camels as they whip the poor beasts and careen through the streets, dust flying and pedestrians running for safety. I hold onto the only strap as the carriage leans into a curve on one wheel. A passenger in the other carriage screams, her face in terror.

We reach an intersection where the driver swerves without warning, cuts in front of a pick up truck, and veers into a left turn off the main road, passing the caleche of his friend. My driver slows, slaps his thigh, leans around, and looks back at me with a toothless grin. He hits his chest, shrieking with laughter, "I'm Ben-Hur, the champion."

"You're *magnoon*, crazy, I yell at him. Stop right here and let me out!" My clothes are mud-spattered and my eyes burn from the dust. "No baksheesh for you, mister," I tell him as I jump down, but he doesn't seem to care. I look around for the other caleche that he was racing to see how the woman inside is doing, but the carriage is out of sight.

CHAPTER EIGHTEEN

NILE DANGER

*Nothing hurts a good soul and kind heart more than to
live amongst people who cannot understand it.*
Arab saying

The idyllic, dimly lit rendezvous for lovers, Badour is
a 1920s houseboat-turned-restaurant. All three
levels are filled with dinner guests nightly and yet it
feels intimate. Mostapha and I, not lovers in any sense of the
word except spiritually, share a *mezza*, an appetizer plate
consisting of tiny bowls of *baba ganoush, hummus, tameyya*,
and *warra eineb*. This is followed by a tableside *shisha*. The
aromatic apple smoke always puts me in a dreamy, giggly
mood, even though there's nothing in it but tobacco. As a non-
smoker, it doesn't take much.

Mostapha maintains his intense demeanor no matter what
the circumstance. My antics will elicit a smile at times, but he

is not a man to laugh easily. I suppose that's why he likes me so much. I imagine I must be like a pet chimpanzee for him, or perhaps a kitten. He looks around to be sure we're alone, leans toward me, and says in a low voice, "I found a contact for a Zar ceremony. By tomorrow I'll know more."

He's not forthcoming with any more information and the details don't really concern me anyway. I'm only interested in experiencing the forbidden ceremony among the powerful women healers of Egypt. The less I know about the illegal channels for our connection, the better. If something were to go wrong and lead to questioning, I would honestly know nothing and I'd be in far less trouble than the local Zar hosts who would be jailed. As far Mostapha is concerned, he enjoys doing things that are forbidden. I've noticed that it's his kind of secret rebellion against authority.

"Soon you'll have your chance to take part in a real Zar ceremony, I hope it's all you expect it to be." He looks at me with his usual solemn expression. "I still don't understand why this is so important to you."

"Of course you do. Don't pretend you're not excited to take part as well. You know that certain music creates a trance state and has been a part of every traditional culture and religious practice throughout history."

He nods as a slight smile begins to light up his black eyes. "Of course, it has always been an important part of every religion. In fact, I plan on going with you."

"Good. What do you think it is about the trance state that is so terrifying to some people? Why would anyone want to ban it? Rhythm and dance are as essential as breath. Nothing else makes us feel so awake and alive."

"Most people don't want to be as awake or as alive as you are," Mostapha teases. "You make them nervous. Sometimes you even make me nervous."

"Oh, really? The energy in that shop of yours is so powerful it creates a force field that reaches out into the street. People are strangely drawn in without knowing why. Some are intrigued and stay, but you see how others almost run back out in fear?"

Mostapha is amused. "It's not me, it's all just energy. What people think doesn't concern me anyway. If they're scared of me, I can't change that. I just try to help the people who ask for my help. I like feeling that I make a difference for the people who come to me."

"I know, and you do help people every day," I assure him.

I'm one of the few he has told about his studies in the Sinai every summer, with a blind Sufi master. Sufism was declared by Islamic clerics to be contrary to Islam and so all parts of the peaceful religion have been abolished in most Muslim countries. He seems grateful for my acknowledgement of his healing work, and that I never mention to anyone that he's a Sufi. We trust one another and there's a bond between us in spite of our differences.

"I can't explain how the stones speak to me, Kara," he says. "My intuition tells me which ones are right for each person and how they should use them." Mostapha opens his hands and shakes his head. "Sometimes the people come back years later and tell me that I helped them. You know I don't go looking for customers, I'm just waiting there in the shop all day for anyone who wants to find me."

"I know, you are a natural healer. And I do understand that

the stones speak to you. After all, they are living entities, each with its own unique vibration."

He leans toward me in an affectionate way that is out of character and takes—my hand. "I like when you're working beside me. We're a good team. We understand each other."

A memory comes to mind of the last time we worked together with a European group all day in the small, crowded space of his shop. I had touched his arm in conversation and he'd pulled back as if he had been burned, his expression instantaneously changing from joy to defensiveness. Something about his mood is different tonight, however.

"You could stay in Luxor every winter with me, get away from the cold weather back home, and work beside me a lot more." He waits for me to say something. "You know I care for you."

I tread carefully, not wanting to offend him. "We might not get along so well if we were to see one other that often. Besides, you know I have obligations back home."

The Nile is dark and moody and the night sky is growing misty as the boathouse gently sways. In the corner, a musician sings a soulful *mawaal*, a pleading, plaintive cry. His head bowed, his body leaning in, he seduces poignant responses from the strings of the oud. The enticing atmosphere washes over me as I imagine a night of passionate lovemaking. It's been too long since I enjoyed the embrace of an attractive man, the thrill of an affair. I have no illusions of it being more than that with Mostapha. An affair, however, is not what my pensive friend is implying. He seems to be looking for something for which I am not seeking. We are of very different natures and I sense we could hurt one another very deeply.

For five years, our twice-yearly meetings have been defined by the tiny space of the gem shop, and long conversations about archeology, religion, and mysticism. The physical attraction has always been there, with the unspoken rule that it would go no further. But why, I wonder? When did we come to this agreement? To others in the restaurant we must appear as a couple in love, enraptured in conversation. I notice the sweep of his long lashes and the wisp of curly black hair that shows above his freshly pressed dress shirt. He has the fit, clean-shaven look I love and the graceful hands and smooth long fingers typical of Egyptians, the hands of an artist and mystic. We're both long-divorced and free, and yet nothing romantic has ever taken place between us.

My thoughts are abruptly interrupted as the waiter approaches with long metal tongs holding a glowing hot charcoal. He leans towards us and places the coal with great care on top of the burning shisha pipe.

"Careful, please," he says as he moves the tall, ornate glass pipe closer to our table. "It is very dangerous." The waiter's serious gaze sets upon mine for just an instant. "Very dangerous," he repeats.

I sense that his comment was meant for me and was in reference to my dinner partner. He then defers to Mostapha with a slight bow and averts his gaze toward the fiery coal. He looks at me again before he leaves, as if waiting for my acknowledgment of his warning and the danger that lurks beneath my companion's calm exterior. I nod slightly and the caution light resumes its steady flash in my mind as I recall the perils of getting too close to danger. The volatile nature of my friend has surfaced on only a few occasions when he perceived an insult from another local and it took three men to hold him back. I never want to be the focus of that kind of fury. I have always sensed a seething pit of pain and rage in my friend. Although I would not be so insensitive as to bring up the topic, over the years I had heard rumors that his mother died in childbirth. They say his father made the small child pay for that loss all of his life with frequent beatings and severe treatment. Whatever painful and dark memories lurk there in my friend's past, I am deeply sorry and I respect the healthy distance between us.

"I must be going, the wine and the smoke have made me so sleepy," I say as I rise from my chair.

Mostapha pays the check and follows to escort me to a caleche and I thank him and say goodnight. He gently pulls me back toward him. "Are you sure you have to leave now? We could walk along the corniche for a while," he says, a smoldering gaze in his dark eyes. He strokes my cheek in an uncharacteristic manner, touching my hair, and I turn away.

I don't dare risk returning his affection, although I do care for him. My instinct for survival is much stronger than my desire for male company. "Yes, very sure." I say as I hop up the step and into the horse drawn carriage.

"*Yalla!*" The driver yells and the horse trots forward. I settle back, breathe deeply, and savor the mild night air on my skin. Out of the spell of the place and the man, I'm thankful to be free of the intensity of it all.

The change of atmosphere has brought me fully to my senses by the time I arrive at my small hotel. I settle into the single bed with a book and a cup of tea and think to myself that the only thing really missing right now is a purring cat beside me. I miss having a cat so much, but it would be unfair to leave an animal for months at a time while I travel. I fall asleep recalling my beloved Scottish Fold Rashid and the comfort of his presence at the foot of my bed. I feel the pad of his feet across the bed and then his warmth as he settles with his head resting on my leg. I am certain his spirit is here with me, guarding me as I sleep. One day he'll come back to me as another big orange cat; he'll incarnate again as a character cat to make me laugh.

As I drift off to sleep, my thoughts turn to romance and I wonder if I'll ever meet my soul partner. I feel certain that he exists somewhere and is searching for me as well. My thoughts must have reached him because he appears in a fleeting dream.

We walk toward each other on a busy city street. He carries a leather valise on his shoulder and is dressed in city clothes, casually elegant. He nods hello and smiles, as in dreams before, those adorable dimples appearing in his cheeks. His eyes tell me to stay, even though we are both rushing to our work places. I have a feeling of being overwhelmed by obligations and distractions, of not enough time. I turn from him and go my way through the tall revolving glass doors of the office building in Boston where I am to collect documents for my next overseas assignment.

THE SOUND OF A KNOCK ON MY DOOR AWAKENS ME WITH a start and I realize the sun is up and I've slept late. Pulling on my robe, I unbolt and open the door hoping it isn't Mostapha offering a mid-morning romantic interlude.

"Message for you, Miss Kara," the young hotel errand boy hands me a folded note on a tray. It's written in the way my friend Mostapha speaks, guarded and cryptic.

"*Thursday, Midnight. Will find you. GO HOME NOW.*"

Why must I go home today? He knows I despise being told what to do. I settle down on the balcony with my coffee and wonder what the rush is for me to leave Luxor. Perhaps there have been more questions or he is in some kind of trouble and my presence here would make matters worse for him. I don't want to cause any problems and so decide it best I leave.

My single bag packed, I take a taxi the few miles to Luxor Airport. In truth, I'm glad to be heading back to Cairo now that my task of locating a Zar has been accomplished. The residents of Luxor, although nice, are even nosier than those in Cairo. I'm accustomed to the curiosity and unsolicited advice of Egyptians, but at least in a big city I have some small amount of anonymity.

My dear Uncle Zacharia will be relieved to know I'm not cavorting with the fierce jinn of Upper Egypt; instead, I am heading back to meet the more hospitable and genteel spirits of Old Cairo in a ceremony this coming Thursday night. I plan to tell my uncles and my godfather about the ceremony when it is over, but for now it must remain a secret.

"One way to Cairo," I say as I approach the ticket counter. Then, looking up at the board, I see there's a flight to Aswan leaving in a half hour and I change my plan. I'm only miles away from the light-filled, high vibration temple of Philae, dedicated to Mother Isis. It's a gentle and feminine temple, which floats like a sparkling gem upon the Nile. It seems fitting that I should make a pilgrimage to Isis and ask her blessing on my mission to contact the women of wisdom who facilitate the Zar ceremony. "Sorry, I changed my mind. Please give me a ticket to Aswan instead, and an open return to Cairo."

In Aswan, I check into a small, inexpensive hotel in time to enjoy a peaceful felucca ride and glorious sunset. As we curve around the first cataract of the Nile, the temple comes into view, bathed in empyrean light. I climb the temple steps and pass groups of tourists leaving. Their guides hold aloft signs and banners to lead them to the waiting boats. In the sacred space, I'm alone with only two silent guards who must linger until closing. They're content to let me wander wherever I like in exchange for a few pounds.

Next to the small birthing temple up on a hill I sit and gaze at the Nile and commune with Isis. The power of the Divine Mother, Isis, Queen of the Heavens, is present in the temple and in the land that makes up this floating island known as Philae. I imagine the soft blue of Isis' cloak being wrapped around my shoulders in a shimmering aura of protection, her hands resting upon my heart. I think of my own sweet mother and how much love and protection I felt from her when she held me as a child. I reflect on all the powerful women I've known and how little recognition they receive for their great contributions to humanity.

Ancient Egyptians revered their many Goddesses and paid homage to them through elaborate rituals and the building of great temples. Royal lineage could only be passed through the female bloodline, and so women held the ultimate power within the royal family. Still, the more aggressive males plotted to destroy and remove the feminine power.

☥

CHAPTER NINETEEN

DESERT DOGS & HELL HOUNDS, CAIRO

The dogs bark, but the caravan moves on.
Arab Proverb

A t the embassy gateway, breathless and parched from the hot, dusty air, I absentmindedly accept the glass of tap water offered by the young errand boy, Sami. I raise it to my lips and then catch myself. In the past, I've suffered fierce symptoms after drinking local water, the curse of all travelers.

Sami is eight years old and from the poor neighborhood of Shubra. He stands leaning on a makeshift crutch, his leg twisted and deformed. His job is to perform errands or bring refreshments to those working in the building. "Sweetie, would you do a big favor for me? Here's five pounds, please bring back a large bottled water and a soda and snack for yourself."

He hobbles back in minutes and I sit on the curbstone

beside him and empty my wallet of all my remaining coins, and then place some chewing gum and a few new pens on his tray as well. It's the pens that most delight Sami and he holds one up with glee.

"I'm learning to write, Miss Kara!" he says with a proud thump of his thin brown hand on his chest. "Soon you will get letters from your friend Sami. Will you write back to me?"

"Of course I will," I say as I hug him and hold his tiny shoulders, looking into his eyes, "and I'll bring you the photos that Noha took of us, too. Promise. Here are some envelopes with stamps on them, you just have to write my name and address and tell me all that's going on with you. What you can't say in English, you can write in Arabic."

I walk inside and greet Noha, the protégé of my godfather. She's a lovely green-eyed diplomat, soon to be posted at the Egyptian embassy in Geneva.

"Come visit me, please" she says. "In a country whose national product is money, I'm sure I'll feel out of place. I need my friends around me."

I'm halfway down the embassy stairs when she calls out, "Oh, and you must return at exactly six o'clock for an outing with your godfather. He said to pack all your belongings, everything." She shrugs, as confused as I am by this news. Intrigued, I wonder if perhaps he's found a quieter flat for me somewhere here in town.

When I return at dusk, I find him pacing outside although I'm on time. He's been stressed and in a hurry for all the years I've known him, except for those years at Harvard when we were easygoing friends. That was long ago, when he was carefree and filled with laughter and fun.

My luggage is placed in the trunk and I'm seated in the black embassy Mercedes with the dark-tinted windows and the Egyptian flag flying on the side mirror. My godfather and I sit in silence in the back seat as we are driven past the embassies of Garden City and through *Maadi*, a large district of expatriates. The ex-pat community has recreated every detail of home, complete with the British Rose Society and AA for Americans. I find this amusing and wonder why people move to this exotic place and then insist it be exactly like home. I prefer to live among the locals no matter where I am in the world.

After a long ride in distracted silence, my godfather finally announces, "Since your visit last year, I started building a place to retire. You'll love it; it's nice and quiet."

"Really? I didn't think you were free to retire. Have things changed?"

He doesn't reply and seems preoccupied and deep in thought. I know there are so many urgent political issues he's dealing with, and so I try not to disturb him with questions.

After a few more miles, we slow down at the edge of the desert where a restoration project is under development. Enormous mounds of sand and metal pipes line the road. It reminds me of the devastated war zones I've seen in newscasts. I lower the window and breathe, swallowing dust and suppressing a cough as I put it back up. The car stops at the last of the faceless buildings. Beyond this, the Sahara looms for 600 miles, all the way to Libya. I wanted more quiet, but not to be exiled to the desert! I keep my thoughts to myself, trying not to let my alarm show on my face.

An ancient doorman or *boab* is startled by the arrival of company and his bamboo walking stick falls to the ground.

Groping blindly for the stick and dragging himself to his feet, he attempts to look alert. His inflamed eyes reveal the advanced stages of *bilharzia* and the *zbeeb* or raisin on his forehead, a permanent bruise, marks a lifetime of devout prayer. I'm doubtful as to his ability to fend off intruders, but in any case, there seems to be no living thing about except for the black Saluki hound that lies by his side. The dog rises and growls and it's evident that the Saluki is the real doorman who protects the premises.

The lifts are not yet working, so we must climb the stairs to the cavernous, dark flat on the third floor. The frail old man does his best to carry one of my heavy bags through the doorway, wheezing and grunting with his first step. Dismissing him with a kind word and a generous tip, my godfather takes the second bag from him. We climb to a dimly lit hallway and enter the apartment. Although all of the windows are taped to keep out the summer *khamsin*, a fine dust has seeped through and left a layer on every surface. Boxes of opened but unpacked household supplies line the walls, waiting for someone to take residence and fill the place with the fragrance of cooking and sounds of voices and music.

We perch on the edge of plastic-covered French provincial furniture, an awkward and uncomfortable style embraced by the Egyptian upper class during the French occupation. Why not the carved wood *mashrabeyya*, the colorful mosaics and richly colored oriental rugs with stories of the people woven into them? I observe to myself that this is a house without soul, a lonely place that no human has inhabited.

I cannot bring myself to tell him I want to leave or that I already miss my noisy Zemalek neighborhood. This is his heavenly retreat from the city and his work, the stress-free future of which he dreams. In a developing democracy, or dictatorship if one is to be clear, there is no option of retirement and we both know this. As much as he disagrees with the direction of the current regime, he isn't free to render a resignation. Besides, he still holds on to his dream of a free nation and social reform for the poor and minorities. The people love and admire him and see him as one of the last of the good and honest leaders. Many times I've joined him as he dashed into a store under the pretense of buying a newspaper or a cigar and then slipped out the back entrance to lose his personal security guards.

"I'm the sacred cow," he once joked, pulling away when I reached for his arm as we walked. The guard stepped between us. "No one can touch me, so don't try." He was making light of a situation, which in fact caused him distress, and I could hear it in his voice.

In the echoing, empty flat, we sit in silence for a moment. "It's yours for as long as you want to stay, *habibti*. The phone is hooked up so you should be able to call taxis whenever you need to. When Adam comes back to Cairo, you can both live here. It's so much quieter than that flat you rented in Zemalek." He glances at his watch, kisses my cheek, and jumps up from the couch, "Now I have to go back to work."

He's gone before I can explain to him that Adam has no intention of returning to Egypt, that he's making his own way in the world now as an adult. The door clicks shut, my godfather is gone, and I am in total silence.

My head is spinning with questions. Was I left alone in this godforsaken cavern at the deserts' edge for my comfort, I wonder, or was it in part to keep me out of mischief? I pick up the phone to call my friend Sherine in Cairo, and am further dismayed that there's no dial tone. I search the cardboard boxes for a teakettle and then find my stash of strong Egyptian Lipton tea and a half package of tea biscuits in my luggage. I didn't bring much in the way of provisions since I had no idea where my godfather was taking me. He has even less attachment to eating than I do and I'm sure it never entered his mind. Tea and biscuits in hand, I light the gas stove with a match. At least the stove is working. I sit at the kitchen table and stare at my dusty, overstuffed luggage and wonder if I can drag it back downstairs and get out of here. I feel less defeated, having been revived by my tea break and decide to check out the possibilities.

Downstairs, I find the boab and his canine companion sleeping again at the entrance. I say hello but the man doesn't stir and so I tap his arm lightly. The saluki hound crouches, half rises and eyes me with suspicion, a low growl emitting from his throat. The animal looks as if it just leapt off the wall of a pharaoh's tomb, menacing and lean with the pointed ears of a jackal. I step back, avert my gaze from his, and fold my arms over my body as the animal ponders an attack. The old man stirs and peers at me with one eye.

"*Estenna ya Anubis*, Stay," he tells the dog.

I speak slowly in Arabic so as not to provoke the dog. "How far is it to a market or somewhere I might catch a taxi?"

"Very far, too far, not possible," the old man replies in a harsh voice, followed by a dismissive flick of his wrist as if I'm a fly that landed on his arm. He adjusts the worn, folded prayer shawl under his head and goes back to sleep. Anubis appears to be smiling in triumph, his teeth slightly bared, his amber eyes narrowed, and his sharp ears at attention.

Relenting, I climb the stairs and retire to one of the dark bedrooms with my second cup of tea and my journal. I find a bag of nuts in my purse from the day before and that suffices as my dinner. For the first time since being in Egypt, I'm lonely. Night has arrived and the howling desert dogs in the courtyard below break the silence. I pull up the covers and shiver, pondering how hungry those poor emaciated creatures must be. I would throw them some leftover biscuits, but the windows can't be opened without breaking the tape. I cannot see them in the darkness, but wonder if they're the medium-sized brown dogs that seem to be everywhere in Mediterranean countries.

There are no other inhabitants of the three-story building from what I can see as I peer out the window at darkened apartments and listen for any sound of people returning home from work. The only other human is the boab who is too elderly and infirm to see or hear any problem that might arise. Oddly, my life is in the care of the saluki named Anubis. Although he has no use for me, I send Anubis my thoughts of appreciation. Uneasy and restless, I realize I must leave this place that has no soul, no signs of life. I feel unsafe and long for the comfort of human presence, even if only through a wall. I muffle the barking of the desert dogs with the soulful voice of Um Kalthum on my headphones as I plot my escape for the following day.

The strategy complete, I settle into writing a long letter to Adam. I describe to him my new situation, careful to downplay the howling hellhounds lest he worry too much. His college roommates, who cannot imagine having such a strange mother, always await the arrival of my letters with excitement, gathering in Adam's dorm room for each installment of the story.

Alone in the empty flat on the edge of the Western Desert, I feel homesick and my heart aches to see my son. I reflect that of all the potential mothers on earth, Adam chose to come to me and I'm so grateful. Yet, I know it's time to let him go, to support him in moving into his own life's path, his own destiny. I just hope he won't conform and become one of the masses of materialistic and shallow people who find no joy in life. I pray I've done a good job in nurturing the qualities of individuality, tolerance, and adventure in my only child. I knew for certain he always felt greatly loved and that he's going into the world with an open and loving heart. Perhaps too open and trusting like his mother. I raised him to believe that it's better to feel too deeply than to not feel at all.

The hellhounds cease their barking and I fall asleep and dream about those happy years when I raised my son and always knew where he was. Whether near or at a distance, my worrying over him never fully ceases.

CHAPTER TWENTY
SEARCH FOR THE ZAR

"It is difficult to free fools from the chains they revere."
Voltaire

Morning arrives at last I'm am ready to bolt out of the flat and get back to Zemalek. Anubis watches me with suspicion as I step out the door, craning his long neck and leaning his head forward as his eyes record my every move. He's a beauty with his silken ebony fur and the rare 'kiss of Allah' white marking on his forehead. I try to talk with him, but he snarls, gives a warning growl, and bares his teeth. "Who's a good doggie?" doesn't work on Anubis, who's taking none of that kind of talk. I step away and bow to him, giving him his full honor as top dog. Employed during wartime, Salukis are known to run up to 30 mph and they are superb trackers. I've never been much of a runner even on my best days and realize I would be easy prey for him.

The half-hour walk from the dusty complex of new buildings leads me into a tree-lined ex-pat neighborhood. The residents, mostly foreign contractors working on the desert
restoration project, speak to each other in German and French.
I'm relieved to hear human voices and to see an actual neighborhood, although I am an outsider. They wave and greet me
as I pass. I continue on for another mile or so to a small corner
market. At a taxi stand outside the market, I negotiate with a
driver to take me back to the empty apartment building so I
can collect my luggage and get back to Zemalek.

When I return in the taxi, the old man and Anubis again
lay stretched out and snoring in front of the entrance. The
driver and I tiptoe past and dash upstairs as Anubis growls in
his sleep. We bring down my luggage, depositing it in the
trunk. The sound of the trunk closing wakens the sleeping
duo and I jump into the taxi and wave goodbye. Anubis
looks relieved to be rid of me, sighs, and puts his head back
down. I know I'll need to explain my quick departure to my
godfather, but he's out of the country and won't return for at
least a few weeks. I feel I've escaped prison as I head home to
the lively *Sharia Mohammed Heshmet* in Zemalek. The
entryway of the apartment building is cool and dark and
smells of cumin and cooking oil. I'm happy to be back in my
own space. The flat is immaculate and the sullen maid is not
there yet. I unpack then go to the kitchen to make a cup
of tea.

"You have garbage today?" The *zabaleen*, the garbage
collector, calls out from the fire escape at the kitchen window.
He and generations of his family are doomed to collect the
garbage of Cairo, turning it into usable items that they sell to

support themselves. Egypt's untouchables, the zabaleen, live in squalor in the City of the Dead amongst the tombs and rubble.

"No, I've been away, thank you," I tell him. The mid-morning adhan begins and I smile at the loud voice ringing through the flat. I must admit I've grown fond of the punctuation of the call to prayer that marks the five segments of the day. I've even begun to feel a sense of order in the regularity of it. For certain, the sound of the adhan is more comforting than that of howling desert dogs and relentless wind blowing sheets of sand from the desert.

The following evening I prepare to leave for the long-awaited Zar ceremony in Old Cairo, the poorest part of town and a place where visitors seldom venture after dark. My stomach is in knots with anticipation and the fear of being caught doing something forbidden. I frequently break rules and it has always been my nature, but I'm not inherently a good criminal. And, I'm certain I wouldn't be a good prisoner either.

I leave the flat wearing loose white linen pants, a long white brocaded shirt, and a blue and green shawl over my shoulders to protect against the night chill. I take only a small purse containing my keys, passport, and photos of family members and my camera in the unlikely event I'm allowed to take a photo of the ceremony. Closing the door and heading down the cement stairs, I turn, dash back upstairs and grab a handful of Bic pens, small notepads, and candy for any children I might see along the way.

It's too late in the evening to call my regular driver, Hossam, who is home with his wife and new baby, so I dial the number on a card I find in the flat inside the Cairo directory.

It's been left there by a previous tenant, who, I assume, was happy with the service. The taxi arrives and the driver looks angry and unkempt. I get in and hand him a piece of paper with the Old Cairo address in Arabic. He pushes his way into the traffic and then turns, shakes the paper, and says in a loud, harsh voice, "This address is a very bad part of town, why are you going there? What kind of woman are you?"

I'm accustomed to the incessant but friendly prying of Egyptians, but not this kind of open hostility. "I have to meet a friend."

He mutters something under his breath about foreign women being *sharmoutas*, whores. I reply in Arabic that he's rude and what I do is none of his business. Embarrassed that I understood his ranting, he turns up the Koran sermon and ignores me as he drives at breakneck speed across town.

After a half hour, we arrive at a desolate street where the only sign of life is a tall, gaunt figure standing in the shadows under a bridge. I realize this must be our contact, fittingly mysterious.

The taxi driver refuses to let me out. "Enti magnouna, you are insane!" he repeats for the third time. "Only a sharmouta walks here alone! I won't let you out here, I'm taking you back to Zemalek."

Just then, I see Mostapha arrive in a taxi that pulls up and stops in front of us. He gets out and assures my irate driver that he is responsible for my safety. Sharp words are exchanged in rapid fire and their voices are becoming increasingly loud. I sense that a *dowsha*, a noisy confrontation, is about to escalate and I know from experience that in seconds the neighborhood will be out in the street to intervene. A noisy outburst is the common and acceptable way for people to let off steam. Still, I find it disturbing and I hesitate to draw attention in this way to our clandestine meeting with the Zar. I sit silently waiting for some resolution, praying it doesn't involve a fistfight.

Back in the States, such minor disputes will sometimes lead to gun violence, and I remind myself that in Egypt such reactions are unknown. The driver gets out and yells and gestures, threatening us with hellfire of Satan and calling us *khanzeer wisak*, dirty swine. Bovine curses are the worst kind of insult, pigs being *haram*, forbidden.

In a flash Mostapha's dark side emerges, his voice grows low, his eyes flash, and he displays all the menace of *Ammit,* the devourer of souls. The driver stops yelling, cowers, and gets back into the car. A loud argument in Arabic is frightening enough without Mustapha's transition into a deranged superhero. I feel my body shaking with fear and my bladder is about to give way.

If the taxi driver were to find out our destination of a Zar ceremony, he'd have valid reason to turn us in to the local police where my passport would be confiscated and a great scandal would ensue.

The *dowsha* contained, Mostapha hands him the fare with a final threatening glare. The driver grabs the money, shouts curses to all sinners and fornicators who meet in the night, turns up his Koranic sermon full blast, and leaves us in a cloud of dust and fumes. It would have been a funny scene if he were not so menacing, and if such instances of intolerance and fanaticism were not becoming ever more common.

Something is changing in my beloved Egypt. I see the emergence of an element of fanaticism I had never encountered before in all my years here. I worry for the gentle, sweet-natured Egyptian people who are just trying to get through the daily challenges of life. They're just as frightened of the extreme religious element as I am and they would be the ones to suffer most from a takeover of the country by fanatics. Poor neighborhoods are often havens for dissidents and I wonder if we have made a foolish decision in coming here.

CHAPTER TWENTY ONE
WOMEN OF WISDOM

"When there is dancing, it is not only the living who are present."
Minianka proverb

The tall stranger approaches us, "*Mesah el kheer*, good evening. Follow me, please." We walk in silence over unpaved roads, dodging muddy trenches and stray cats and dogs, through a bleak and desperately poor neighborhood. I've always felt safe anywhere in Egypt and am also reassured by the confident stride of my friend Mostapha who is fiercely protective of me for reasons I don't fully understand. My white clothing is mud-splattered as I maneuver past craters of stagnant water in the road. The sound of drumming and the wafting scent of myrrh and frankincense become the trail we follow.

Our escort taps on the door of a small mud brick house. A

young woman appears and stares out a crack in the door with wide, dark eyes, assessing us from head to toe without a word. She wears all black except for a hot pink and yellow flowered hijab, the edge of which she grasps between her teeth, her head down. The cloth hides her lower face and she holds a baby on her hip. The child is exceptionally beautiful and there's a tiny blue *feance* bead on a string around her neck, as is the custom, to protect her from the evil eye. I refrain from exclaiming at the child's beauty, as this is considered a bad omen, especially coming from a stranger. The woman turns and motions to others in the house while we wait on the landing outside. After a few moments of huddled and furtive discussion among the residents, we're invited inside and told we are the only newcomers to the Zar group in many years.

A dark entryway leads to a small makeshift shrine lit by votive candles. Above the candles are three photos: One of a Sufi saint, and on either side are photos of JFK and Anwar Sadat, surrounded by a collection of faded plastic flowers and Koranic verses written on small bits of paper. In front of the photos, lying on a prayer shawl, are a Koran and a wooden cross.

"We love this man, JFK," the young woman touches the photo with a gesture to her heart.

"Me too," I reply. She at last offers a smile and the edge of the hijab drops to reveal a sweet face and gentle beauty. It's the kind of face they call *Qamr*, round and pale like the moon.

"He cared so much for the people. You know him?"

"I loved him too," I reply, "but no, I never met him, although I live near his family home. And Sadat too, I loved him so much and I cried when he was killed."

"Yes, we respect these two the most, JFK and Sadat. Always the evil ones steal the good ones away from us, but we must be strong and remember what they taught us. Inshallah their dreams for us will come true someday." Her dark eyes are filled with sorrow and I sense a well of both sadness and compassion within her.

She offers her hand while hugging the baby close to her, "I am Badriyya, and this is my baby Yasmina,"

The young mother then closes her eyes and kisses the baby's curly dark hair and breathes the scent of the baby's head, the scent of hope; the shared sacred gesture among mothers everywhere. We talk for a while when it dawns upon me that we're conversing entirely in English. She reads the surprise on my face.

"Your English is excellent."

"Thank you. We lived in Suez for 3 years. My husband was training to become a teacher. When he was killed, I came back to Cairo to live with my family. My boy, Mohammed, he died with his daddy. He was seven years old. They are in heaven now together, praise Allah."

I hold back tears at the thought of this young family so painfully separated. "I'm so sorry"

"Do you have babies?" Badriyya asks.

"I have one son, not a baby any more. He's in college now in the States. He was here with me in Cairo for a while, but he wanted to go back home. It's crazy, I miss him all the time, even though he's grown up and has his own life now. I'm trying to let him go and accept that he's a man now, but I haven't been able to."

"Do you have a photo of him?" she asks, the inevitable question among Egyptian women.

To Egyptians, there is nothing more precious than a child, and the sharing of photos of children and other family members is a source of great joy and bonding among women. I reach into my purse and hand her my plastic photo wallet, which is filled with photos of Adam, my family, and my cat Rashid.

Badriyya takes the photo of Adam out of the plastic, looks at it with intensity, then kisses it, saying, "Allah bless him, he looks just like an Egyptian boy, so handsome. My boy would have grown up to look just like this. So beautiful." She's silent for a moment. "But, no husband? Where is your husband?"

"He died a long time ago. Adam and I have been on our own for many years, since he was a baby," I tell her.

"You must be very proud he goes to college," she said, "Someday he will take care of you. That would make your son very happy if he can take care of his mother."

I have my doubts about that, but I say nothing and nod in agreement. Badriyya puts her arm around me and pulls me close. "We are like sisters, so much alike. We both love our children too much."

She leads me to a small room that is apparently shared by all the young women in the household.

"Here, please hold Yasmina for a minute." Badriyya hands me the baby and I'm surprised to be given this honor. I look into the wide eyes of the baby, my own eyes welling up with tears again. I wish I were not so emotional. Badriyya, being sensitive, as are all Egyptians, is unfazed by my tears as she opens a tall wooden wardrobe and pulls out a faded white wedding dress, laying it carefully across the bed.

"This is mine," she says with pride. "And, it was my sister Soha's and my mother's too when she was a girl and much thinner."

I admire the delicate wedding dress and the photos on the bureau as she points out family members as if I should know them. "Here's uncle Abdallah from Shubra. He's the brother of my Umi."

"Come, the drums will start now," she says as she takes my arm. "You have to meet everyone." We move to the main room of the small house.

"First, I want you to meet my Umi, my mother," Badriyya says as she reaches out to a round figure dressed in black.

A kind-faced brown woman steps forward and embraces me in her great cushion of flesh, pressing my head to her bosom for far longer than is comfortable. She then lifts my chin and looks at me as if I am a small child. I wonder if I have something on my face. She continues to stare and I begin to realize she is reading my soul. After a few more awkward minutes, she nods her head.

"Now I understand why you wanted so much to come to the Zar. You have the gift," Umi says. "I see it in your eyes. You have felt alone all your life because you've been different. You see the spirits and they talk to you. The jinn will come to you tonight and help you with your heartache, I promise you."

"Thank you for allowing me to join," I reply.

She pats my cheek. "Don't be afraid, our jinn are good spirits, not the evil jinn. Even your grandmother, she is here. You look so much like her." I'm startled at her words. She takes my arm and leads me into the room, "All your spirit family have been waiting for you, come."

I want to explain to her that I am not so different, that in my Irish family generations of women, and men as well, have seen into other worlds and spoken to spirits. I was just one of the few who listened and learned how to deal with it instead of drowning out the voices and visions with drink. I had begun early to explore those misty realms of spirit, the realms that are near for all people of Celtic descent. Still, the sensitivity that goes with the ability to travel between the worlds is often marked by a constant sense of anxiety and depression.

I think about this so-called gift and all the pain it had caused me throughout my life. As much as I tried to avoid it, it would often happen that three days before the passing of family members and friends, I sensed something bad was about to occur. The person about to pass over would be bathed in a soft golden light and I'd watch the changes in the energies around them. I learned early to keep my revelations to myself if I were to avoid another trip to the priest followed by a lecture on the evils of spirit communication. After the talk with the priest, I'd be given a number of Hail Mary's and Our Father's to recite, followed by the Act of Contrition and the Apostle's Creed. To me it was all just a waste of time, time that I could be outside playing.

"I know it never seemed like a gift," Umi says, reading my thoughts. "All of us have to take care and use our gifts to help each other." She holds my hand. "You're safe here with us, don't worry."

Drumming signals the start of the ceremony and drowns

our voices out. Everyone moves into the small living room, or main room. I look around at the gathering of women and a few older men who play percussion and all seem so natural and at ease with the circumstances.

The objective in Zar ritual is to surrender to the rhythm, to move and sway to the point of exhaustion, until all sense of identity and separation has dissolved. Percussion becomes the catalyst for the journey into the labyrinth of sound and it takes us where we need to go. Young people back in the States do a similar thing with their "raves" where they dance into a state of ecstasy.

Judging by the distinctly similar features, I guess that most of the group members are related. Two of the men are dressed in street clothes, while the others wear white gallabeyas and prayer shawls over one shoulder. The younger women wear bright, flowered gallabeyas reminiscent of 1960s hippie clothing, or what my elite Cairene friends would refer to as *beledi*, or unsophisticated. The married women are dressed all in black and their hair is covered in black headscarves called hijab.

The scene would be, by most cultural standards, an odd family gathering. Yet it feels friendlier and more relaxed than any holiday gatherings I recall back in the States. There is no bickering over who sits where, who's late again, or how someone has forgotten to bring some key ingredient for the dinner. Most striking to me is the fact that no one is drinking anything stronger than tea. Although the mood is festive, not one person is being loud or unruly. There are outbursts of joyful laughter in contrast to the seriousness required in religious rituals.

The meager collection of wooden furniture has been

pushed against a wall to make space for the gathering and the room has become is a sea of movement; heads swaying, eyes flickering in ecstatic trance, all lost in their own inner worlds. Women drape large black cotton scarves over their heads for privacy and their tent-like swaying figures create an eerie silhouette. The few men present provide the repetitive trance-inducing *Ayub* rhythm, each holding a *doumbek* or *riq*, the traditional drum, and tambourine and chanting a repetitive phrase.

A sightless man, his eyes rolled back in his head, plays the nay, the Egyptian flute. To my surprise, Mostapha is there among the musicians, drumming and chanting as if this is his regular gig. His usual pensive and suspicious expression is gone and he smiles and laughs while calling out the chants in a strong and pleasant voice. He looks like a child, the way I imagine he might have looked before life became so difficult for him. In our many years as friends, he's never mentioned that he's a musician, and he's a good singer as well.

Sleepy-eyed toddlers watch the adults from the pass-through of the kitchen area, heads resting on their dimpled arms. In the back of my mind, my mothering instinct says to help put these little ones to bed. How will they function tomorrow at school? None of my business, I sharply remind myself. I am here at the Zar to loosen the mothering ties, not to form new ones. Besides, these people are so poor that the children probably don't go to school - another concern that I must release for now.

The power of the music overcomes me and I'm magnetically drawn to surrender to it, allowing the rhythm to move my body as my mind is blissfully suspended. There are no steps to learn, only to give oneself over to the hypnotic repetition of drums and chanting. The music dances me as I let it take over my being. Beyond all thinking or self-consciousness, I move in a way that is deeply familiar, instinctual, and primal.

My eyes close and the inner landscape opens to brightly lit pathways. I've been making this journey for a lifetime alone through my dance, music, and art, but the sense of community in this family makes it all the more powerful. The synergistic energy of the group multiplies the power available to all of us, and that power surges outward and creates a vortex. I imagine it travels out into the city and beyond, bringing peace and healing wherever it travels. All because some dedicated women refused to give up what empowers them. I'm deeply grateful for the openheartedness and fierce passion of these women who defy the law and continue to run these ceremonies. If caught, they would be imprisoned or worse.

There's a loud thump as a heavy figure drops to the floor, a black mountain of fabric writhing and trembling. The *sheikha*, the spiritual leader of the group, drops to her knees beside the writhing woman and calls out to the spirit that possesses the woman, exhorting the jinn to speak. In spite of the alarming appearance of the scene, there's no panic, no attempt to rouse the woman, only to calm and appease her as she wails. The sheikha leans over the writhing mass, places her ear to the woman's lips, and asks the jinn what it wants.

To my great dismay, this jinn demands a cigarette and a heavy dousing of a cloying, sweet perfume. Other attentive women administer the requested vices and all the while the group moves and chants around her. Contented, the woman stops convulsing and she rocks back on her haunches, smoking and talking to herself/her jinn in a low, gravely voice. She continues to hold up both sides of the conversation until it becomes apparent from her gestures that some sort of understanding has taken place. She nods in agreement, holds out her hands for help in getting up, Her friends help her rise and she continues the chanting and ecstatic swaying of her head.

My allergies are flaring up from all the smoke and perfume and I move to an open window to breath in the cool night air. Badriyya joins me and we stand and chat. I take my rose quartz heart from the silk pouch that I wear in my bra. "Here, this is for you. It will help heal you," I tell her. "Keep it over your heart whenever you can."

"Thank you, my sister," she says tenderly as she tucks the quartz heart under her clothing.

Umi calls to us, comes over, and takes our hands. "*Yalla Banat*, come on girls, we're not done yet." I wonder where Umi gets so much energy at 3 in the morning as we follow her. We join in again, swaying to the movement and I struggle to keep my eyes open. Hours pass, tea trays, tiny glasses, and pastries come and go, and the call to prayer echoes over the city. I turn to Badriyya and Umi to say goodbye and thank them for the honor of being invited into the circle, dropping some pound notes into the donation basket that sits upon the table in the hallway.

"Come back again, you're family now," Umi says while crushing me in another embrace. "And bring your friend Mostapha with you. He's a good musician and singer."

I look across the room at him as he hugs the other musicians. "I never knew that about him until tonight. He really seemed to enjoy himself. He didn't want to do this at first and I was surprised he decided to join in."

Umi leans close. "You know, we women are the ones who lead men to what they need, but we have to pretend they had the idea all along. Someday he will admit you were right. Women are the ones who should lead the world. Then there would be peace." I look at her and smile in agreement and for a moment her face becomes that of my grandmother, as if an image superimposed; she has transfigured into a sparkling-eyed old Irish woman with a white chignon. A second later, I see only the dark, joyful face of Umi. This transfiguration catches me by surprise and I wonder if it really happened, or if I'm just overtired. It seems I'm the only one who has seen it. Umi smiles knowingly and I understand. Only a few seconds have passed. The women begin to laugh and nod their heads in agreement with what Umi said about women and our power. There is no doubt among them as to which sex is the stronger one. I've been given entry into a sisterhood of wise women: maidens, mothers and crones, and I'm so grateful. I've noticed that Egyptian women view me with a mixture of curiosity and admiration. I'm an oddity, an independent woman who moves about the world without the supervision of a man. Despite the differences in our lives, we are linked as sisters, mothers, and friends. Each of the women embraces me and says goodbye, invoking the protection of Allah.

Mostapha and I follow the rest of the guests as we silently file out into the morning haze, all going their way without a word. Our gaunt and mysterious escort walks ahead of us, leading us back to the underpass where we first met, which now seems like days ago.

He turns to us at last and begins to speak and share his story. He talks of a time of near blindness, which was cured by his taking part in the Zar ceremonies weekly. From the way the old man walks, as surefooted as a gazelle in the early morning haze, he is far from blind. In fact, it appears he has the sharper vision of the three of us. We thank him as he smiles a toothless smile and bids us goodbye. "*Maasallamah*, May God go with you."

THE STATUE OF THE GREAT PHARAOH WELCOMES OUR arrival at Ramses Station. Mostapha and I agree to talk when we've both rested and had time to integrate all that has taken place. He walks away with a spring in his step that I'd never seen before, shoulders relaxed and arms swinging. The Zar seems to have given him back years of his life and released his inner turmoil. He reaches the platform and waves, and I continue to my flat in Zemalek.

Exhausted, I fall into bed as the hypnotic sound of the drums still resonates in my head and I am plunged me into a hallucinatory sleep. Dreams arrive filled with colorful geometric shapes and sounds that generate kaleidoscopically from some deep place within my brain. My observing self notes that this must be what taking hallucinogens feels like, except that my own body produced the chemicals that caused the experience. The sound of traffic outside weaves into the rhythm, and images swirl into a vortex as I'm suspended in a multi-dimensional, timeless place. My conscious mind is aware and witnessing the visions, yet I am in the blissful mystical state between waking and dreaming. I relax and let myself be carried further still on this healing journey into my own past.

A labyrinth draws me to my childhood and the liminal world in which I so often dwell. I'm experiencing a life review as one does upon death, yet I am calm in knowing I am not dying but being born anew. I'm integrating so many aspects of my life that had never made sense until now. Not just thinking of my childhood, I am living it in full detail and vibrancy with all the emotions it stirs. Sobbing comes in waves, interspersed with indescribable bliss.

CHAPTER TWENTY TWO

AWAKE IN THE DREAM - BOSTON

"All that we see or seem is but a dream within a dream."
Edgar Allen Poe

I t's fall in Boston, a sparkling time of year, and I'm on my way to Rome. For most people this would be thrilling, but I have only one day to digest the vast history, geography, and architecture of Italy before leading a group of forty-two American tourists through the art and religious sites of that great nation.

An upscale hotel bar in Copley Square is the meeting place for my hour-long briefing with another tour manager, Jane, who has just completed three rounds of this same Italy assignment. I've never met her, but when she arrives she has the familiar glazed, burned-out, jet-lagged look that all tour managers have during peak season. Autumn, it turns out, is the best time of year in every place on earth and therefore all of us are straight-out busy. I'm seldom assigned foliage tours of New England since I'm of more help to the company I work for if they send me overseas. The few New England tours I have done made it apparent that I know about as much history of my own birthplace as many visitors do. Tour companies trust me, however, because I've run my own small tour company for five years, specializing in sacred site tours of Egypt and North Africa. Being both a tour operator and a tour director, I know all sides of the industry and I fit the category of international madwoman who will take on anything. The fact that I also have infinite patience with people and their idiosyncrasies is another bonus.

The years of leading senior tours has allowed me to visit 25 countries with scarcely time to repack, study a new destination, and leave again, my carry-on heavy with tour books. In an effort to appear knowledgeable about the destination, there is constant study and memorization of places, dates, and maps. Jet lag and anxiety are my ever-present travel companions, along with a host of inexplicable symptoms that I chalk up to stress. My premenopausal moments cause my passengers to question just who among us is experiencing dementia. This daily situational comedy delights the group members and they look forward to my taking the microphone each morning and sharing my latest misadventure.

Jane and I sit at a table in the empty bar and begin our rundown of each and every minute of the 14-day program, with a careful review of the correct pronunciation of the major towns and sites. I take notes furiously on a clipboard, hoping I can decipher them later. We've created our own network of Boston-based tour managers and these briefing sessions make all the difference when we venture out into unknown territory.

I know I take my work too seriously, always trying to get everything exact and to fulfill each item on the program. But I think, after all, this could be the only time in their lives that my passengers take such an extensive journey. It may be their anniversary, or even the last trip they will ever go on if they're ill or elderly, which is often the case.

My gaze wanders to the young black-haired, well-groomed bartender who is polishing the mahogany bar to a shine. He then arranges the napkin holders and condiments in precise right angles to each other, stepping back to view the bar from different angles, taking obvious satisfaction in his work. He then leans over and lifts a white plastic bucket to fill the stainless steel ice bin, offering me a view of his taut physique and cute behind.

Jane calls my attention back to the map of Italy on the table before us. "I know he's cute, but we only have a half hour left and you surely don't have time for him."

"Of course not. He's beautiful, but much too young for me. Just dreaming while awake," I blink my eyes and refocus. "It happens a lot since I started in this business. Sleep deprivation does that to me. I find lately I'm often dreaming with my eyes wide open."

"Well, I think we just had the same dream," she quips.

The handsome bartender comes over to our table. His manner is slow and his voice is low and soothing. "Drinks, ladies?"

It's only 9AM, but in a large hotel catering to wealthy foreign guests, it's bound to be evening for someone.

I look up at him. "Just water with lemon for me, please."

His sweet smile creates dimples on his cheeks. My colleague orders black coffee to put a fresh edge on her edginess. He returns in a short while to refill her cup, still smiling just enough to show those dimples and to catch my eye. I gaze at his name badge and my mind goes to angels, archangels, and other heavenly things. His name seems perfect for him, although my foggy brain doesn't register exactly what that name is.

An hour passes and he offers us the menu of lunch specials from the restaurant. We're still the only customers in the bar, but I'm losing concentration and we're out of time as well. There's something in his eyes that I feel drawn to - I have to look away. In just a few hours I'll be boarding an international flight for another demanding tour and I have so much to memorize.

Jane stays firmly in her managerial persona and her stern voice pulls me back to reality. "Thank you, we have to leave right now. Could you please just bring the check?"

Nurses and tour managers learn from necessity to be hyper-efficient and bossy. I hope I'm not becoming that way. The bartender looks hurt by Jane's abruptness as he tears off the check and places it in front of her. I smile at him again to make up for Jane's impatient tone and he smiles back with a sparkle in his dark eyes. "Have a great day in the city. You'll love Boston."

I don't reply that I was born in Boston and still love this beautiful city. Casual conversation is seldom on my agenda these days as all my focus is on work and the endless to do lists that I carry in my head.

Jane and I walk out to Copley Square and stand in front of the Boston Public Library. The sun is creating brilliant slanting patterns on Trinity Church across the plaza from where we stand. I wish I could relax and take a walk through this favorite part of the city, but there's no time.

"You were spacing out and staring at him again."

"Was I? I'm so tired I don't know what I'm doing."

Jane is getting on my nerves. "You'd better get some sleep on your flight; you're going to hit the ground running in Rome."

This statement raises my anxiety level and I feel a tension headache coming on.

"And remember," Jane continues to drive home her point, "before you meet up with your group, go outside the baggage claim and look for your driver to brief him on the day's program, then go back inside to help your passengers collect their luggage off the carousel. It will be much too early for check-in at the hotel. You'll have to take them on the 3-hour city tour directly from the airport." She breaks into a sinister laugh, "You'll want to grab a large coffee at the shop on the way out of the airport. Believe me, you'll need it."

I have a few last minute errands to run before heading to Logan Airport, the most important being a call to Adam, to say goodbye and tell him how much I love him. He's managing a Vermont Inn, and as it is peak foliage season, I'm not surprised that he doesn't answer. We've always shored each other up in our ventures and I need to hear his voice one more time before leaving. My son loves Italy, where he studied language and Tuscan cooking in Florence. I wish so much he could join me and help on the tour, but it's against company rules.

I give Jane a hug. "Thanks for all your help. You know how to reach me if you get assignments to any destinations you're not familiar with."

"For sure," Jane replies as she crosses the street toward Boston Common. "In fact, I may be assigned to Morocco in a few months. I'll need all the help I can get, especially with Arabic greetings."

The Alitalia dinner of pasta and red wine makes me drowsy. I set up my pillow against the window, drift into a deep sleep, and experience another dream of the same mysterious man I'd dreamed of in Cairo, years earlier. This time we're not on a train, but in a large, empty room.

THE DARK HAIRED STRANGER STANDS BEFORE ME AND WE LOCK gazes and begin to move slowly. We flow together, never touching, yet moving as one. Although no words are spoken, I have a feeling of being seen and understood on a deep level. It's a strange and disconcerting intimacy after years alone in my own private world. Our eyes seem to open a world of memories of our love, our time together somewhere else. He seems to be trying to tell me something as his eyes search mine. There's a humility and gentleness about him and I want to stay there longer, but the dream vanishes as I awaken to the cabin lights going on.

THE LANDING GEAR DESCENDS AND THE SOUND OF announcements in Italian jolts me into the present as my anxiety about this tour returns full force. Through the porthole window, I look down at stucco buildings and red-tiled roofs that are surrounded by gently rolling hills. Tall, slender cypress trees dot the landscape and it seems we're descending into an idyllic painting. If only I were on a relaxing, romantic holiday, I'd find Rome a lot less intimidating. I wonder if I've packed the right clothes, my umbrella, and sunglasses, items that would cost a fortune to replace here. My tour manager's salary offers no room for luxuries or last minute purchases of any sort.

All my adult life, I've kept a journal and given titles to my dreams in order to recall them more easily. I cannot reach my journal in the overhead bin without provoking the wrath of the flight attendant who has already scolded me twice to remain seated. I scrawl a few quick notes on the back of my ticket stub so that I won't forget the dream. I title it 'Dream Lover. '

☥

CHAPTER TWENTY THREE
THE GOOD SHEPHERD - ITALY

"When you are born in a world you don't fit in,
it's because you were born to help create a new one." -
Johnny Stores

The warm, sensual air is heavy with the fragrance of freshly baked garlic bread as I exit the airport. Within an hour my passengers, all Americans seniors, and their luggage are piled into the waiting coach and we're off on our whirlwind tour of downtown Rome. The itinerary is formidable: two or three visits to a church, cathedral, or museum every day, and a different hotel every other night.

"We have a full itinerary today," I say with a cheerful tone that I'm not really feeling. I look around and see that my passengers are overcome with jet lag and barely awake. Half the group is sound asleep in their seats as we whizz past the coliseum. I continue my commentary about the ancient landmarks for those few who are listening. This was poor planning on the part of the home office, but the itinerary only allows for the city tour today.

Nothing has prepared me for the madness of the city of Rome where people are driving dangerously fast. Italian drivers are nothing like the drivers in Liberation Square in Cairo, who simply don't use signals or obey lights. The Roman drivers are aggressive and verbally abusive toward one another. I watch as a Fiat swerves onto the sidewalk to pass our bus, barely missing pedestrians.

In every group, there are a few clients whom I immediately fall in sync with, and a bond of friendship develops between us. In this group, I instantly connect with an elegant older couple, Sophia and Martin, who are interested in Italian art, but more focused on enjoying their honeymoon. At seventy-five years old, they giggle like teenagers as they confide in me that they only met six months ago and eloped against the wishes of both of their families.

"We figured, what are we waiting for at our ages? It's now or never," Sophia laughs.

As we drive through the streets of Rome, Martin explains that he and Sophia lost their spouses shortly after retiring to an assisted living facility on a California golf course.

"God's green waiting room," laughs Sophia, "We weren't waiting, but just beginning to live again after all the years of caretaking."

I feel wistful as I listen to the story of their meeting. Martin had been playing golf when Sophia's shapely legs distracted him. He'd hit his ball into her shin, and then had to half-carry her to the golf cart and take her to the Stamford clinic. "Fate, and my bad swing got me this gorgeous new bride," he beams.

"I had to wear a cast for two months and so this rascal took advantage and proposed while I couldn't get away." Sophia wraps her arm around him. "This is the third marriage for both of us and we couldn't be happier."

This couple is inspiring me to believe again in the notion of devoted partnership and I so want for this, their honeymoon, to be perfect in every way.

At breakfast the next morning, half the passengers have constipation and the other half have indigestion from the rich Italian food they enjoyed at dinnertime. I reach for my large carry-on bag and pass out Rolaids and Maalox as we drive to the next destination, the first of many churches where priceless frescoes adorn the walls. For five days we visit numerous sights throughout Tuscany before heading north to Venice.

By the time we reach Venice, the group is so exhausted that many vote to skip the evening gondola ride on the Grand Canal in favor of the comfort of their beds or a seat outside a café at St. Mark's Square.

Sophia and Martin are snuggled up in the back of the gondola, their faces flushed with passion. Venice is awash in warm coral light and jeweled palaces appear suspended atop the sparkling water. This panorama of water and architecture combines to create a world of mirror images.

The smell of liniment from my little tour group mixes with the brackish scent of water gently caressing the bow. The newlyweds appear to have always been together, with their matching pleated khakis, white polo shirts and sunbaked skin. Word spreads amongst the gondoliers that the couple is on their honeymoon and everywhere we go they call out their charming translation of a honeymoon greeting, "Happy Sugar Moon!"

Something about Venice reaches into my heart in a way no other place has and it rouses all the dreams I keep hidden in the vault labeled what could have been. Venice is heart-wrenchingly romantic and it alternately makes me sick with sadness and elated with new hope. How can I be in such a place and not be in love? My romantic artist self, no matter how much I try to subdue her, has reawakened in Venice and I long for someone special to love, to travel with, to come home to.

My mind drifts to the dreams of the stranger, the dream lover. He's now appeared to me in three dreams, which have left me longing to see him in reality. I move to the back of the gondola, close my eyes, and put out a call in my mind to my soul partner, wherever he may be. With all my focus, I imagine an arc of pink light flowing from my heart to his, a bridge to connect us. I invite him to come into my life and I vow that at last I am ready to accept a real partnership.

The reality is, I'm in yet another romantic locale, chaperoning happy couples and helping make their dreams come true. That's my job, to take care of every detail behind the scenes so that all goes smoothly according to the hour-by-hour itinerary given me with each assignment. Back at the home office in Boston, a twenty-something employee who's never left the country sits snapping her gum and writing these idyllic itineraries. Then, we tour directors, most of us older women are handed the detailed itinerary. We're expected to single-handedly make it all happen exactly as written. Any emergencies while on the road are put through to an answering machine in the home office thousands of miles away, which promises to get back to us later. If it happens to be a Friday afternoon, we'll have to wait until Monday for a reply. We have to think on our feet, problem-solve and multitask, all the while pretending to be calm and to know the destination as well as any local would.

Although I've never settled well and love traveling, I've recently begun wanting a dream for myself, a place to safely land after years of wandering. Independence has become empty as a goal in itself, and I often feel like a satellite, spinning in deep space alone. Sometimes I imagine looking down on the festive lights of the earth below, forever destined to roam solitary among the stars. As much as my friends and family envy my life of travel, I long to belong somewhere, to rest a while in someone's arms and let go of being in charge of every moment. I'd love to just show up somewhere and have a relaxing time without having to organize every detail--that's a luxury I dream of.

THE GROUP HAS RETIRED TO BED AFTER DINNER AND I linger over coffee with newlyweds Sophia and Martin. All of us are reluctant to leave the relaxing warmth of the stucco hotel dining room with its colorful mosaic walls. The tour is halfway over and I'll miss this couple that have taken me under their wing from day one. They radiate an aura of contentment and easy companionship as Sophia leans her head on her husband's shoulder. He strokes her arm with tenderness. I wonder if they ever bicker the way my own parents do. My parents were a united front and provided a secure and loving home for us kids until a series of deaths and other crises in the family. Then things fell apart and the drinking and discontent escalated.

Sophia seems to read my thoughts as I gaze at them in admiration. "Come visit us in California and meet Martin's son. He's been divorced for two years and he's ready to fall in love again. You two are perfect for each other."

Martin adds, "You'd be a great addition to our family. We're Jewish, but you wouldn't have to convert. I kind of like the idea of an Irish/Egyptian daughter-in-law. Mix it up; see what happens; that's what makes life interesting, right? All of us love to travel, dance, go to museums - you'd fit right in."

"I know it's beautiful in Stanford where you live," I reply, "I was there for a while years ago, but I didn't get to see much of the area. To my own surprise, I find myself sharing with them the reason for my stay in Stanford, a topic I seldom share with anyone, least of all my tour passengers. "My second husband, a gifted artist, had been one of the first in the US to receive a heart and lung transplant, The surgery was performed on Easter, and he lived exactly one year longer, although he never left the hospital or enjoyed any quality of life again. They listen in silence. "So you see, it was a sad time. We only had five years together. But, I do recall enjoying the beauty of the area as I walked each day from my hotel to the hospital."

Sophia reaches for my hand and says in a quiet voice, "I'm so sorry, dear. Now you can come stay with us and have a happy experience. We would love to be your hosts."

I'm scheduled for two more months of back-to-back tour assignments, the final one being in Egypt. Following the last of the tour assignments, I'll take a break and wander the temples and tombs along the Nile. Although touched by the couples' kindness, I decline their offer. Besides, another long-distance romance is not what I need. I know I would be miserable living so far from my son, family, and friends.

"But how will you meet a man and get married if you're never in one place?" Sophia says, "All this traveling may be interesting for now, but you need someone to go home to, to make a life with."

"I have my son to go home to," I immediately realize how foolish and pathetic I sound.

BY DAY EIGHT OF OUR TOUR, MANY OF US ARE IMPATIENT listening to docent lectures all the way from Rome to Milan, and viewing religious art in every far-off chapel with an important painting on its wall. No matter how exquisite the paintings in each place we visit, the repetition of theme and subject becomes unbearable. We shuffle from one opulent, massive space to the next and endure endless versions of the Virgin Birth, our feet aching. I begin to believe that at any moment there could be a spontaneous event among us--- a visitation and Immaculate Conception among my elderly passengers. I cannot take any more. I was raised Catholic and spent years looking up at a suffering blond Jesus nailed to a bloody cross. It never made me feel uplifted or joyous, only burdened with Catholic guilt.

Our final stop is a daylong tour of the Vatican. I long to sit this one out and join Sophia and Martin in a cafe somewhere. Ever tactful and kind, Sophia explains the reasons for not accompanying the group to the ultimate Catholic pilgrimage. "It was the art that drew us to this tour, but we cannot take any more Christian doctrine. We are Jewish after all."

I laugh in agreement. "I understand completely. See you at dinner tonight."

The weary group is corralled into the enormous St. Peter's Square where the late afternoon sun is blinding and heat rises from the stone slabs beneath our feet. In pious determination, my passengers have marched across the wide plaza and into the souvenir shop, purchased their medallions and prayer beads, and mailed postcards bearing the official stamp of the Vatican. What my wilting group and I desperately need is a large drink of water and a place to sit down out of the sun.

I realize that in the process of toileting the incontinent among them, I've neglected to use the facilities myself. I look at the long line for the bathroom and back again at my waiting group who stand in a tight huddle like obedient sheep. They need to be herded back to the waiting coach, but I know I won't make it across the wide courtyard and down the street to the parking area. I feel sorry for them, so frail and still trying hard to keep up with the absurd schedule of this tour. They're nice people and I've grown to care so much for them and to admire their fortitude under duress. A nasty bronchial virus has run through the group since day three and we're like a pathetic traveling TB clinic seeking a cure at the Vatican. I'm worried that all my passengers might not make it to the end of the trip and back home to their families.

In my years of leading tours, I've only lost one passenger, an eighty-five-year-old man who announced he would take up snorkeling before his time on earth ran out. He then rented gear, stripped off his trousers and shirt, and dove into the

Caribbean. His time did in fact run out as all of us watched in horror as he choked and expired before us. That had set the tone for that entire nightmare trip through the Panama Canal. The day after the snorkeling incident, everyone on board had come down with a norovirus, which lasted right through to the end of the cruise. I tried to put that particular disaster out of my mind, although I had a bad feeling about leaving my group unattended.

It's risky, but there's no other choice. I call out to them, "Everyone, please stay right here, don't move. I must dash to the restroom or I won't make it to the bus."

They nod in agreement, or at least that's what it seems. My voice simply doesn't travel no matter how I try, so I'm always left wondering if I've been heard. These old people are so polite, they agree to everything I say, leaving me wondering what their real thoughts are.

I take my place in the long restroom line after requesting, in three languages, to be allowed to cut into line. Desperate, I perform what is surely obscene sign language in my enactment of my problem. All my attempts are met with blank stares or smirks. Twenty minutes later, I emerge to find every one of my passengers has disappeared.

I race across the half-mile wide courtyard, locate the waiting coach, and deliver the news to my surly Italian driver who smokes a rancid-smelling Bide cigarette.

"Madonna Mia," yells Luigi, repeatedly hitting himself on his forehead with his meaty hand. "You lost everyone? Madonna Mia, how can you lose all of them?"

"I did, that's all. Now stop saying that and just drive. We have to find them before someone gets run over in this rush hour traffic." I toss my purse and clipboard onto the front seat and press my hands to my temples in terror as I imagine the faces of my forlorn, sweet-natured passengers.

"Some of these people shouldn't even be out alone," I say, to myself more than to Luigi.

"I know," he nods. "So why did you take them so far from home?" He glares at me as if I'm a monster.

"I didn't take them. My job as a tour manager is to execute whatever ridiculous itinerary some kid in the home office dreams up. I don't get to review it first or find out which passengers are capable of joining any given tour." I'm trying not to show how defensive and angry I am, grasping at any decorum I have remaining. "The sad truth of it is that these people's grown kids figure out it's much cheaper to send their parents on a budget tour than to pay for a nursing home."

Luigi's expression is both astonished and disgusted. He stares at me as I rant. "I meet them for the first time at the airport and take my chances that they're lucid and mobile enough to get around without assistance. As you see, some are, and some are not at all."

I can tell he's overwhelmed with frustration as he rubs his eyes and lets out a growl. He shakes his head as he drives in circles in the rush hour traffic. I think I see tears streaming down his face, but it could just be copious sweat and olive oil.

My emotions are out of control and I feel my blood pressure rising. "Some of these dear old people just keep traveling endlessly with no idea where they are." My voice catches and I choke back tears. "One little woman asked me yesterday how much longer we would be in France. She said she took French for years in school but she couldn't understand a word anyone around her was saying. There was no point in telling her yet again that we were in Italy, not France."

"America doesn't make any sense to me." Luigi says in a low voice. "Here in my country, everyone lives together in one small house and we take care of each other. We make sure the old people aren't in any kind of danger, even if we have to stay with them all day and night. We don't try to get rid of them or send them far away from us, no matter what. They're the most important people in the family."

I lean toward the front window of the bus and search the crowd as we drive in frantic loops around the roundabout until the sun is setting. One by one, or two by two, we spot the wandering group members, beep, and cut across lanes to collect them. They look relieved to see us, but not entirely certain of who we are. They're just grateful for the ride

"There are three more all walking together!" Luigi calls out as he swerves toward the sidewalk.

I jump off and on the coach until the last of my wayward charges had been retrieved. My polyester company blazer is suffocating me and my feet are blistering in my pumps. I know if I remove my heels I'll never get them back on again, so I try elevating my feet against the handrail of the front seat. My skirt rides up clear to my crotch, but I am sure Luigi is much more interested in getting home to his sultry wife than eying my pale American legs.

The shepherds in those idyllic paintings we've been viewing all week come to mind and I imagine the life of a real shepherd. At least they had those pretty black and white herding dogs to help them round up the renegade or senile sheep. I have a disgruntled driver who only wants to get home to a nice meal and the comfort of his big family. No doubt, he'll relate the day's events to his loud, happy brood and they'll laugh and then suck their teeth in disgust at American *stunatas*.

I can't blame them. I'm pretty disgusted with the ways of Americans myself, especially those who entrust the care of their ailing parents to a complete stranger with no medical training and no assistance.

By the following morning, both my heart rate and sense of humor have returned to normal. A ride through Tuscan countryside has a calming effect on all of us as we settle into an easy pace. Like a little, mismatched family, we're on another outing. It's true that not everyone knows where we're going; some still think we're in France, some that I'm their daughter taking them on a bus ride. To a few, I'm their long lost sister who had arrived to bring them home as they hold my hand and thank me for coming to get them. One lady kisses me tenderly on the cheek as she introduces me to her seatmate as her sister and I hold back my tears.

It's senseless and cruel to argue with the delusional. I let them think whatever outlandish thoughts make them feel happy. I break company regulations and I don't try to explain the day's itinerary or how many transfers, site visits, and hotel check-ins they will have to endure in the remaining few days. It has been a different hotel every night and a full day of touring each day. They've never complained. The schedule is killing me and I can only imagine how they are suffering in their silence. I think they must be true Christians; martyrs, maybe. I take out my humor folder, as I do every day, and read some new jokes from my collection. I hear them twittering.

Half way through the four-hour drive, I sit up front alone

and watch the exquisite countryside and focus on my breathing. The upcoming day trip to Milan looks promising. We'll have a private tour of La Scala opera house and a relaxing outdoor lunch. I feel infused with gratitude and relief that everyone has survived the previous day. The coughing has even subsided with most of our entourage and the sun is breaking though the clouds. We are all contained in one vehicle. A few passengers, the driver, and I know where we're going, and we're making good time. I can't ask for more.

CHAPTER TWENTY FOUR

THE GLAMOUR OF TRAVEL

*"If I had no sense of humor, I would long
ago have committed suicide."*
Mahatma Gandhi

In Lisbon, Portugal, I place a call to our next hotel in Paris to confirm the arrival of my latest group. I'm told that the home office in Boston cancelled all our rooms the day before, no reason given. In my panic to track down enough rooms at an alternate hotel, I've forgotten I'm in the process of frosting my hair. An hour passes before I resolve the crisis and glance in the mirror. Wispy chartreuse strands float down the drain when I stand in the shower and remove the frosting cap. At the nearest drugstore, the closest thing I find to a head covering is a white terrycloth turban.

"So exotic today, Kara," a passenger teases as I board the bus at 7AM "Where are you taking us?" I consider telling them

I've had an overnight epiphany to join a cult, but then I relay the story of how I left the frosting cap on for an hour during a crisis and my hair went down the drain. Their faces register a mixture of both horror and delight.

Once checked into the next hotel in France, I remove my turban and look in the bathroom mirror. Over the course of the day my hair has become a few shades greener and now looks like a St. Patrick's Day skullcap. After a frantic race to the nearest hairdresser, I pay a substantial, and still unknown, sum of francs to have all my green spikes cut off and any remaining hair restored to its strawberry blonde color. I leave the salon looking like a newly-shorn lamb. The hairdresser says I look "tres chic," but what else can she say?

In my hotel room, I'm finishing the bookkeeping on my tour when a call comes from the US operations manager. "Can you take over a last -minute cruise assignment to the Black Sea? The scheduled TD bailed out due to exhaustion and someone has to lead this group."

"I can relate to that," I said. "This assignment has me completely fried, even my hair got fried. I don't know if I can hold up for another tour right now."

"This one will be easy, it's a cruise," she says, "It won't be nearly as demanding as all of the over-the-road coach tours you've been doing. And you'll have local step-on guides at every port, so you don't need to learn too much about the destinations."

I think about it for a few minutes. I have nothing urgent to go home for, it's cold back home, and Adam is away at college.

"Sure, I'll take it. But only if you can promise my cabin won't be next to the engine room this time." I hear myself saying yes at the same time my aching, tired body is shouting no. "As long as I end up back in Cairo after that. Book my return flight to Cairo and not Boston.

"And please, I add, "This time I need a non-stop flight, not one of those roundabout routes they give us tour managers in order to cut costs. These inter-Europe flights should only take only a few hours, not two days."

The agent chuckles. "Oh, so you don't enjoy flying in cargo, is that what you're telling me? "

For the next few weeks, I'll cruise the ports along the Black Sea and only unpack once. How bad can it be? Then, I'll be back in Egypt where my heart will sing again.

☥

CHAPTER TWENTY FIVE

THE BLACK SEA

*"I wish I could show you, when you are lonely or in
darkness, the astonishing Light of your own Being."*
Hafiz

Since the fall of the Soviet Union in 1991, the economy
of the entire region continues to reel. The ports of
Yalta, Odessa, and Constanta, although empty and
depressed, are oddly comfortable and familiar to me. There are
few other tourists, no crowds at the historic sites and every port
stop offers gorgeous views of the Black Sea. In the economi-
cally depressed city of Odessa, all the cruise passengers on our
boat are invited to a ballet performance of Giselle in the
Odessa Opera and Ballet Theatre. The dancers are grateful to
have an appreciative audience and they pour their hearts and
souls into the production as if dancing for a full house.

I sit in the highest loge alone and relive the joy and excitement of my childhood dance recitals. I recall how much I love to dance and how few chances I have to do so any longer. I'm working too much, leaving no time for things that once made my heart sing. It's true that one never stops being a dancer. If ignored and stifled for too long, it catches you when you least expect it and pulls you back. I know that I need to dance again soon or I'll lose my spirit.

On the daylong tour of Odessa, I form an immediate kinship with our local historical guide. Irina is a divorced mom with one small child and we bond over our love of our sons and the difficulties of raising them alone. The auburn-haired, green-eyed beauty is resigned to old age at the "advanced" age of forty and Irina's voice resounds with defeat, "I know it's true, I'm old now. I'm forty, and I'm finished. My husband tells me he wants a younger wife, and then right away he runs off with our babysitter who is 16. She's a Russian immigrant with no family here. That's why I hire her and try to help her. Now, I don't know whether to be mad at her, or adopt her and protect her from him. Anyway, it's too late, he's already slept with her and told her he will marry her."

I can't believe what I'm hearing. "I would be confused and upset too," I tell Irina. "These young Russian girls have wandered everywhere since the fall of the Soviet Union and they're so vulnerable and naive. As a mother, I wish I could protect them from their situation. In Egypt their presence has upset society and broken up countless marriages."

One of the mini-skirted young girls wobbles by in high-heeled red boots and we stop talking while she passes. I notice bruises on her slender arms and legs.

"In Egypt," I continue, "the people blame many problems now on the arrival of the Natashas, as they call them."

Irina is on the verge of tears, "I know it's more his fault than hers, but I'll never trust either of them again. The girl is only five years older than our son Sasha." Her hands tremble as she pulls her sweater sleeves down to cover the frayed cuffs of her blouse. "How does he expect us live in this way? If I didn't have a child to think of, I would kill myself. I have tried already once, but I couldn't do it. I think if I die, then my boy will be raised by this Russian girl who won't take care of him."

The desperation and hopelessness in her voice makes my heart ache. I want to help, but don't know how. I touch her shoulder. "Listen to me, Irina, I'm forty-two. Do I seem like I'm finished?"

She smiles. "No, not at all. But this is what they believe in Ukraine. It's not modern here like in America."

"You can't believe the stupidity you hear," I tell her. "You and I are not old; we're seasoned women; sophisticated, and far more interesting than teenaged girls."

"Maybe for you," she says, "you come from a different world. Here we women are all used up by now. What do I have to offer anybody?"

I put my arm around her. "Look at you, you're bilingual, educated, much better company than young girls, at least for any man with a brain."

Unlike in the West, consciousness raising and women's liberation have not yet reached this part of the world and the notion of a woman's worth without a man is a new one to Irina. As we talk, her eyes glisten at the possibility that her despicable husband might be wrong, that perhaps she's not useless and unattractive now. Irina's coveted new job as a local city guide offers her a small glimpse into how the rest of the world lives and she's eager to hear about women her age in other parts of the world. We come to the town center and sit on a bench while the passengers take a lunch break. It's what we call in the tour industry a "scatter lunch" where everyone goes in search of what they like, returning at a designated time and place.

Irina turns to me. "Tell me everything about this women's liberation and your life back home," she says, "Can single women really find work and raise children without a man?"

I hesitate before answering, "It's not easy and you have to work twice as hard to earn a fraction of the pay, but it can be done," I don't want to delude her about the realities of being a divorced mother in the States. I struggled financially for many years, dealt with groping bosses and creepy landlords, and received no child support or assistance from anyone.

We talk all day between Irina's lecturing at the museums and historic sites within the city. To lift her spirits, I point out one of my single passengers, a middle-aged gentleman who is escorting his mother. All day he's been glancing her way with appreciative eyes and has asked me about her. Embarrassed, Irina is unaware of the effect her beauty has on men and seems determined to keep her eyes focused down unless speaking directly to someone.

"I never notice any men watching me. Those men must be looking for prostitute. My husband says this is what I should do now to make money. He says he'll help me get customers. Maybe I'm even too old for that. I never was very good at the sex anyway. That's why he looks for someone younger."

I stifle a laugh at the absurdity of her turning to prostitution with the assistance of her low-life, cheating husband. "Oh no, please don't listen to him! There has to be another way."

The daylong tour is over and everyone tips Irina shakes her hand, and tells her how much they've enjoyed the day. I want to bring a little gift for her, but I need time to race back to the cruise ship to find something.

I motion to a rundown coffee shop, the only one nearby. "Meet me right here in a half hour, I'll hurry. Order whatever you want, I will join you and pay."

On the cruise ship, I gather armfuls of magazines and newspapers from passengers and put them in a tote bag. Then I race to my cabin for a few uplifting books and a pretty turquoise print scarf from my suitcase. I hurry back into town, hoping my new friend has waited for me.

Irina is sitting at a café table, head down, looking forlorn and tired. I join her, kiss her cheek, and put the scarf around her neck. "Thank you so much," she says as she clutches the stack of reading materials to her chest. Then she places the books and magazines back in the tote bag. "We're only allowed to read what the government wants us to, and it's all lies anyway. You're so lucky you can read anything you want; express yourself without being punished. I wish for the freedoms you have."

"I'm so sorry. I hope soon you'll have that freedom and your life will be less difficult." I write down my home address and phone number and hand her my card. "If you ever find yourself in the States, please call and come stay with me for as long as you like. And bring your boy too."

"Thank you, I will call you if I ever get out of here, for

sure. And I'll try to remember what you told me today." Irina rises to leave, "Maybe I can find a better life for myself and my son. Thank you for cheering me up today. You made me laugh and you gave me hope."

"I have to run to make it onto the ship before sailing time," I tell her as I pay the check. "When we meet again, I hope you'll have some happy news for me. You're beautiful and intelligent; please don't ever give up on yourself. And don't listen to that stupid husband, just let him go. He doesn't deserve you. Someone better will come to you."

As I stand on the bow watching the coast of Ukraine disappear, I hear my own words in my mind and wonder if I believe all these things of myself; or have I begun to give up on my own happiness? Why do we women so easily abandon ourselves? I think of the tender young girls in the park, wobbling in their high heels and miniskirts with bare legs, ready to sell their bodies to the highest bidder in order just to live. I think of the evil pimps who put them there, and the selfish, heartless men who use these innocent children. Equality for the women of the world is still a far-off dream and this fact had distressed me throughout my life; even more so as I learn how desperate existence is for so many women and children in the places I travel throughout the world.

A sense of sadness washes over me. Was I now destined to live out my own life as a wanderer and an exile? I could identify with Irina's sense of despair, having felt that way many times in my life as a struggling single mother. It's heartbreaking to me when another woman shows such little regard for her own worth. I know how a negative relationship can erode all sense of self- esteem; I have been there before and will never allow it again. I hope that my brief time with Irina has made some difference in how she views herself. I'm touched at having deeply connected with a new friend, although in reality I doubt we would ever meet again. Yet, sometimes it helps just to know that someone in the world sees us and cares about us.

I know Irina is one of my tribe, those souls with whom I have an instantaneous bond. I have met quite a few such soul mates over my years of wandering, male and female, young and old. Always, we recognize one another and there's a feeling of being reunited.

In my thinking, each of us on earth has many soul mates, those with whom we made an agreement prior to this lifetime. Sometimes the plan is just to meet for a moment or a day, sometimes to circle in and out of one another's lives. In the end, all we need do is recognize them, bless them, and give silent thanks for sharing the journey with us for a while. As Ram Das said, we are all just walking each other home.

CHAPTER TWENTY SIX

ISTANBUL

"Fear does not prevent death, it prevents life."
Naguib Mahfouz

The cruise of the Black Sea stops in one of my favorite cities, Istanbul. The ship curves into the Bosporus as the Golden Horn comes into view and the sun casts an iridescent shimmer on the minarets of the Blue Mosque and the Aya Sophia. I stand on the top deck as we dock at Kusadasi and marvel at the beauty of life. My sadness has lifted somewhat from yesterday's visit to Ukraine and I am less worried about my new friend Irina.

The sight of Istanbul is one of those magical moments that make me long for someone to share it with. Not even my passengers are around. They've found lounge chairs where they sit enjoying cocktails and chat among themselves. The itinerary for the day ahead is easy and includes only a three-hour visit to the sprawling Topkapi Palace. My plan is to steal away to the Grand Bazaar after the tour and bargain for dance costumes and scarves in the sprawling covered marketplace. There are over 4,000 shops, but I have a good idea of where I am going, having been here in Turkey before.

After my visit to the Bazaar, I consider going for a pummeling at the Cemberlitas Hammam, the oldest existing bathhouse, built in 1584. There I will likely find the same unsmiling, stocky women who stand waiting each day to take out their aggressions on foreigners. I went for a massage just a year prior and it was an experience I could never forget. I think of the hefty, bare-breasted masseuses who were so intimidating and I almost turn back at the memory of their scowling, mustached faces. This time, I decide, I will be forearmed with a few Turkish sentences learned from my taxi driver, "Please don't toss me around on the stone bench." "Please don't throw water up my nose," "In the name of Allah, stop, that is enough." If they would just grant me these few polite requests, a visit to the hammam could do wonders in releasing the knots in my shoulders from hoisting luggage for so many weeks on the road.

The driver drops me off after a reinforcement of the key Turkish phrases to use if I get into trouble. I enter the dark foyer, walk over to the table, and ask for a massage. I take out my change purse, heavy with hundreds of dirham coins and pay the equivalent of 10 USD. Then I change into a thin cotton robe given me by a small woman who sits in the locker room with a resigned, sullen expression. As I strip off my panties, the hearty, muscled masseuses lumber past and the floor shakes. I begin to doubt as to whether they're really female and so I put the panties back on for some small sense of modesty.

There's no one else in the women's section of the spacious hammam and I enjoy a quiet, relaxing lie-down on an enormous heated, circular marble slab. The 18th century building has a domed ceiling complete with star-shaped cutouts that look to the open sky. I am almost asleep when a door creaks and two sumo wrestler figures enter wearing only the tiniest of black thongs. Their large, pendulous breasts and bellies form an overhang that nearly obscures the bit of cloth. They stand with arms crossed and eye me with unsmiling expressions. I wait for something to happen, hoping it won't to be sexual or violent in nature.

"You want massage?" croaks the larger one.

I find my voice and stand up, clutching my towel around me. It's too late to back out now. "Yes, please."

The shorter woman grabs my towel and gestures for me to lie down on the stone bench where they both proceeded to dump buckets of ice water on me and then rub my body from head to toe with black mud. Grey bubbles rise and billow all around me. When I start to slip off the soapy bench, they pick me up and flip me like a wet dog onto my stomach. My cheekbone hits the stone and I move my jaw around to be sure it's not injured. Large, strong hands ply a rough hemp loofah over my body, deftly removing the first two layers of my delicate, fair skin. When they start on my upper chest, I flinch and indicate that it hurts. To my surprise and great relief, they lighten up on the loofah. Then, starting from either end of my body, the two women administer a deep massage with a lotion that smells of animal fat, while talking in low voices to one another. Each time the pitch of their conversation rises, they massage more vigorously until I can endure it no longer.

I love deep bodywork and it's what I need, but I don't want the assault and waterboarding I'd received last time I was here. I sense that their heated conversation is leading them in that direction. The massage is followed by a drenching of more ice-cold water from metal buckets, which hang on the walls behind them. I begin to shiver and gasp as each bucket splashes over me. This time the masseuses note my discomfort, seem to take pity on me, and ease up.

The bigger woman with a grasp of English looks at me and gives a flick of her hand. "You done, you get up now." I hold onto her arm to avoid slipping on the soapy marble floor as I struggle to stand up. She makes no effort to assist, only stands like a rock while I grope my way to a standing position, catching my fingers on her thong.

"Thank you, that was very good, *merci, tres bien, Shukren, azeem awi, gracias, muy bien.*" In my muddled state of mind I can't recall the Turkish words, so I instinctively use whatever non-English words I know. As I slip toward her, she hugs my head to her breast in a chokehold to catch my fall. I struggle to breathe against the hot, soapy flesh as it envelops my face. I fear I will pass out. When my feet are at last steady underneath me, she releases my head, takes my shoulders and turns me toward the door. I ponder what the protocol might be for one naked lady tipping another. I'm wearing only wet panties and I have no money on my body. I always make a point of being a generous tipper and it doesn't seem polite to just walk out. I hesitate but no solution for tipping comes to mind and they are both staring at me. I creep out of the room one tiny step at a time, to avoid slipping on the wet floor.

In the dimly lit dressing room, I pull the curtain and put on my clothes. I roll the wet panties into a ball and stuff them into my trench coat pocket, comb my wet hair with my fingers, and put on some lip balm. I slide out the dressing room door and escape past the masseuses before they can get me for a second round.

A few doors from the hammam, there's a café with the delicious aroma of spices and fresh baked bread. It has an exotic atmosphere and live music and to me it feels like home. The drum rhythms are Turkish, not Arabic, but it's close enough. A tall host in black Cossack-style pants and striped silk vest welcomes me with a wide smile. Unfazed by my dripping wet hair and smudged make up, he leads me to a single table with a full view of the dance floor.

I'm weak and dehydrated and the scents of cooking make me aware I haven't eaten in many hours. "First, I would like a very large bottle of water please."

"Ah yes, you have been next door, and you survived your massage," he laughs. "They are tough ladies, yes? You did very well to get through it." He walks away and I sit and wonder what becomes of those who don't. Following the waiter's recommendations, I enjoy the most perfectly spiced traditional Turkish dish, *Imam Bayildi*, Turkish for "Fainting Imam," and a glass of local wine. Turkish food is always fresh and delicious and I'm ravenous from all the pushing and pulling of the masseuses. No one seems to notice that I eat everything on my plate in less than 15 minutes, something so uncharacteristic of a cat-like fussy eater. I feel much better as I relax and observe my surroundings.

The band begins to play a dramatic prelude as a young dancer emerges and swirls in pink silken veils, her long black hair flowing. She is soulful, classy and skilled, not the 'anything goes' dance so often found in Turkey. The entertainment is so entrancing I forget about being a pale, panty-less foreign woman out on the town alone.

Seated at the table next to me are the mother and two young sisters of the dancer. As the evening goes on, we talk and I learn that the sweet twenty-year old dancer is the sole support of her mother and siblings. Between sets, she comes and sits with us and we have a wonderful time speaking in English about the art form and music that is our shared passion. The young dancer's dream is to go to Cairo and maybe get a job dancing, and so I write down the names and phone numbers of my Cairo contacts for her.

I feel so relaxed and at-home that my self-consciousness dissolves and during the break I am on the dance floor with the women. I thoroughly enjoy my free night in Istanbul, returning by taxi to the Bosporus Hotel after midnight. I find my tube of arnica cream and cover each of the red loofah welts on my chest, then sleep soundly, deeply cleansed and prepared for my upcoming time in Egypt.

In just 4 more days, I will reach Cairo and a badly needed rest from passengers and their endless chatter and questions. The cruise will stop in Mykonos, Athens, and then end in Venice; all of them are places that I love.

Still, I long for the silence of a dark, comfortable room and the sight of the Giza Plateau outside my window. In the Istanbul newspaper, I read of yet another excavation underway in the desert outside of Giza and I plan to explore it. Yes, I'm going home again at last.

☥

CHAPTER TWENTY SEVEN
RITUAL OF AWAKENING - CAIRO

"Do you know that Egypt is a copy of Heaven
and the Temple of the whole world?"
Egyptian scribe, c.1400BC

Desperate for a quiet, solitary place to decompress after so many months of leading tours, I plead and bargain with the hotel manager to rent me a room for an extended stay in the palace section. The Mena House is my favorite hotel of all the places on earth I have travelled.

"Of course I can give you a very good rate for a long stay, but won't you be afraid up there with no one else around? The entire palace is closed for renovation."

"Don't worry," I reply, "I like being alone."

The manager persists. "All day there will be construction, dust, and terrible noise. What will you do up there by yourself for a month? It's not good for a woman to be alone like that."

I hate it when people encourage me to be afraid and tell me what's "not good for a woman." The word 'alone' sounds blissful to me after months of taking care of passengers.

"I'll be out exploring all day, so none of those things will affect me. The workmen will be gone before I return."

Frustrated, he relents and hands me the large brass key to room 124. "Aha, number seven, my lucky number." I turn away from his confused stare and hurry toward the lift before he can change his mind.

As I approach my room I notice that there's sawdust everywhere, but all I care about is dropping my cases on the floor, taking a shower and falling into bed.

A week passes as I reacquaint myself with Cairo and my many friends in the city. My dear Hossam drives me everywhere and waits for me and it feels like old times. I stay up late studying symbols and practicing writing in hieroglyphs. My dreams are filled with images of life in ancient Egypt and morning arrives with the sounds of the plateau outside.

It could be a tomb, my hotel room so dark and silent as I lay savoring the stillness, reviewing the night's journeys. Which was dream, which reality? It must be almost time for the second muezzin call to prayer; I can hear it off in the distance as each minaret begins its message.

A light tapping startles me and I rise, pulling on the enormous white terrycloth robe that trails on the floor behind me.

"Made special for Americans," Samia from housekeeping had told me with pride. "You're not American. Americans, they are all tall and big," she had insisted, spreading her arms to describe rotund Americans as if the point was not clear.

"No, I really am American. There are all kinds of Americans, all colors and sizes." I reply.

I open the heavy wooden door to find Ahmed from room service balancing the fragrant tray, which bears my breakfast. Stepping inside, he stands tall and statue-still and waits for his eyes to adjust to the darkness, exaggerating his difficulty. His magnificent classic features barely visible, he could be a Pharaoh stepping out of the shadowy past. "Please Miss Kara, could you let some light in so I can move?"

"*Tayib*, okay. Wait while I open the drapes." I relent, turn, and drag my white train across the carpeted floor. I remove just one clothespin, allowing precisely two inches of sunlight to enter, just enough for him to make his way across the room and set down the heavy tray.

"*Shukren ya Sitti*, thank you," Ahmed surveys the room with a frown. His dark eyes light upon the opened book and the map, and he shakes his head. "Back to pyramids again today? No make shopping at *Khan el Khalili*? I worry for you, Miss Kara, why can you not lie by the pool today, do easy things? I think maybe you're not a normal woman."

"This is normal, Ahmed, normal for me," I reply. I lead spiritual tours and there's no end to new discoveries beneath the sands of this ancient land. Descriptions in the Book of the Dead of higher planes of existence and the journey through the astral plane into spirit fascinate me. I find there is little interest among Egyptians in their own mythology or monuments, and so I don't attempt to explain what I'm doing.

Ahmed smiles as I hand him five pounds extra for his extreme good nature in enduring me every morning. "Shukren, enjoy your day, Miss Kara." He leaves without any further discussion of my abnormal ways.

Awakening rituals must be performed in a certain order; this is made clear in the Book of the Dead, more accurately translated as "The Transformation into The Light." A worn copy lies on my nightstand, transliterated in Arabic and English.

Every two days, management leaves a gift of fruit and fresh roses. The scent of tamarind hangs heavy in the room and the tantalizing array of fruits begin to spread their sticky ripeness over the sides of the silver tray onto the garlands of late summer jasmine I wore last night.

Today I will perform the 'Ritual of the Eating of the Fruits', I determine, but with great care so as not to invoke again the dreaded mummy tummy. The barren desert is no place to have diarrhea. After careful washing with bleach, I will remove the peels and dissect each fragrant, ripened fruit. On second thought, I had better wait until evening, just in case. Diarrhea in the desert is disastrous and today will be a long day beneath the sands of Saqqara.

I open the outer and then the inner drapes, carefully moving aside the intricately carved *mashrabeyya* shutters. I turn the handle of the old casement window and it creaks with age to reveal the dazzling world outside. The sight of the pyramids takes my breath every time, and the nearness and beauty of them is almost too powerful to bear.

The morning air carries a rich bouquet of scent and sound; along with a fine dust that dances into the room on rays of sunlight. The clip-clop of hooves, the braying of donkeys, shouting of vendors, honking of horns, blaring of Arabic music, the scrawny desert dogs barking, all heading in a great colorful parade up the curving road to the Giza Plateau.

Pulling table and chair closer to the window, I turn to the tray and slowly open the thick white linen napkin, revealing a basket of fragrant pastries and 'aish baladi, local bread. I reach for a chocolate croissant. The *Al-Ahram* newspaper with its stylized red pyramids logo lies folded on the tray, waiting to shatter the magic of this moment with world news. "World Leaders Convene in Cairo to Discuss Hijacking." No, I will ignore the newspaper as if it is an unrecognizable object from another world. I toss the Al-Ahram to the floor.

Focusing instead on the perfectly designed square silver teapot, I lift its solid weight and pour with both hands, inhaling the steam of strong, black tea. I then sit back in the ornately carved, red velvet chair to gaze at the pyramids, praising Allah that I am alive in this moment. I was raised both Catholic and Muslim and I honor and respect both. However, I dispensed with the middleman long ago and now just follow my own spiritual path.

Omar's stable across the street is chaos. Busloads of tourists are descending, demanding camels or Arabian stallions immediately as if they have urgent business meetings to attend across town. American women in bright and clinging polyester attire, giddy with excitement, bravely climb up on the high saddles as the camel heaves and pitches back and forward to struggle to its feet.

"*Yalla, yalla!* Let me help you," the camel guide calls out, lovingly cupping and pushing up on the derriere of a woman who hangs sideways on the beast. Mute husbands stand aside in velour jogging suits, baseball caps, and white Nike running shoes, holding their wives purses and cameras. They watch as handsome stable hands in loose-flowing gallabeyas coax the women onto camels. They seem wary of releasing their wives into the looming desert but there is no stopping the fun-seeking women now and off they go.

"Camel for you too, sir. No miss the fun. Two for one!" From my experience in leading Egypt tours, it's often the men who are hesitant to let go of control, to leap into the experience and enjoy the journey. I think of how many of life's adventures I once held at bay because of men like those who wanted to suppress my joy. Never again, I think to myself. Freedom is worth all the sacrifices I make for this life I have chosen.

I watch with delight as a few of the husbands are pushed forward by their friends, hoisted, and cajoled against their protests. The newly mounted men give the 'thumbs up' gesture to the camel boys, a gesture that in this culture means 'up yours.' A stable boy calls back with a laugh, "You too." The travelers at last fall into line as a caravan, shouting and taking photos of one another; evidence for someone back home that they did, in fact, ride a camel to the pyramids.

It is day one of their high-end tour, which always begins with a textbook overview of the Giza Plateau, nothing of the mystical aspects of the site. The cliché has already been documented on Kodak film. If they allow the magic to touch them, by the time they return to Giza in two weeks for their final stay at The Mena House, they'll be forever changed. Some for better, some for worse, depending on whether they are willing to surrender to the enduring, maddening mystery that is Egypt.

CHAPTER TWENTY EIGHT

SAQQARA

*"The courage of the poet is to keep ajar the
door that leads into madness."*
Christopher Morley, writer

"*Sabah el Warda*, Good Morning." The red-jacketed
bellman greets me on the front stairs in the
morning.

"*Sabah el Ishta, Sabah el Full,*" I reply. Morning of flowers,
morning of cream. morning of jasmine. There are endless ways
to say hello. My Arabic is improving each day. I'm now fluent
in calling out absurd phrases to relative strangers in passing. I
must move quickly before the bellman can respond with yet
another flowery greeting; this could go on until afternoon
when protocol requires it all be repeated again.

My driver, Hossam, is waiting at the end of the driveway in
his black and white taxi. We head south to the Necropolis of

Saqqara and the vast rock-cut underground burial chambers of the sacred Apis bulls.

"You don't have to wait for me today, Hossam. Just leave me at the entrance and come back at closing time."

"You'll be down there all day, underground in the dark with dead bulls? This is important to you?"

"Of course," I say. "To ancient Egyptians the Apis bull contained the divine manifestation of the god Ptah, and later of Osiris. You know Osiris, right? He shakes his head. "Come on Hossam, you must have heard of Osiris. Didn't you learn some Egyptian history in school?" He gives me a quizzical look and shrugs, then turns up the radio and begins to do a shoulder shimmy to the beat. Like most Egyptians his age, he's never been inside a pyramid or tomb and takes no interest in the ancient past. It's Western culture, American in particular, that young Egyptians aspire to. We ride a few miles on narrow roads past green fields of alfalfa, date palms, and dried-up canals clogged with debris. A large black water buffalo walks in a circle in the field, turning a shadouf that draws up water for the alfalfa crop. Children play alongside the animal and try to jump on and take a ride on the wide wooden wheel of the shadouf, something I have done myself in the past. I smile at how much fun they are having with such a simple activity.

Hossam turns and tries again to dissuade me. "How about the museum today? Nice and cool in there."

I lead forward. "Would you like me to explain the mythology of Isis and Osiris? It' a great story, really, and one that every Egyptian should know." Hossam is no longer even pretending to listen to me as he searches for another pack of

Cleopatras in his glove compartment. An oncoming truck swerves to avoid us and I gasp, sitting back.

"No problem, you are home now," Hossam assures me. The rhythm of Egypt begins to sink into my being. The noise, the chaos, the alarming lack of normal caution all become oddly acceptable. I begin to entrain to the sounds, as a child in utero to its mother's heartbeat. Hossam is right; I am home now in the arms of Mother Egypt. The much-loved Egyptian song goes round in my mind, "*Um el Dunya*," Mother of the World.

We park at the entrance and he turns to face me. "You will find me right here when you come up at closing time. Have a good time with the bulls." He then adds in a more serious tone, "Oh, and be careful. It's dangerous for a woman to be in there alone. I know you have no fear of spirits, but there could be someone alive in there who is not as nice as the dead bulls."

I lean in the window and reply, "That's true, I'd be terrified if someone living stepped out of the shadows. Spirits, though, don't scare me in the least. Thanks for your concern."

Hossam laughs and shakes his head, waves, and begins to turn the taxi around. I head towards the entrance of the *Serapeum* where two guards stand in loud and heated conversation. They don't notice me, and so I pass by them and disappear through the entrance. No one will know I'm inside and that works out better since I won't be disturbed.

I take small steps down the long, sloped shaft entering the 3500 year old chamber. The interior lights aren't working and so I stop and crouch down to search my pack for a flashlight. It seems no one else has taken an interest in visiting the Apis bulls on this beautiful day and I am alone in the vast, dark space. The dark, 110-foot space is lined on either side by rows of 24 two-ton black granite sarcophagi, which supposedly once held the sacred animals. Each carved from a single piece of granite quarried 500 miles away, the boxes have perfect right angles to 1/1000th of an inch and fine depictions of ceremonial rites on the outside.

The air underground smells of dampness and dust. The flashlight falls from my pack and rolls away under a sarcophagus. I crawl onto my stomach and reach for it, but my arms aren't long enough. My heart races as panic takes over and so I lie on my back and take a deep breathe to calm myself. Then, as if from an unseen hand, it rolls back to me. I grab the flashlight, stand up, and whisper thank you to spirit.

As I continue to inch along, I pray there are no pits ahead that could swallow me into the darkness. My mind flashes to the gruesome details of a recent story in the Al-Ahram of a foreigner who fell into an open hole in the street and drowned in sewage. I hear my mother's voice inside my head, "You never did listen to anyone, stubborn child, now look what you've gotten yourself into." I implore Mom to please be quiet and just help me get out of this alive. My jaw tightens and I keep my gaze focused on the small beam of light as I walk further.

What was I thinking, entering a cavernous underground chamber with only a small flashlight? I'm no Indiana Jones for sure, although I'm totally at home crawling around under the earth. I've spent a good deal of my life at sacred sites, sitting in stone boxes, sarcophagi, and tombs. I can sense the energy of the places and times, and often I see scenes of events that took place in the location long ago. I do believe that events are imprinted on places and can be experienced by those with sensitivity and open minds.

Each enormous stone coffin looks exactly like the next and I become disoriented the further I walk. I'm almost to the end of the chamber and there's only one way in or out. I assure myself that and all I need do is retrace my steps when ready to leave. I put my jacket on the floor and settle in to meditate, my back against the cool stone. A presence hovers in the chamber, a presence both ominous and welcoming at turns. The stone chamber resonates with vibrations of what took place here thousands of years ago. As my teacher, Hakim el Awyan, once told me, "all the memory of human existence on earth is contained in stone and bone."

I imagine the procession of solemn high priests, shaven heads and white robes, carrying censors of myrrh and frankincense, as they honor the sacred animals, the Apis bulls that represent the great master Serapis. I feel the protective arms of my guide enfold me, the way a loving husband or father might do.

After a while, the heavy air underground begins to feel oppressive. I stand and brush the dust from my clothes and give thanks to all the unseen ones who dwell in this place. Hands on the stone sarcophagi, I feel my way back up the sloping shaft towards the opening, keeping my eyes on the one ray of light in the distance.

The sun is blinding as I emerge into the desert. Two hours have passed since I arrived at Saqqara and now there are a dozen busses unloading hoards of dazed travellers. The architecture of Saqqara looks like Art Deco, not like one of Egypt's most ancient sites. This confounds people and they stand in awe.

Vendors have set up stalls where they sell oranges and the ubiquitous Coca-Cola and Snickers bars. I buy a large orange and bottled water and climb to a shaded outcropping of stone where I sit and watch the passing crowds. Some German tourists call out hello and I wave back at them. I love the sense of camaraderie amongst travelers throughout the world, especially those who are spiritual seekers. Finishing the orange, I put the peels in my pocket, take out a wet wipe and wash my hands of juice and dust and climb down from my perch.

Nearby is a table strewn with colorful clay *shawabti* dolls, reproductions of the minions of the royal families. The concept of burying the dead with legions of tiny clay servants to take care of their every need in the afterlife seems a clever plan and I wonder if it proved to be helpful to those ancients in the afterlife. My desire for *shawabtis* is not so much about the purchase, or even my fondness for the figurines, as it is for the sheer joy of interacting once again with the living. I've reached my quota of time among the dead for today and enjoy being social again.

I despise bargaining and I hesitate to begin the game. To my relief, this vendor is funny and gracious and he doesn't push for sales at all. Because of his pleasant nature, I purchase two-dozen *shawabtis* instead of just one. He carefully wraps each one in yesterday's Al Ahram as we chat and then hands the black plastic bag to me with a broad smile and a thank you. As I place the bag in my backpack, a kitten rubs against my leg and cries, her spotted black and grey coat soft and silky. She begins scaling my leg, tiny claws sharp as pins as she makes her way to my shoulder. The Egyptian Mau recently made centerfold of 'Cat Fancy' magazine as a prized and costly breed. Here the spotted grey cat is a common sight, just another stray cat in a land with too many people, and too many cats. I hug her and then kneel down and offer her water from the upturned peel of my orange. She crawls back onto my shoulder where she purrs and perches like a tiny royal feline. I sneeze repeatedly. As much as I try to deny it, I'm severely allergic to cats. Still, I cannot live without them.

I call the kitten Bast, after the ancient cat goddess of the arts. We take a walk along the half-mile perimeter of the Step Pyramid of Zoser. Bast holds her head high, enjoying the view. She proves to be an excellent conversationalist and she chirps and purrs in reply to my questions, chewing on my hair and licking my cheek. She rubs her head against mine and claims me as her own.

Saqqara is believed by scholars to be the oldest of the known pyramid sites, predating even Giza, and yet it is not known why the step pyramid was built in this stairway fashion and without deep inner chambers as the great pyramid has. So many things are conjecture, which is part of the mystery of Egypt.

A large Japanese tour group huddles together, much closer than would be comfortable for other nationalities. Each one wears a surgical mask and holds a brightly colored parasol to block the afternoon sun. They stand listening to their Egyptologist guide, my friend Sherine, as she recites facts with an astounding command of Japanese. A French group passes by and she seamlessly switches to French as she stops to chat with her colleague.

My brilliant friend Sherine transitions to Arabic and

English as we greet each other and walk along. I request her as our site guide for every tour I lead, but she's in great demand and booked a year ahead. Sherine has the characteristic demeanor of a highly educated Cairene and her classic beauty captivates men and women alike. As with all cosmopolitan, educated women of Cairo, she doesn't wear hijab and she moves with calm self-assurance, her long black hair secured by a barrette. We stand outside the entrance of the step pyramid while her Japanese group is inside. We talk of our lives and the choices each of us has made and I tell her how I wish I had come home with my godfather and attended Cairo University and studied languages.

"Ah, but that was not in your soul plan. You did well with your education while raising your beautiful son," she says. "I don't have any children yet and I'm starting to be concerned that I never will. I don't want a husband so much as I want a baby."

"I do believe in fate or destiny," Sherine says, "as well as the free will of each individual within the plan the soul has made."

At the same instant, we both look around to be sure no one can overhear us as she lowers her voice and continues. "My soul plan could have led to a number of outcomes. I feel I have lived in every culture in past lifetimes and have been of every religion and race. All of it seems so familiar to me." Sherine's thinking is clearly not in alignment with traditional Islam, which rejects the concept of reincarnation, and of unmarried women bearing children. She has thus far resisted all attempts by her family to push her into an arranged marriage. Instead, she's pursued her doctoral degree and become an archaeologist guide.

"I agree," I reply, "I believe the only essential part of my plan was to have my wonderful son."

We continue in easy conversation about free will and destiny and the beliefs of the ancient Egyptians compared to those of Islam, in particular concerning women's rights.

"In ancient Egypt," Sherine says," women were equal to men in every respect and royal lineage could only be passed through the maternal line. This only makes sense since one is never entirely sure who the father is, but always we know who the mother is." We both laugh at this indisputable fact.

Sherine's Japanese group finally emerges from the temple and they stand waiting for her. We hug goodbye and make a plan to meet later that evening back at the hotel for dinner.

She turns and calls back, "*Fifi Abdou* is at *Abu Nawas* tonight. We can dress up and have some fun. And, you can get up and dance with her again while I take photos."

"No, please don't draw attention to me. I just want to enjoy the show."

Sherine laughs. "It's so odd how you get singled out to join the dancer everywhere we go. There must be some dancer energy that makes all of you recognize each other."

The sun is setting and the muezzin call can be heard from the minaret of the nearby village of Abusir. I continue walking in silence with my feline friend who sits regally surveying the scene from atop my shoulder. All the tour groups have gone back to the bus lot and the mau kitten and I walk alone through the vast courtyard space of the Saqqara complex.

As Bast and I cross the final wide expanse of stone courtyard, a tall male figure appears seemingly out of nowhere, dressed in pharoanic clothing and wearing the blue and gold striped nemes headdress, over which is a golden uraeus crown. The flared hood of the cobra on his forehead represents enlightenment and power. Only a pharaoh would be allowed to wear such a headdress. There's a light emanating from him and he moves within a shimmering gold mist.

I wonder to myself if there's a theatre production going on and I think perhaps he's returning from rehearsal. The man's short white kilt is girded with a wide belt. Broad-chested and caramel-skinned, he embodies strength and masculinity. His stride is determined and I slow down and waver, uncertain which way to step to avoid crashing into him. He doesn't seem to even see me or to make an effort to step aside, but walks right through me. I gasp aloud and shiver as a bolt of electrical energy rushes through my body. The kitten screeches, leaps off my shoulder, and races away. I turn to address the man and reprimand him for his lack of manners, but he is gone. The courtyard is empty.

Shaken and confused, I sit on a low column of stone and wait for my heartbeat to steady and my knees to stop trembling. Thinking perhaps I have heatstroke and am having hallucinations, I find my bottle of water, drink some, and splash the rest on my face and neck.

The man was magnificent. Had he not been so imperious looking, I would have found him attractive. But how could I be attracted to a phantom? There was something oddly familiar about him; it was as if I had seen him somewhere before, but that makes no sense at all. I wonder if I have just entered through a portal into another time/space and walked for a moment in the ancient past. Such things are not unusual in

Egypt, at least not for those who come here with minds open to other realties.

The kitten reappears, jumps down from a rock and pads back to me. She tilts her head and watches with narrowed turquoise eyes, the scarab beetle pattern on her forehead clearly outlined in the light. She comes closer, stares and then and blinks slowly, a sure sign that we have become friends. When satisfied it's safe to return, she hops back up onto my shoulder and purrs and chortles until we've returned to the entrance of the Saqqara complex.

I bring my little spotted friend over to the *shawabti* vendor. He's a kind man and he promises to look after her. I kiss the kitten goodbye and cuddle her once more. We've bonded over a strange paranormal experience and I wish she could give me her opinion of what happened. If I see her again, no doubt she'll be grown, yet I feel certain we'll recognize each other. In one graceful leap, Bast hops onto a pile of tapestries and kneads the fabric frantically until she finds the perfect spot to nap in the shade. She yawns, stretches, gives me one last flash of turquoise gaze, and falls asleep. The vendor and I laugh.

"Don't worry, she will be well cared for until you come back," he says. I'm grateful that the treasures above ground have proven at least as valuable to me as those I went in search of beneath the desert today.

Hossam is leaning against the car in the same spot where he left me early that morning. He waves and opens the door for me. I stumble into the back seat with a strange, other-worldly feeling still possessing me and toss my head back onto the headrest.

"Why do you look so pale?" He asks, "Did someone bother you? Are you alright?"

"I'm fine, Hossam" I take out my tissues and wipe my face and neck. "In the course of this long day I made new friends and fell hopelessly in love with a Mau kitten which I just had to say goodbye to."

He laughs and shakes his head. "How is it you find cats everywhere you go?"

"They find me. They sense I'm a crazy cat lady. Animals recognize those who love them." "I love them too, but I they don't find me or follow me everywhere," Hossam says. "That's because you're always driving, they can't catch up with you," We both laugh and he starts the engine. Turning out of the parking lot, we head towards Saqqara Road. I think for a while in silence and then lean forward and tell Hossam, "Some other things happened today. Things so strange I cannot begin to explain right now. Maybe later I can talk about it. But no, no one bothered me at all. *Mafeesh mushkelat*, no problems."

"Good," he replies, "You know how we Egyptians can sense things," he says, "I can always tell when something is bothering you. We are friends, yes? We can talk about anything."

The strange encounter in the courtyard with a being from the pharoanic past is too bizzarre to articulate. I've not begun to sort it out in my own mind and wonder if perhaps it is all due to the heat and lack of sleep in recent weeks. The handsome pharaoh wasn't hostile or unpleasant; in fact, he was intriguing. His image stays in my mind and serves to shake up my reality far more than being in the dark chamber with the dead bulls. I can still feel his energy and see the steely determination in his gaze as he strode toward me. I can't quite shake his presence and wonder if a part of his spirit has lingered with me. I smudge my room with sage when I get back to my hotel room and take a long shower to remove the desert dust. Then I take a nice nap. Clean and rested, I order *Umm Ali*, my favorite traditional dessert made with crushed pastry dough layered with hazelnuts, toasted coconut and sultana raisins, and warm milk. That and a pot of hot strong tea revive me for the night ahead.

At the hotel's Abu Nawas dinner club, Fifi Abdou, an icon of Egyptian dance, will perform at 2AM. I learned Egyptian dance over the years, primarily from watching Fifi, and dancing with her whenever she coaxed me to join her. I look forward to the evening and to discussing the events at Saqqara with Sherine, especially the encounter with that alluring phantom pharaoh. I'm sure she won't find it frightening and perhaps she might recall having seen him before, maybe depicted on the wall reliefs or statuary. She's been studying the pharaonic dynasties for decades and so should know.

A call comes from the lobby at 10PM and Sherine whispers, "There's a problem. When my brother Farouk saw me dressed up to go out, he insisted upon accompanying me. He says he's interested in the show, but I know he really hates our dance and just wants to be sure I don't sit with any men or discuss forbidden topics with you. I think some of his boring religious friends are coming too. They'll listen to every word we say."

"Oh, no," I reply, "Does this mean we have to behave all night?"

"I'm afraid so," my friend says. "Since our father died, Farouk has become a religious fanatic. He's even telling our mother how to behave now. She's become afraid of him when he starts yelling about women and the word of Mohammed."

"Oh great. He must not be pleased about your meeting up with me tonight."

"He just told me he likes you very much and he would like to get to know you better, but that you're a dangerous influence on me. So it seems you're good for him, but not for me."

"No problem, I hear this often. Seems fanaticism has risen everywhere over the years, I've become that dangerous blue-eyed devil the imams preach about. And, to make matters worse, I'm a dancer, a disreputable profession now in Egypt."

"Please, I hope you will still come down and sit with me. I cannot take this long night on my own. We can sneak away to the ladies room and talk, although there's always that crow sitting in there, the elderly lady in black *niqab*, listening for gossip."

"I know, your brother will probably pay her to report every word of our conversation. Don't worry, I'll stay with you all evening until the show ends."

"Yes, please. I'm dying to hear more about the handsome pharaoh spirit you met in Saqqara. Maybe he's my future husband coming to rescue me at last and I'll be saved from an arranged marriage."

"Oh, maybe so," I say. "But we'll have to share him whenever I'm in Cairo, he was so gorgeous and mesmerizing."

Our moods lighten at the idea of the phantom pharaoh coming to whisk my friend Sherine to freedom before the descent of the Dark Ages that are encroaching on Egypt.

In spite of the somber, condescending faces of Farouk and his friends, one of whom is wearing a traditional *abeya*, with a prayer shawl on his shoulder, the dinner show is well worth losing an entire night's sleep. Fifi Abdou and her band are spectacular and the audience showers her with adoration. Of course, not one person in the audience would approve of her marrying into their family, so split is the consciousness concerning art and religion.

Music of all kinds, as well as dance, is now frowned upon by self appointed 'good Muslims.' Cairo has been the music and entertainment capital of the East for a century, but now in recent years the creative spirit of the great city is suffocating under religious repression. The happy times of sophisticated Cairo nightlife and of women's freedom are becoming a thing of the past.

☥

CHAPTER TWENTY NINE
RENDEZVOUS WITH SERAPIS

"Everything you see has its roots in the unseen world.
The forms may change, yet the essence remains the same."
Rumi

I return alone to Upper Egypt two years later, where I imagine that my spirit guide Serapis awaits my arrival. The new Luxor museum has been constructed to house the collection from the astonishing 1989, excavation, which my group and I had the honor of witnessing.

Within that three-month period, 25 magnificent statues and various smaller artifacts, all from 1405-1367 BC, early 18th dynasty, have been unearthed. I feel as if I'm revisiting an old flame and I eagerly await the sight of him. My heart flutters as I ride in the caleche, past the Luxor Temple complex and to the museum. As we near the entrance, I adjust my scarf, smooth my wind-blown hair, and freshen my lipstick in the tiny mirror of my lipstick case. What am I doing? It's ridiculous to be primping for a long-deceased pharaoh. I smile to myself at the sheer absurdity of it, but this is the life I live while hovering between ancient and present-day worlds.

As I had hoped it's early enough that he museum is still empty of tourists. I look around with a sigh of relief, thankful the pharaoh and I will have the privacy we need. The six-foot high pink quartzite statue depicts the king standing on a sledge and wearing the double crown of Upper and Lower Egypt. The flawless statue of my dear spirit guide that has been unearthed completely intact transfixes me. His eyes seem to observe me, his royal demeanor steady and sure, his hands by his sides in a pose of power. I'm locked in his gaze. Beside him is the life-sized statue of his wife who is precisely my own height and build. I amuse myself in imagining we once had a past life together. Her eyes are wide and gentle and she radiates a sense of calm and ease as she stands next to her beloved husband. Serapis/Amenhhotep. They're radiant as with the delight of loved ones reunited after a long absence. I feel his presence enfold me, so familiar and welcoming. I make no effort to stop the tears rolling down my face as I stare into the eyes of the statue, the eyes of my long-time spirit guide.

The imperiousness disappears and his expression becomes kind and infinitely wise. I recall the phantom male figure that had walked toward me two years ago in the courtyard at Saqqara; it's that same determined gaze and regal presence. The pharaoh's head tilts slightly as he looks at me with tenderness. It could be the angle of the light, but to me it seems real. Then, so subtly, he smiles and nods his head in greeting.

CHAPTER THIRTY
LONGING - CAPE COD

....You who never arrived
In my arms, Beloved, who were lost
From the start...
Who knows? Perhaps the same bird echoed through both
of us
Yesterday, separate, in the evening...
Rainer Maria Rilke

I awaken from another image of the dream lover with a sense of sad longing. I haven't met anyone I care to spend time with, or who even remotely resembles my dream lover. A part of my heart still belongs to Naim, although we officially ended our affair three years ago. I wonder if this dream lover could be as wonderful and kind as my former love. And I wonder when I will meet him face to face in the physical world. I am growing disheartened by the dream meetings and I want something real.

The dreary weeks following my father's death on New Year's Eve of 1994 drag on and I move as if in a daze, my sleep void of all dreams as my body struggles to recover from a deep exhaustion. Then, out of the bleak tunnel of grief, one snowy morning in late January I'm surprised to receive phone calls, hours apart, from three women friends.

First it's Tina, "Who else would I go with? You've been enticing me with stories of Egypt for years and now it's time. What do you mean you're not going? You have to go, I already told my boss I was taking time off to join you." The calls keep coming from women who don't even know one another, but know me.

Next, it's my pragmatic friend, Carol. "Whatever crazy metaphysical tour you have scheduled this time, I don't even care. You know I'm not into all this spiritual stuff, I just want to see Egypt with you and I happen to have the time and money right now to go,"

"It's a good one," I tell her. "Conscious Immortality; Life, Death and Reincarnation."

"That's it," Carol replies with sarcasm, "I need that."

"Sorry, but I've been so sick with the flu I can't go further than the local pharmacy, let alone lead an international tour. Since my father died, I just don't have any desire or energy to go anywhere."

The following day, I have a surprise visit from Adam's closest friend, Molly, a girl I love as if she's my own daughter. She's been away at college studying international law and world religions and is now eager to experience the most ancient culture on earth.

"Great news!" she calls as she rushes in the door, stamping snow off her boots. "I'm coming to Egypt with you this time. Can we room together?"

"You know I despise rooming with anyone. Besides, I am not going this time."

In her unstoppable enthusiasm, Molly overlooks the second sentence and surges ahead.

"Come on, I'm not just anyone. You know how much fun we always have."

Her excitement and sparkling Irish eyes force me to reconsider. This girl is so special to me, how can I disappoint her like this? She's almost family, as well as a loyal friend.

Something odd is going on with this Egypt tour and it's eerie how things are unfolding. This feeling of pre-destiny happens often enough with spiritual tours, I remind myself, and in spite of great expectations, the higher plan often turns out to be some dreadful karmic lesson. I'd had enough travel mishaps and fated experiences. I've learned that just because something feels fated does not mean something wonderful is going to happen.

Still, I really like all of these women friends who've resurfaced and the thought of introducing Molly to my second home appeals to me. I can just imagine Molly's delight at being in Egypt.

THE ANNUAL INTERNATIONAL CONFERENCE ON metaphysical topics is a complicated production that my California colleagues and I somehow manage to pull off each year. I call the West Coast in between coughing fits to tell my California colleagues that I've changed my mind.

"There's been a change of plans. A group of ten has formed out of nowhere, so I will take part in the conference after all. I'm too burned out to be a presenter this time, but I'll bring a group and help out wherever needed. And, I'll teach an Egyptian dance workshop. That's always easy for me since I've taught it so many times."

More than a hundred and fifty spiritual seekers have signed up from various parts of the world, the largest conference my tour colleagues and I have ever led.

Getting out of the U.S. in a blizzard and two feet of snow is an initiation in itself. Logan Airport is closed and a frantic chase begins for trains and taxis to get to JFK on time for the Egypt Air flight to Cairo.

My little group convenes just in time for final boarding, all except four women who are still missing. As I pace, boarding passes in hand, I spot them strolling down the long hallway toward the gate, laughing and not seeming at all in a hurry. A dark-haired man saunters along with them, loaded down with suitcases, as he basks in the role of shining knight. So that's why they're so late, I think to myself as I stride to greet them.

"You're just in time, boarding has begun." I hand them their boarding passes and check off their names on my list. The only remaining problem is this handsome young man who doesn't seem to be leaving. I turn to him, clipboard in hand, and inquire in my most professional tour manager voice as I attempt to suppress my annoyance. "And who are you?"

"My name is Raphael. I'm a member of the conference. I

signed up last week from Boston, called the main number in California and got the last space." He's much too pleased with himself, I think, as he gets in line to board and my group welcomes him with open arms.

Apparently, he has shepherded my ladies to all their connections and assisted them with the absurd number of suitcases they were checking in. They seem quite taken with this stranger, huddling around him and chatting as if they've just reunited with a long-lost friend. I overhear talk of architecture and sacred temple complexes built to align with star systems. He appears to be well informed about the sacred architecture of Egypt.

So, he is one of those self-absorbed architects who just read the latest book from Robert Beauval and John Hancock. He seems the kind of left-brained guy who travels to sacred sites to measure God with a slide rule. I wonder if he has any idea what he's getting into with this spiritual tour, or just how far-out a New Age conference can be, especially when there's a large southern California contingent. We shall see how long he lasts among these crazy new age seekers, I think to myself with a smile.

On board the Egypt Air craft, everyone is seated, announcements made in English and then Arabic, and we lift off into a snowy sky. Relieved to settle in with my headphones, earplugs and eyeshade, I take a handful of vitamins and a melatonin and begin my well-established ritual of getting some sleep on the long flight. In my wooly plane socks, my shawl wrapped around me like a cocoon, I close my eyes. Just as I begin to doze off, Molly taps my arm.

"He's calling you. Raphael is calling you from back there!"

"For God's sake, this isn't a damned school bus; it's an international flight! We can't just stand up and call other people out loud."

I remove my eyeshade and earplugs and get up, but cannot see over the headrest. I climb onto my seat to look back to where his voice is coming from, flinging my Pashmina over my shoulder in frustration. It catches on the armrest and I pull it with a jerk. A glass of cold Riesling topples onto the lap of the German businessman next to me who's in the act of pouring it.

Instinctively, from many years of caring for children, I lean to rescue the glass and then to sop up the liquid on his legs with my shawl. The indignant German refuses my attempts to dab at his wine-soaked crotch, muttering some remark about crazy American women. My apologies have no effect on the man's seething mood and his red-faced glare is frightening.

I apologize one last time and turn my attention to Raphael who's foolishly standing up waving at me as if I cannot already see him. I lose all patience with the situation and my frustration can be heard in my voice.

"What is it? Why are you calling me?"

"I remember now, I'm sure I met you before."

Rolling my eyes, I reply, "And I am certain I've heard that line before."

He persists, "We met the September before last, at the Terrace Lounge in Boston. I tried to serve you, but you only wanted water - a lot of water with lemon. You were wearing a white blazer and carrying that same clipboard with the Arabic decals on it." He's determined to jog my memory of our meeting. "There was another woman with you and she had a clipboard too."

I had to concede his small victory. "You may be right, I was there last year on business. Can we talk about this later?"

I shrug and sit back down, leaning as far away from the seething German as possible. I hide my head on Molly's shoulder, mortified at my having lurched toward the crotch of a stranger. Molly and I hope the sound of the engine is muffling our giggles as we whisper about the odd chain of events.

I at last calm down, close my eyes, and try to recall that past September and any further memory of that annoying man.

"So do you remember meeting him before?" Molly asks.

"Yes. All right, I was in that hotel bar with another tour manager who was briefing me for my next assignment. I was intent upon learning the major points of Italy in the few hours before going to the airport and my focus was on memorization of an itinerary and a city map. I do vaguely recall a bartender who refused to accept the fact I wanted nothing to eat and I that I don't drink alcohol in the morning."

Molly smiled as I went on. "He had tried to strike up a conversation, but the last thing I needed at the time was a flirtation with a young bartender."

In that moment, his gold name badge flashed into my mind, 'Raphael.'

"Yes, I do remember thinking at the time that his name had an angelic feeling and it went well with his appearance."

Molly is all eyes and grinning widely, "Aha!"

"So it's true, he and I have crossed paths before. This doesn't necessarily mean anything in a busy world."

"I think it does," she says. "I think both of your guides have been trying for a long time to hook you two up. The problem was that you weren't paying attention and he was. Or at least now he is, that's for sure. He can't take his eyes away from you."

"Hook us up? For what purpose? He's too young and immature for me. I think it was all arranged so that you would meet him and fall in love, not me. He seems closer to your age than mine."

Still, I questioned why he would have remembered me, except for my utter lack of response to his persistence. Maybe I was the first to refuse his attentions, his Latin charms failed him for once. Enough thinking - I put my travel pillow in place and pull my damp Pashmina over myself like a blanket, taking care not to infringe on my seatmate's space. A few desperately needed hours of sleep will clear everything up and I'll be back on keel with my emotions.

Again Molly shakes my arm, this time much too hard. I wince, "Your grip is like a vice, stop it!" The girl is working out too much and doesn't know her own strength.

"Wait! I don't understand it, she says, "Why are you being so rude toward this nice man?"

Exasperated, I remove my earplugs again to answer her. "I don't know. Something about him just bothers me. He thinks he knows me. And he's so arrogant. He's cute, but immature in a way that grates on my nerves. Altogether a dangerous and annoying man."

Settling back in my seat, I ask myself. What it is about him that so annoys me. I reflect on this for a while and then dismiss it as the effect of a long travel day. I drift in and out of sleep, awakening intermittently to sneeze, blow my nose, and use my inhaler. The flu from hell is still hanging on and I cringe with embarrassment as other passengers glare at me. I don't blame them, as I'm often the one obsessively using my hand sanitizer and cursing those travelers who sneeze on everyone around them. I feel like a pariah and want to be home in the safety of my own bed, in the dark confines of my room with all the shades drawn. What have I let myself be talked into now? I should learn to say no and mean it.

CHAPTER THIRTY ONE
IN THE SHADOW OF THE PYRAMIDS

"We travel, some of us forever, to seek other states, other lives, other souls."
Anaïs Nin

T he Mena House is the perfect setting for the international conference. Every inch of the hotel is kept polished to a sparkle and each detail exquisitely crafted due to the loving care of the British woman who had restored it back in the early 1900s. The aristocratic woman imported materials from every part of the world to create this gem, which was meant to be a retreat for her friends. It later became a meeting place for dignitaries and the site of the signing of many international treaties over decades.

Chandeliers cast intricate patterns on the walls and ceilings. It's a scene from an Arabian Nights tale brought to life, a setting so intriguing and so rich with beauty and refined elegance. It speaks of former times of great opulence combined with good taste.

I'm greeted upon arrival by the bellmen and front desk staff as they echo, *"Ahlen we Sahlen*, Miss Kara. Welcome home."

"Ahlen bikum," I reply, as the old-world glow of the place begins to weave its magical spell. The front desk is staffed, as always, with an array of gorgeous, dreamy-eyed young men. In all my world travels, nowhere have I ever seen so many beautiful men in one location as in Egypt. The women in the group are commenting on this phenomenon as well.

My weary and awe-struck group gathers on the front steps of the lobby, beneath a 20-foot white plastic banner kindly created by the hotel staff. In large bold letters it stated, "Welcome to Conscious Immorality." That missing "t" makes all the difference in meaning and the humor is not lost on us, or any passing guests.

"Do you see that?" Egyptian guests exclaimed as they paused beside us and looked up. "These Americans just go too far! They are actually proud of their immorality. *"Mish Maoul!* Unbelievable!"

The travel-weary conferencees gather around, gasping and exclaiming to each other at the splendor of the hotel and the surreal sight of the pyramids in the distance. They waited for instructions to their rooms, in the garden section, a short walk from the main palace. This is always a hectic part of the tour for me, as so many things have to occur immediately. We have a team of five assistants and we gather to sort through the details. Suitcases tagged with room numbers, morning room numbers and keys issued, schedule posted in the lobby, all is at last in order.

The night air is uncharacteristically balmy and my hair frizzes up into a wild, uncontrollable mane and I'm at my wit's end with yet another annoyance. I'm self-conscious and insecure in the gaze of that handsome young Raphael and he's eyeing me and maneuvering to get closer to where I stand. I refuse to let him get the best of me and I regain my composure, push my hair back, and walked over to him.

"Here's your room key, up one flight and with a view of the pyramids." As I hand him his key, he holds my gaze for a second too long, as if expecting I'll say something else. I quickly pull back, turn away, and join my women friends who stand watching and waiting for the next directive from me. Like everyone else, they're too tired to think of where they should go next and they need explicit guidelines to get to the front desk of the garden section of the hotel where they can drop their bags in their rooms. We agree to meet back at the main lobby.

After a half hour, I escort my disoriented but happy group of women upstairs to the coffee shop and get them settled with menus. I then excuse myself, and dash down the hallway to visit my Uncles, Zacharia, and Mohammed in their small jewelry shop. I pass Raphael in the hallway and he's headed for the coffee shop.

"Raphael, come join us," I hear Janet calling, "We're all too charged up to go to sleep, we're in Egypt! Egypt! Can you even believe it? I feel like I'm in a dream. Look at this view!" The pyramids are illuminated against the night sky. The other women chime in and urge the interloper to take a seat with them. It seems they cannot be without his company for a moment.

My heart drops with disappointment when I find the door of my uncle's shop is closed. This is the busiest time of evening, yet there's no note on the door. Returning to the group, I sit down and try to focus on the conversation, but I have a strange feeling that something is wrong. An hour passes as I absent-mindedly listen to conversation, answer questions about the next day's schedule, and watch the door for a familiar face.

Uncle Mohammed enters, dressed elegantly in a dark suit, white shirt, and tie. He holds a long-stemmed pink rose and his expression is solemn and pained. I get up and walk over to greet him and I see tears in his eyes.

"I am sorry to tell you this, but our dear Zacharia died suddenly, three days ago, of a heart attack. I thought it best to tell you in person. I was in the backseat of the taxi with him on the way to the hospital with my arm around him. He praised Allah, closed his eyes, and he was gone. The funeral and burial, of course, took place the next day, as is our custom."

It takes a moment for me to comprehend what I've heard; it all seems surreal and I'm unwilling to hear those words—the painful words I've been trying to dislodge from my mind: death, funeral, burial, goodbye. Too many goodbyes. Mohammed and I hug while others look on.

"Come visit me tomorrow, after you get settled, and we can talk more," He hands me the rose and then leaves with a slight bow, his right hand to his heart. A silence falls over the group as I return to the table, explain what has occurred, and then say goodnight to everyone. Raphael stands and offers to walk with me to the garden section of the hotel and, in a daze, I consent. He's quiet, except to say he's sincerely sorry for my loss.

"Sounds like you've been having a rough time lately, losing your father and now your uncle."

Upon observing this more mature and caring side of his personality, my feelings of annoyance toward him begin to soften. Maybe I just need to be alone, get some rest, and comprehend the loss of two of my beloved father figures in the short space of just one month. Perhaps with a good night's sleep I may find this Raphael character less disturbing. Raphael touches my shoulder lightly and opens the door for me as I make my way to the lift and the peaceful darkness of my room.

My suitcase has already been placed on the luggage rack by the staff, but the thought of even opening it overwhelms me. I can unpack in the morning. For now, I just need to sleep. I take my essential items from my carry-on and get ready for bed. Before turning off the lights, I light a candle to Zacharia and pray he will move quickly into the light and be healed. I imagine Dad greeting him and the two loveable charmers walking arm-in-arm, exploring new worlds. Exhausted from travel and grief, I fall into a deep and dreamless sleep.

☥

CHAPTER THIRTY TWO
THE DANCING HORSES - CAIRO

*"Life isn't about waiting for the storm to pass...it's
about learning to dance in the rain."*
Vivian Greene

Horses are psychic; of this I am certain. Egyptian
horses perhaps more so than others since they live
in the shadow of the pyramids, where they are
being constantly bathed in all that powerful psychic energy.

With loud drumming and great fanfare, six of the famous
dancing Arabian stallions arrive on schedule in the driveway in
front of the lobby, bright tassels, and bells adorning their regal
forms. The small, wiry trainer leads the way, followed by three
local percussionists, all dressed in colorful Ottoman garb traditional brocade vests, pantaloons and turbans. The whining
sound of the *mizmar* begins, loud and jarring.

The dancing horse shows is spectacular as the stallions trot and prance in perfect time with the drums. My group is delighted and the horses seem to sense the approval and hold their large and regal heads high as they glance at the crowd A few minutes into the performance, someone blows on what I think could only be a shofar, a sound I've heard before in Jewish ceremonies. Brilliant, Omar, I think; this will bring you a bigger tip than usual. There hasn't been a Jewish element in any of our past ceremonies, yet there are many wonderful Jewish tour members among us every time. This would be a nice treat for them and I make a note to keep this as part of every welcome ceremony in the future.

THEN, AN ENTIRE CHORUS OF SHOFARS SOUNDS, followed within seconds by a perfectly executed torrent of excrement from all six of the horses. I realize with panic that the sound had not been a shofar, but a forceful projection of horse gas. The crowd begins to jump aside as brown liquid sprays in all directions. Cameras are dropped and chaos ensues as everyone scrambles to a safe distance, tripping over one another.

I watch in horror as odiferous brown fluid splatters onto Gucci shoes, manicured toes, designer clothing, and crystal ankle bracelets; no surface is spared. Amidst much shrieking, the dignified red-jacketed attendants rush forward in unison with long-handled brooms and dustbins. They do what they can, but what's needed is a high-pressure hose. Someone runs for the fire extinguisher on the side of the building and soon white foam sprays over the scene like snow on a slippery country road. Putrid foam billows and the revolting sight rolls toward us. The irate manager shouts orders to his staff as they run around apologizing profusely to the guests. In the noise and chaos, the manager can barely be heard and his hand gestures and dramatic expressions of regret add to the absurdity of the situation. I step back and enjoy the hilarious scene and snap a few photos, then go back to my room to take my second shower of the morning.

The start of the program is delayed an hour for all of us to clean up and recover from the early morning welcome celebration. I send the housekeeping staff to each of the guest rooms to collect the soiled items and I pray this isn't a preview of what the week ahead will bring. On the other hand, the scene has lifted my mood and my sides ache from laughter. It's a fitting, if disastrous, start to yet another tour of this crazy, funny country. The never-ending humor of Egypt has already begun its potent healing effect and I cannot help but laugh as I walk to the conference room. I make a mental note to find an alternate welcome ceremony for future tours.

CHAPTER THIRTY THREE

CENTERING HOME

"The whole problem with the world is that fools and fanatics are always so certain of themselves, and wiser people so full of doubt."
Bertrand Russell

We're seated in the historic Mena House Hotel within the shadow of the pyramids, bathed in the energy of the most ancient and mysterious spiritual center on Earth. The ringing of Tibetan *tingshas* marks the start of the program and brings stillness to the conference room. The anticipation in the room is palpable as my tour colleague from California glides up to the microphone, adorned with colorful beaded Egyptian jewelry and wearing a flowing purple dress. She addresses the group in a warm greeting.

"Today we begin our journey through the ancient land of

Egypt. Let's breathe together, arrive, and be fully present here in Egypt."

Everyone takes a deep breath and there's silence except for the sounds of quiet sobbing. The sacredness of the moment catches up with me as well and I become aware of how much I need this time of healing after the past months of loss and grief. For many, a dream of a lifetime has been realized.

Opening introductions are going smoothly and some late-arriving panel members straggle in due to the effect of continued East Coast snowstorms. The keynote speaker is a well-known author and much loved inspirational teacher. The gracious woman's luggage had been lost en route yet she maintains her calm composure. Her professionalism is in glaring contrast to that of some of the others on presenter panel.

The California contingent of self-proclaimed ancient masters and channels has made their calculated arrivals. Each one carries a stack of promo materials and 8x10 pre-signed glamour shots of themselves for distribution. In contrast, the sincere and dedicated spiritual seekers are alert with anticipation, their open expressions radiant with love toward everyone. Seated in the front row, the returning temple priests and scribes have arrived earlier to get settled, notebooks open and eyes closed.

As if on cue, the reincarnated Nefertitis enter late, heads held high, haughtily claiming their sections of the conference hall, while already magnetizing a following of admirers. A door slams and announces the arrival of the five resurrected Ramses who scan the room with an imperious air, searching for potential conquests, shirts unbuttoned to reveal opulent chest hair.

The alluring Cleopatras are still making their slow and

dramatic entrances, pausing at intervals to peer through black bangs and gauge the effect they're having.

It's perfect; the stage is set for another unforgettable New Age conference and all the characters are taking their places. Thus far, there are three Nefertitis, two Cleopatras, and five Ramses. I have no doubt that more royal family members will emerge as they awaken to their past incarnations at the temples along the Nile.

Amused and delighted, I reflect on how much I really love this work of bringing people of like mind together. I vow to put my own problems and grieving aside and focus on playing my part as well. The atmosphere of reverence and anticipation, the incense, the resonant sound of the tingshas and crystal bowls all are comforting and I begin to look forward to the times ahead with the group.

I sigh a deep sigh of relief; I too have come home - to Egypt, to myself, to my true nature as a spiritual seeker and leader. I remind myself to suspend judgment when a channel from Los Angeles sways to the microphone and pontificates for twenty minutes about her "powers." The woman's mangling of royal names and ancient temple sites, even the name of her supposed royal husband, is beginning to annoy me. 'Suspend judgment,' I tell myself again. I know I have the power to shift my focus, and so I choose instead to stare at the five-pound crystal hanging from her neck. I wondered if it gives her a cervical subluxation as it would myself. I imagine how she must look forward to removing it at the end of the day in the way all of us women look forward to removing our bras at night.

The crystal energy healer announces to the audience that

past life recall is guaranteed if one gazes into the crystal long enough - that's how she knows that she's the reincarnation of the illustrious female pharaoh Hatchepsut. Of course, she reassures us, we will recall past lives just by staring at her dangling crystal. Every man in the front row is fixated on the faceted stone resting snugly on her large and unharnessed breasts. They are obviously recalling something. Their faces change before my eyes, so it must be working.

I suppress a smirk as Molly and I exchange glances. My sweet young friend is a novice in the New Age world and is constantly both amazed and delighted. I cast a cautionary look at her not to giggle, or we both will go into fits and have to leave the room.

I imagine Uncle Zachariah, his spirit hovering in the corner enjoying the scene, his coffee-stained smile, and big grey eyes filled with mirth. He always looked forward to meeting my groups and I know he wouldn't miss this, no matter how heavenly Paradise was. It's good to be home in Egypt and I feel all the layers of my being drifting into the conference room as if I'm arriving in stages.

My head cold is hanging on, but at least I can now breathe when I'm not choking with laughter. I give thanks for my returning health and all that is being renewed and restored in my life. My energy field relaxes and expands beyond my body. The tension and jet lag begin to ease, along with my impatience at the phoniness of some of the panel of "experts" being introduced. My colleagues in California who hire these people apparently have very different ideas of what a spiritual teacher is. I actually enjoy the humor in all of it and of just being in the moment with whatever might take place.

However, that man seems to appear wherever I turn. As I rush to find tissues to blow my constantly running nose, there he is, nonchalantly leaning against a column next to the rest rooms or standing by the conference room entrance, stylishly dressed and smelling like woodland spices. Rushing back into the ladies room, I wait and double check that he's gone back to his seat, only to have him appear beside me, as if an apparition.

He seems never to run out of corny, romantic one-liners, all delivered with a dimpled, innocent smile. After a few days, I become amused at how he can say such absurd things with such sincerity. I wonder if Egyptian men are coaching him, since American men of our generation don't talk this way with such ease. My father said such romantic things to my mother, but only when he thought we kids couldn't hear.

Besides, American men seldom show the slightest interest in me. To them I'm always too 'foreign', too small, not thin enough; I had once even been told I was 'too feminine.' They always found me to be too much of this and not enough of that. I gave up years ago on meeting a man in the States and now only date Egyptian men.

At break time, we head out into a perfect sunny day. As I give him directions to the outdoor café where lunch will be served, Raphael comments, "You have the most beautiful eyes I have ever seen. They're as deep and blue as The Nile." Flinching, I wonder how he's failed to notice my red nose and the circles under my eyes from so much crying and coughing. I feel I'm truly a mess, and the last thing I need is some strange man directing this kind of attention toward me.

"Have you really taken a good look at the Nile? It's dark with pollution. It's only blue in Upper Egypt in Aswan."

"I guess I only see your blue eyes everywhere I look," he replies.

To add to my self-consciousness, my self-highlighting mishap while on assignment a few months ago has left me with a haphazard sort of blonde dreadlocks. Yet, as he opens the conference door for me, I don't detect a bit of sarcasm, only an awkward nervousness as we part and return to our seats. I see him looking over at me and I turn away from his gaze. I think he's not as bad as I believed at first, and he does seem guileless and quite innocent. He even reminds me of my father in the way he blurts out the soppiest remarks.

Still, I have my reasons to avoid him. In fact, I run through the list daily to be certain I've not overlooked a single one. After all, I'm working now; he's at least a decade younger than I, and excessively handsome in that dangerous, Latin way. He moonlights in an upscale bar in Boston and he's a big city architect. Plenty of opportunity there for casual affairs, I decide. No, I'm just another potential conquest, a 'yellow tail' as I hear white women referred to in the Caribbean. Surely, they have a similar saying in South American countries, or wherever he's from. Where is he from, anyway? I should have looked closely at his passport when I had it in my hand at check-in. I overheard him speaking Spanish to another group member, but his English is without a trace of a Spanish accent.

No, I will not allow myself to be another of his conquests, nor did I have the slightest desire for a quick affair with a young American man. In fact, I cannot recall ever feeling less inclined toward an affair in my entire life.

Besides, from the way women are vying for his attention, he's sure to find plenty of willing lovers right in this group, most of them 'yellow-tailed' as well, whether by nature or double process blonding. I further determine that he's likely married and wildly promiscuous, a carrier of STD or even worse. I repeatedly work myself back into a state of annoyance with him, although he's not said or done a single thing to warrant it.

My friends urge me to go to dinner with him, saying we're perfect for each other. Why they imagine that, I cannot understand. I begin to suspect that they're all in on this match-making scheme now and probably betting a Stella beer on whether I will relent. No, I'm certain he's a bad risk and entirely unsuitable. So what if he is caramel-skinned, clean-shaven and has the most luscious full lips that tempt me to kiss him just one time . . .

CHAPTER THIRTY FOUR

THE CAMEL CARAVAN - FEBRUARY 1995

When a boat runs ashore, the sea has spoken.
Irish proverb

As with teenagers, we never hear about the good camels, only the troublemakers who capture the spotlight and give all the rest a bad name. We've all heard stories of nasty, smelly camels that spit, lie down and quit midway across the desert, and generally behave like all-around jerks. My camel, Sayeed was not like that. He was a gentleman; a good natured, smiling model of a camel, a camel anyone would be proud to be seen with. Those who depend on camels for survival refer to them respectfully as 'the ships of the desert'. Equipped with double eyelids to protect from sand storms, and the ability to walk in heat for days without water, they can glide along through all adversity like ships upon the sea. I love camels, especially my tall and noble Sayeed.

On the morning of our caravan, my camel has gone out with an Australian tourist, a large man whose girth demands an equally large camel. Did I mention that Sayeed is the tallest, strongest beast in Omar's stable? I like to think he protested against leaving with the Australian and insisted upon waiting for me. I'm sure that in the end, he didn't have much choice but to carry that rotund man all the way to Saqqara. A taxi to Saqqara would have taken a fraction of the time, but the Australians are an adventuresome lot and the man insisted upon riding my Sayeed the entire way.

Omar, the stable owner, laments, "Sorry, I had to let him go. The man was too big for any of the other camels," he motions toward the stable. "Here, my boy Mahmoud is bringing another camel for you. We just got this one and he's a good boy. His name is Rambo."

"Why Rambo if he's so good?" I observe the skittish camel approaching me.

"He's like an American, he never gives up. Fast too, like Rambo," he adds.

I shake my head, "I don't want fast, I want slow and relaxing. I want Sayeed."

The young Mahmoud walks over to me, dragging behind him a tall, snarly-looking camel with a devilish look in his eyes. Omar excuses himself and continues to organize the rest of the group onto their camels.

"No worry, he like women, specially small women with blue eyes."

The young Mahmoud, already a salesman at his tender age, tries in his fragmented English to justify the switch. I doubt a camel perceives eye color or height, and besides, none of this forced reassurance is helping. Rambo snorts, gives me a side-long glance, and then spits something disgusting in my direction. He's obviously not a civilized, genteel fellow like my Sayeed.

I jump backwards and grimace. "Ugh. Keep him back, he scares me."

"C'mon, you not scared, you from Dallas! Dallas girls they ride all time." Mahmoud pushes on the camel's rear end and commands him to sit. Rambo drops his front legs and then his hindquarters down onto the sand with a grunt and a moan, as if resigning himself to being ridden, even if the rider happens to be a small, blue-eyed female.

"I'm not from Dallas. I'm from Boston. You're watching too much American TV. Not all American women are from Dallas."

Egypt has become obsessed with American soap operas and movies. "I've never ridden a horse or a camel in my life, and I've never been to Dallas either."

"No problem. See, Rambo like you very much," the boy says as the camel looks at me, shakes his tasseled head, and sticks out his long tongue. "See, he stick out tongue, he want kiss you."

I'm not warming to Rambo and I turn away from the revolting image, take out my wet wipes, and clean my hands.

The group is being assisted onto the waiting line-up of camels, a gallabeya-clad boy assigned to walk alongside each of them and hold the reins. All is coming into order except for a commotion toward the back of the line. There's one extra woman without a camel and she's becoming upset and starting to whine in a high, nasal voice. I know that voice, I've been hearing it all week; it's the California actress-turned-channel who believes she's the reincarnation of Cleopatra. I feel certain the real Cleopatra, powerful stateswoman that she was, had never been given to whining. A great leader, Cleopatra would have been a take-charge, no whining woman.

I lean to the side to look back as I see Raphael get down and offer his camel to the Cleopatra knock-off. He then gallantly helps her climb up and hands her belongings to her. She puts on her wide-brimmed red hat with a flourish and holds her hand out as if inviting him to climb up, but he shakes his head.

Rather than join her, instead he turns and begins sauntering toward me in that annoying, loose-hipped way he walks. What is it about the hips of Latin men? Do they have an extra joint that allows that rolling motion? It's not unattractive, not at all. Still, it makes for an unhurried, languid gait that never seems efficient in the face of the task at hand.

We have a caravan to move, a schedule for the day, I think with impatience as I watch and wait until he reaches me. He's wearing a black-and-white checkered keffeya wrapped around his head, and with his darkening tan he looks as if he belongs here in the desert. I'm reminded of the young Omar Sharif in Lawrence of Arabia and try to block that connection between Raphael and my favorite actor from my mind.

"Would it be okay if I ride with you?" He smiles that charming smile up at me and shields his eyes with his hand from the glare of the sun. How many dimples does he need? He doesn't own a pair of sunglasses, he had told me earlier in the week. Never has. The man has no common sense. I marvel at how he's lived this long with so little regard for his own well being.

I quickly weigh the options, and there are none. As a tour director, I can't stay back and release the group across the plateau alone. And given the popularity of Raphael among the ladies, there'll be an insurrection if I leave him behind. Not that any one of them wouldn't be delighted to share her saddle with him. Still, it would be awkward to refuse as he stands there waiting, and besides, we're wasting time.

"Sure," I reply as I motion for him to climb up and sit in front of me.

"Thanks," he says, "I can't miss out on a chance to ride a camel today."

"This camel is called Rambo," I tell him. "He's the newest addition to the stable. I'm a bit nervous about him. I hope you have more experience with riding than I have. I've only ever ridden Sayeed in my life and he's calm and a real gentleman."

Raphael doesn't respond but looks at me with a confused grin.

"Sayeed, my regular camel," I clarify, "He's taken off with some Australian to Saqqara today."

With colorful blankets and an elaborate saddle piled onto his back, Rambo stands close to two stories high. The camel springs up and straightens his front legs as we lurch backward, then forward again as the snarly creature gets his back legs under him. My body tilts forward as Rambo steadies himself onto all four feet and shakes all over. I feel safer having a man seated in front of me on the saddle, my arms around his waist. As Rambo jerks about, I press my head to Raphael's back. He smells of fresh laundry and Drakkar Noir, the current popular cologne among Egyptian men. I appreciate how nice he always looks and smells and observe that he's becoming more like an Egyptian man every day in so many ways. He's even picked up a few words in Arabic, although he uses them in odd and nonsensical ways. He's taken to hitting his forehead with his palm and exclaiming *mish maoul!* unbelievable! at every opportunity, leaving everyone around him to wonder what unbelievable thing just happened. His sense of humor is immature, but I appreciate the way he can laugh and play. I can't decide if he's childlike or just plain childish, but I notice lately I feel happier when I'm around him.

After a half hour, we reach the top of the highest vantage point and the caravan comes to a stop to enjoy the breathtaking view before us. The three larger pyramids, as well as the three smaller ones, lay ahead in all their glory. The last of the ancient wonders of the world never fail to create a sense of awe and wonder, no matter how many times I view them.

Molly, in her sporty, quick-moving way, jumps down from her camel and runs over to us.

"Stay there while I get a few shots of the happy couple. You two look so great together." I flash a scolding look at her, but she ignores me. She's relentless in trying to get me involved with this man. Like a paparazzi stalking us, she takes photos from every angle.

"Smile," she calls out. "Wow, that's a great shot. You're going to love it. Now, Kara put your head on his shoulder and your hand on his chest. Perfect!"

I can't help but smile, I'm feeling so happy. It's a good day; the sun is shining but not scorching, we're nearing the end of the tour, and it's been a laughter-filled and healing experience.

The group members have bonded and forged new friendships. It's turned out to be one of the most successful and hassle-free of all the many Egypt tours I've led.

RAMBO DROPS TO HIS KNEES WITH A GRUNT LIKE A petulant teenager to let us down and Raphael and I walk around to take more photos of the sun setting in the desert sky. All of us pause before heading back and we gather on a hill for a group shot with the backdrop of the pyramids. It's a moment for all to remember, a moment that will be etched forever in the minds of each and every one.

For me, it's exactly the healing I need after the heartache of my father's death, followed by the news of my Uncle Zacharia's passing. I feel the stirring of feelings toward Raphael as he stands beside me, the sun lighting up his handsome face. In this light, now he somehow reminds me of my sweet-natured and handsome father.

I notice Rambo lying off to the side with his head down and he looks sad and listless. I walk over and speak to him in a soft voice, telling him how good he has been. I pet him on his neck and he stares past me and shows no response except to snort and moan. I sense that he's ill or in some sort of discomfort. Feeling guilty, I apologize for comparing him unfavorably to the noble Sayeed. He was just a teenage camel after all and maybe in time he would achieve a regal stature and become top camel in Omar's stable.

When it's time to return, we take our same places in the caravan and head out across the desert toward the smog and dust of the city. The call to prayer begins, today louder and for longer duration than usual.

"Why are they so noisy today?" Raphael shouts to me.

"It's Friday, the holy day, as well as it being the holy month of Ramadan. There are extra prayers and sermons as the country slows its pace. During Ramadan, Muslims fast from dawn to nighttime, then they have a great feast at night.

"I could never do that, I'd get too hungry and grouchy." he says.

"It's a time of reflection and compassion when everyone shares food and money with the poor." I respond.

Our boy guide Mahmoud lightly holds the reins, his worn flip-flops making a clapping sound as he steps along beside us. He announces with pride, "Rambo is good Muslim, he fast all day like me. He know call to prayer mean end of day. Soon he get water and food. That's why he hurry."

I was incredulous, "You mean this poor animal hasn't had anything to eat or drink since dawn? No wonder he's so miserable. That's a cruel thing to do to an animal."

"No problem. Rambo like to fast for Ramadan. We both hungry and thirsty, but we don't mind to fast; we do for Allah because we good Muslims. No problem."

I'm reminded of a former friend who is a dog breeder in the States and how she's taken to advertising her French bulldog puppies as "Christian" following her own "born again" experience. Prior to her being saved, she just bred cute puppies. Now I find both the woman and her puppies obnoxious. Another acquaintance, in spite of all research that dogs and cats are natural carnivores, had announced with smugness that her dog had become a vegan Hindu, like herself. A year later when I saw her, she was wearing a sari and the dog was dead.

The "Muslim camel" was a new concept I was trying to wrap my head around. This idea of assigning religious affiliation to animals struck me as self-serving. The pure, loving nature of animals surely must absolve them automatically of all need of religion.

The Friday call is growing louder as it spreads throughout the village. Rambo begins to speed up, snorting and bouncing us about. At first we're delighted. I laugh at the excitement, never having experienced a camel running like this. He then lowers his head, crouches, and sets out in a determined gallop, leaving the rest of the caravan in the dust behind us.

My throat is tightening and my voice cannot hide my fear. "Maybe he knows a shortcut home and that's where he's headed. Hold on tight."

"He must be hungry for his dinner," says Raphael, "I know how he feels. I'd be in a hurry too if I didn't even get a drink of water all day in this dry desert."

The camel is gathering speed. We stop talking as we concentrate on just staying on the saddle. Rambo is wild and out of control, breaking away and taking off to the left and down a steep, rocky slope.

"Hold on tight," Raphael yells, "It's a long way down."

Rambo then sets to galloping at an even more frantic pace and nothing will stop him. Raphael and I panic, leaning forward and pressing our legs into the sides of the camel. The starving animal has enough of people on his back slowing him down and he begins bucking to throw us off.

In the next moment, we're hurtling vertically through the

air and tumbling toward the earth. We collapse to the ground with a thud, a cloud of dust scattering our belongings across the sand. Raphael lands on his back, I on my left side with my ankle bent under me. We hear the commotion of hoof beats as all the animals begin panicking and running around us as we lay still. Raphael tries to shield me and we curl up together in fetal position and cover our heads, to avoid being trampled to death. All we can do is wait for whatever will happen next.

After a few minutes of shouting and running about in panic, the young camel guides bring everything to order, swat the camels with whips, and round them up into a line. Our friends arrive and help us to our feet.

"Wow, what a sight that was as you were shaken off and thrown in the air." Molly shouts as she gathers our scattered backpacks and their contents. "That was a long fall, I'm glad you both can still stand up."

I try to walk. "Well, just barely, I don't think I can put my weight on my left leg."

We brush our clothes off, rinse our mouths with water to get the sand out of our teeth, and then check for injuries. My ankle is swollen and painful and Raphael holds onto his lower back with a grimace.

"We'd better get some ice for both of you right away or you'll be in trouble," Molly says.

After a few more minutes of battle with Rambo, the stable boy Mahmoud is able to retrieve and bring him back to us. "Sorry, I couldn't hold him, he's too strong." The boy looks scared. "Maybe I should not make Rambo fast for Ramadan, he make big problem for you."

"You're right, it's a crazy thing to do," says Raphael. "We

could have been killed." His face registers pain and I hold onto his arm for support as lightly as I can.

Rambo, on the other hand, doesn't appear the least bit contrite, only defiant, and resentful as before. We know we have to get back in the saddle or walk the rest of the way, and walking that far in our condition was out of the question. My entire left side is painful and we are both too shaken to think of any other way to get back so we climb up onto the camel and trot our way to the stables.

At my friend Gouda Fayed's house near the pyramids, a neighborhood doctor assesses our injuries. My leg has turned dark purple right up to my hip and it's painful and swollen. Raphael's back is bruised and clearly out of alignment. The doctor suggests both of us go to the hospital for further evaluation, but we have doubts about entering any foreign hospital.

We recline on adjoining low couches with ice packs on our injuries while the rest of the group watches the sound and light show from the rooftop. There's laughter from upstairs on the roof as the outdated 'Son et Lumiere' audio show blasts across the plateau.

"Not a happy ending to our caravan, that's for sure," I say as I check the darkening bruise on my leg. "Still, it could have been much worse. We could have broken our necks or ended up like poor Christopher Reeves. I just thank God we're alive to talk about it."

"You find something positive in every situation, don't you?" He looks pained to see my bruises. "I'm so sorry I wasn't able to control the course of events. To tell you the truth, I have no riding experience, even though I grew up in the Southwest. My childhood didn't afford the luxury of horses or riding lessons."

"Neither did mine. I only rode the flying horses when we got to visit an amusement park once a year, and those horses never went astray. Don't blame yourself."

I adjust the ice pack and try to get comfortable. "I don't think anyone could have stopped that poor camel from running home for his dinner."

Raphael sits up, leans toward me, and holds my hands, looking into my eyes. "Are you sure you're alright? Your pupils are so dilated I can barely see the blue of your eyes. Do you think you might have a concussion?"

"That's a normal reaction. When our pupils dilate it just means..." I stop.

"Means what?" He waits while I mull over how to answer.

"Everyone's pupils dilate when we're looking at something we like, that's all."

"Oh, that's a relief. I thought it meant you're of those aliens we've been hearing about all week. You know, the ones with the big black eyes."

The conversation has taken a weird turn and I decide it's gone as far as it needs to. "Don't worry about me, I'll be fine. I'm sturdier than I look, thanks to all the dancing I do."

"I noticed. Very nice muscle development you have, especially for an alien." He gives me a mischievous smile.

I gaze at his tanned arms and slim torso. "You're in great shape too, for a human."

We're blessedly interrupted when Mrs. Fayed brings us a tray with hibiscus tea and the traditional bowl of fresh dates for *iftar*, the breaking of the Ramadan fast. We sit up and pretend to enjoy a steamy bowl of *mulaqayya*, a slimy green soup I have never gotten used to although I know how healthy it is. This is followed by *kushari*, a local carbohydrate extravaganza of elbow pasta and lentils, topped with fried onions, served with hot local bread, or *aish beledi*.

After dinner, we're both feeling able enough to get up and move and so we hobble out to a taxi and ride the short distance back to Mena House. Seated in the elegant piano bar like two dusty desert dogs, we enjoy an icy Stella Export Egyptian beer. Raphael looks at the beverage menu. "Why didn't we order the Stella Local? It's twice as big for half the price."

"That's true," I reply, "but it often comes with a long camel hair and that ruins it for me. I found out the hard way, years ago, when one of those camel hairs got stuck sideways in my throat."

"Oh, I don't need my beer to be that authentic," he laughs.

The Stella and Extra Strength Tylenol help take the edge off of the pain for both of us. Feeling grateful, we toast to having survived the fall with only minimal injuries. Our shared experience of a camel stampede has brought us closer and we laugh as we recount each scene as it unfolded.

I'm enjoying Raphael's company when a loud and ominous rumbling begins in my stomach, accompanied by the all too familiar woozy feeling that signals the start of mummy tummy. I'd been struck with it many times in spite of carrying a supply of every natural remedy ever known to protect the GI tract. Once it hits, there's nothing to be done except stop all food, take the local drug called Entocid, along with lots of hot tea and bottled water, and then wait it out while remaining close to the toilet.

"On no," I say, leaning forward and clutching my stomach, "I'm going to be sick. I knew I shouldn't have eaten the local food. Even though it was cooked, it was still made with tap water. Sorry, I have to run," I say as I jump up and limp toward the lift, not even giving him a chance to reply. I race as fast as my injured leg allows, down the hallway to my room and just make it in the door. The night is spent alternating between worship at the porcelain throne and icing of my swollen ankle.

Molly is out with the women–on a mission to buy a water pipe and smoke shisha at the *Khan el Khalili*, leaving me alone with my thoughts for the evening. I review the events of the day. It had been a peculiar day from start to finish. Although feeling miserable, I reflect on how sweet and concerned Raphael had been. Being close to him all day and evening was nice, even if we did get thrown in a frightening stampede and the day ended with a fierce attack of mummy tummy.

In spite of my prejudices, Raphael isn't proving to be the Latin Lothario I'd taken him for. I'd even heard that he was born and raised in Arizona, of Spanish and Mexican heritage. I'm growing increasingly fond of him, although I still feel we're unsuited to each other. As I fall off to sleep, I wonder how Raphael's cute backside is after that fall. I make a mental note to ask him as soon as I see him in the morning. Then I smile to think of how he'll blush at my directness. First his neck, and then his ears will turn red as they do whenever he's embarrassed. It's become evident to me that he has a shy, insecure side to his personality. I add that to my growing list of likes. The ledger is tipping. I am falling in love.

CHAPTER THIRTY FIVE

INITIATION INSIDE THE GREAT PYRAMID

"To face a real daemon, you must first look inwards and conquer your own darkness."
Luis Marques

There is perhaps no place on earth darker or more powerful than inside the King's Chamber of the Great Pyramid. Each of my tours ends with a nighttime ceremony in the largest of the 3 major pyramids on the plateau. It's a time to integrate the energy and experiences of the temples, pyramids, and tombs we have visited along the Nile. No one returns unchanged from the journey along the Nile where we tap into the energies of the chakra system represented by the temples ascending from Aswan back to Cairo.

Although we have the great pyramid to ourselves for four hours, the length of our stay is determined by how much intensity the group can take. Some find being in the chamber oppressive and are terrified by at being in such deep, enclosed darkness. Most people, once settled, find they're enjoying the trance state evoked by the chamber and want to stay as long as possible. Once relaxed, a feeling of being suspended in time takes over as one drifts into the ancient past. The amount of available oxygen varies as well, according to the number of people in the chamber. Memories of previous Egyptian lives often surface, as well as spontaneous healing of body, mind, and spirit.

The only person I had ever met who could speak with authority on both the scientific and metaphysical aspects of the pyramids and many other mysterious sites in Egypt is my long-time teacher, Hakim Awyan. A Sufi master and mystic, Hakim has earned the title of "wise elder and wisdom keeper" and is content to live simply in his small house, near the plateau, with his wife and children. Dr. Hakim studied abroad in his youth and earned degrees in archeology and engineering, a surprise to the Western skeptics who underestimate him and attempt to catch him up in argument.

Tonight, we're blessed with the presence of the Khemit wisdom keeper Hakim as we stand before the entrance to the Great Pyramid. He's been conducting interviews all day for the excellent documentary 'The Pyramid Code' by Dr. Carmen Boulter of Canada. The unassuming, quiet man finds all the attention focused upon him amusing and he delights in sharing stories of the land he loves. The generations of his lineage have been the 'eyes of Egypt', the keepers of the wisdom from as far back as anyone recalls.

Hakim begins our pyramids visit by addressing us at the entrance of the pyramid in his low, raspy voice. His blue-grey eyes sparkle with enthusiasm born of his great love and pride in his country. His tall frame is outlined against the setting sun as he gestures with long, slim fingers, his garments fluttering in the night breeze that rises off the desert. There's timelessness about his image with the pyramid as a backdrop. We could be in any period in Egypt's vast history. Hakim's words flow with deep wisdom and we're transported to a far distant time when super-human beings from other dimensions worked side by side with the ancient Egyptians. Hakim speaks of the power of sound and the mastery of vibration and explains how the high initiates of old were able to move the enormous slabs of stone and create the masterpieces of architecture such as the temples and tombs of Upper Egypt and other structures throughout the world.

"Why did the Egyptians build the pyramids?" He poses a hypothetical question, no doubt having been asked this hundreds of times. "There was a time period in history when pyramids were built in every hemisphere and major energy center or vortex of the planet, all at the same latitude, the 27th parallel North or 'the zone of silence'."

"What does that signify?" Molly asks.

"The zone of silence refers to the phenomenon by which radio waves cannot function. It's theorized to be due to high iron content in the area." Hakim replies.

Hakim asserts that the great pyramid is both a receiving station and a giant transmitter of energy, its signal reaching for miles in all directions, including deep space. If we could repli-cate these advanced technologies of the ancients, we could help our world today in so many ways."

"I just watched a documentary showing satellite images of

the pyramids. It's amazing that they can be seen so clearly from space," says Raphael, "I've visited pyramids throughout South America and Mexico, but nothing like this."

It seems Raphael and I have both been on the quest for ancient truths for many years and have been to many of the same sacred sites. Knowing we share this most important quest, I become aware I haven't really given him a chance and I need to know him better.

Hakim continues, "In each culture where pyramids are found, there are legends about the great beings, visitors who later became known as gods and goddesses. In Egypt we call them the 'Neteru,' the pantheon. They represent aspects of The One Creator. Only one," he repeats, pointing heavenward, "One God, many aspects. We are able to translate directly from hieroglyphs and so we know what the ancients had to say about the mysteries. The truth is coming into the light for all to see because humanity needs it now more than ever." The beloved Hakim continues, "For many years, classical Egyptologists maintained that the pyramids were merely grandiose tombs to commemorate dead pharaohs, built by slave labor, and laid out in a relatively unstructured manner. However, recent work by our writer/researcher friend Robert Bauval has shed an intriguing new light on the issue."

Hakim sits down on a block of stone in front of the entrance and continues, "Beauval realized that the relative sizes and detailed positioning of the Giza pyramids were a faithful representation of the stars that form the 'belt' in the constellation of Orion.

For the benefit of those who haven't heard this information, I add, "Bauval has written many fascinating books about this which I've listed in your pre-tour handouts."

"I just read about the recent discovery of supposed 'air shafts' in the pyramids which point directly toward Orion, Molly says, "They speculate that these shafts were built to guide the soul out and towards the constellation in it's journey home."

"That is correct, and all these discoveries are rewriting our understanding of the motivations for building the pyramids," Hakim replies.

Raphael adds, "We've heard about a robotic camera that was sent into the shafts, leading to the discovery of a door to a previously unknown secret chamber. And the door is made of metal!"

"Metal? Another member of the group questions, "They didn't use metal that far back in time."

"Apparently they did, Raphael says, "yet another mystery unfolds."

Molly leans toward me, "That Raphael has done his homework."

I nod, "Yes, he certainly has. I'm impressed"

Rumors abound that imminent discoveries may even more radically change our perception of ancient civilization. Our heads are swimming with all the possibilities as we say good-night to our beloved teacher and watch him as he slowly walks away across the desert toward his home.

As a group, we enter the pyramid, ducking down for just a few feet before standing to ascend the enormous grand gallery, all the way up to the topmost chamber. It is a massive interior and not the claustrophobic space people fear; no crawling or struggling to reach the top. I hear the group exclaiming at the vastness of the grand gallery as we climb. The excitement in their voices always makes me so happy.

As each person reaches the top of the grand hallway and ducks to enter the chamber, we form a circle and lie on the floor and breathe deeply for a few moments. This act brings about a hushed sense of awe and reverence and each settles into a spot to acclimate to the energy. After twenty minutes, we rise in silence, hold hands and encircle the sarcophagus and begin to sound and tone. Then, one at a time each person lies inside with the crown chakra toward the east while the group intones and sends love and healing to the one inside.

The experience of being inside the sarcophagus is both stirring and enlightening. For some, it's a time of emotional release and weeping, for others, it stirs visions and memories of the ancient past. The experience is different for each person, but always it is powerful and unforgettable. Those who come along only at the coaxing of partners and with little interest in the metaphysical aspects of the tour are often the ones who have the most profound experiences. Even when they claim nothing has happened, the others in the group notice the effects in the days following. They often become more compassionate, more accepting of one another and the world around them. Couples have insights into their partnerships and decide to make changes; they either become closer, or realize it's time to move on, blessing and releasing one another.

I am brought to tears in the moment the sounding begins. I know I'm safe in this group, even if we are of many differing backgrounds and beliefs. Our group is made up of every religion and none. No one knows or cares what religion others follow, only that they are reverent and sincere in this sacred space. Everyone is here because they're seeking to know deeper truths. We don't have to agree in order to honor the soul presence in one another.

We gather afterwards under the stars and talk about our experiences inside the pyramid. There's no resisting the overpowering healing force of the pyramid and lots of tears are shed as we discuss the effects of the experience.

"Does it ever get to be commonplace for you?" Molly asks.

I laugh, "Oh no, never. I learn something new every time. Some part of myself, a part much wiser than my conscious mind, knows what healing I need.

Raphael had connected with Hakim from day one of the conference and has been invited to his home for tea the following day and he asks me to come along. As we sit in the simple, unadorned space of Hakim's living room, the wise elder shares his insights on the wonders of Egypt's ancient architecture. We're enraptured by his explanations of star systems, correlations between sacred symbols, and the human body. He talks of the initiation chamber, now erroneously called the "King's Chamber," the place of culmination of the mystery school initiates' journey.

Hakim explains more about the process of the initiation in the pyramid, "If the initiate survived the final test of being closed in the sarcophagus for three days and three nights, they emerged fully enlightened."

"How did they breathe inside a sealed sarcophagus for that length of time?" Raphael asks.

The mischievous old man raises a gnarled hand and places it over his nose, mouth, and eyes,

"An initiate must have full control of all the faculties and be able to shut them down for the required length of time." He breaks into a laugh and his eyes twinkle with glee, "and, if when the cover is removed, the initiate doesn't rise, no problem. It's still a success, they have reached enlightenment. The soul goes home and meets the Creator." Hakim slaps his knee and laughs at his own joke and we laugh with him.

To me, the hallmarks of a true enlightened master are childlike humility and a lively sense of humor. I've met a very few such masters in my life, but always they are animated with a sort of joyful irreverence and complete lack of pretense.

CHAPTER THIRTY SIX

FAREWELL PARTY

"To love someone is to learn the song
That is in their heart
And sing it to them
When they have forgotten."
Arne Garborg

The farewell party at the end of each tour occurs on the rooftop of my friends' 3-story villa overlooking the Sphinx. We can enjoy the sound and light show over the entire plateau from this vantage point, spared the outdated commentary that blasts from crackling speakers. Musicians begin arriving from throughout the small village of *Nazlet el Samman* and the dancing and feasting begins. The stars seem close enough to touch and the cool, dry air is charged with a special energy. The thrill of being here rushes through my body, and for a moment, everything seems possible again. My heart aches as I look over the familiar scene of the pyramids, recalling the many magical years I've spent here. So accustomed to being in Egypt, I sometimes forget the power of the place until I bring a group and see the effect it has on each person.

As I watch the sky, I imagine Dad and Zacharia as sparkling souls among the stars and say a prayer of thankfulness for all the years of love we shared. The veil is thin between the worlds and I feel all of us celebrating together, on earth and in the heavens.

The caterer and his staff arrive with huge platters of fragrant food, which they line up onto a long table decorated with hibiscus flowers and roses. The chef beams with pride and announces in a loud voice, "I've prepared many traditional foods for your welfare dinner." The group laughs and applauds, the chef smiles, and everyone lines up at the buffet table.

Across the room, I see a raven-haired woman slither and wrap herself around Raphael like a serpent. The Nefertiti look-alike writes something on a business card and hands it to him with a seductive gaze through the black fringe of her bangs.

I make my way along the edges of the crowded room and almost reach where Raphael stands talking with Nefertiti when I'm detoured by the diehard line of dabke dancers. I let myself be drawn in, knowing it will be a while before I'll again have the thrill of dancing to live music in Cairo. The line dance ends and the music shifts to one of my favorite songs, *"Bint el Sultan,"* 'daughter of the sultan,' and I'm lost in the ecstasy of dancing, giving myself over to the drums as I close my eyes. *Tarab,* the ecstasy and enchantment one reaches through music and dance, has taken me over. Tears roll down my face but I don't care, it feels so delicious to shimmy my hips and snake my body. I'm intoxicated by the music and it dances me as I surrender to it. I forget about my mission to reach the other side of the room where Raphael is fending off Nefertiti. My body is absorbing all the healing energy it so badly needs after these past months of grief.

I love Egypt, my other home, so much and regret having to leave soon. Only two weeks have passed since that first day of the conference when all of us met. We've journeyed the length of the Nile, laughed and cried together, shared our hopes for humanity. We've become family, pilgrims on a quest, closer in ways to this newfound family than to our own loved ones at home. The group begins saying their goodbyes as the dawn arrives and the magical spell is broken.

The musicians are putting away their instruments as the muezzin call echoes across the desert. The sound brings a nostalgic hush over the group as they fall silent and look about in despair, as if dropped into the spot from a time tunnel into reality. Everyone gathers their belongings and moves toward the stairs.

Across the room, I notice that Nefertiti has left and the over-processed blonde channel from Hollywood is leaning in, her crystal glinting in the candlelight, her large new breasts pushing against Raphael insistently as she kisses him goodbye. Good God, is he really falling for that? Can't he tell they're fake by the way they bounce against him, or does he just not care? My 34Bs can't compare, but at least they're real.

Raphael steps back from the kiss with a look of confusion, searching the room. His gaze falls upon me and I detect a hint of relief in his eyes. The channel tosses her hair, throws her head back, lifts the girls higher, and walks away, her bottom swaying as she balances in her crazy neon platform shoes.

Crossing the crowded room, I finally reach to where Raphael stands and our eyes meet. I try to sound matter-of-fact through the confusion and odd jealousy that I'm feeling.

I look up at him and reach to embrace him goodbye. "It was nice meeting you. Have a safe journey back to Boston."

"Oh, I am not leaving Egypt yet. I booked extra nights at the Marriott Palace. I get that great Marriott employee discount, remember?"

Stunned, I think this must be a joke and my friends are again setting me up.

"You're joking, right?"

He searches in his backpack. "No, I'm serious, look." He hands me his hotel reservation and air tickets. We had each booked 4 extra nights downtown at the same hotel, The Marriott Palace, before leaving the United States, weeks before we had met. To make it even more implausible, we're booked on the same return flight to Boston and in the same row. The room is closing in. I feel my hands shake as I give him back his documents and I start to hyperventilate like a trapped animal.

At last I find my voice. "I always stay on at that hotel after a tour. It's so beautiful and peaceful, almost as nice as the Mena House, but not quite and of course without the view of Giza Plateau." My head is spinning as if I just had three Turkish coffees and a double shot of tequila. I think I might pass out.

"Really, so you've stayed there before?" he says.

"Almost every time after I drop my group at the airport. Lot's of great restaurants and shopping nearby and the Khan el Khalili is a short taxi ride from the hotel." I'm chattering like a ditsy schoolgirl, my normally low voice has become someone else's voice, squeaky and high-pitched. "You could go back to the souk and stock up on that apple tobacco you like, maybe buy one of those tall, ornate shisha pipes to take home with you too."

I can't seem to gain control as the room sways. I blink and look down at the intricate pattern in the oriental carpet in hopes that something will stabilize me before I fall over into a Victorian-style swoon. I despise women who talk in a high pitch and behave this way. Get a grip, I tell myself. He watches me with an expression of concern that turns into a stifled grin.

"Well then, I guess you've run out of excuses. Can we at least have dinner sometime in the next four days? You can't be that busy. Besides, you have to eat sometime."

"Dinner? I'll have to see, I've promised lots of people in Cairo a visit before I leave. How about we meet up and talk about it once we both check in at the Marriott Palace?"

"Sounds great, ring me when you get there." he says, "I just heard that Molly and Suzie have decided to extend their stay for a few days too. Maybe we can all go out tomorrow during the day? There's so much more I want to see here in Cairo."

My tour manager self kicks in - now this I can handle. I can arrange a day of sightseeing in the city for all of them with no problem.

"Oh, really? That's an excellent idea. I'll arrange an itinerary and a car to take you to the souk, the Coptic district, and to the area called Old Cairo. It's not to be missed."

"And you?" he asks, "Will you join us?"

"I'll see if I can get free, no promises." I think of Naim and our standing lunch date at the Nile Hilton in Midan el

Tahrir. We make a point of meeting in the same place every time I visit Cairo and open old wounds that aught to remain closed. The usual plan is to drop my group at the Egyptian Museum with the museum guide and then walk across the square to meet Naim in the Nile Hilton cafe for an hour. This time, however I cannot have anyone with me since I have something to tell him and it may take time. This attachment to each other long after our break-up isn't healthy and we both know it, but we have such longing to see each other, if only briefly. The public setting assures that it will go no further than lunch, although each time we're both unable to eat a thing out of nervousness. Although his cosmopolitan family doesn't object to me, they much prefer he find a Muslim woman close to home rather than travel so much to meet a foreigner in other countries. As is believed throughout the world, it's always best to marry within one's own religion and social group. I'm too free and independent to blend into an Egyptian family and Naim never asks me to change in any way. In fact, he's endlessly pleased by our differences and the new points of view I bring to his life. Tomorrow I'll go to meet him and bring our affair to an end so we can both move on with our lives.

I accompany the rest of the group to the airport for their return home to various parts of the world. Then, I check into the Marriott for a few days of rest and my much-needed quiet time alone. Molly, as usual, is eager to go exploring the city and seems never to have need of rest. She goes on about meeting Raphael for day trip around the city, urging me to join her.

"You're sounding like a love-struck teenager, Molly, always talking about Raphael."

"No, no, no! I'm in love with the idea of you two getting together, I'm not in love with him, no way." she says.

It's forbidden for unmarried couples to share a hotel room in Egypt, a rule that can only be enforced if one of them carries an Egyptian passport. I have both American and Egyptian status, but don't want any hassles and so pretend Raphael is my husband to avoid questions. At the front desk, I ask if my husband has checked in yet. When asked his is name, my mind goes blank. I'm a very poor liar and seldom can get away with it. I reply "Romeo, no, Raphael." What was his last name anyway? It had lots of letters and four syllables. In a fog of confusion, I cannot recall his first or last name with any certainty. Why didn't I pay closer attention to these important details about the man I had spoken with so many times and who had pursued me relentlessly?

The desk clerk and I play a guessing game until the right name and correct spelling is found on the guest register just as it comes into my mind. My apparent stalking of a young male hotel guest brings some sidelong looks and a few smiles as they ring his room. I step away from the counter and wait until Raphael walks into the reception.

He greets me with a mischievous look in his eyes. "Oh, here's my little wife."

"I forgot your name. I hope you're not upset?" I ask.

"No, but why did you ring my room anyway? Did I invite you?" He winks. "Just kidding. I'm just glad you're here and we can spend some time together. I made reservations for tonight at a place called 'Eastern Nights.' It's here in the hotel." He looks apprehensive as if he wants to please me. "Is that a good choice?"

"I have no idea, but let's try it," I reassure him. We part with an awkward giggle and kiss on the cheek and I head outside to walk in the remaining daylight before taking my afternoon nap in preparation for the evening. I've adapted to this late afternoon naptime tradition and realize it gets me two days in one.

CHAPTER THIRTY SEVEN

SEDUCTION

"The night, the world, the wind, spin out their destiny."
Pablo Neruda

I put on my close-fitting black dress with the discreet thigh-high slit, the one I haven't taken out of my suitcase yet the entire trip. The slit is on the right side and nicely hides my bruised left leg. Until this moment, I have not felt like a tight black-dress, seductive vixen, but suddenly I'm excited to dress the part of an all out, authentic cougar. I put on high-heeled sandals, a gold ankle bracelet, and my collection of gold bangles, diamond stud earrings, nothing too obvious. Understated elegance with just a hint of seduction. It's a challenge to walk without limping on my injured leg, but we'll only be staying within the hotel and I don't plan on much walking. I take out my most treasured shawl, a large piece of black linen with hammered strips of fine gold, a unique fabric made by hand in the town of *Assuit*. It shimmers and drapes softly, giving me a sense of calm and comfort. My philosophy is to never be without a shawl or scarf, no matter the occasion. A woman's safety blanket, it can become a demure cover-up, modest headscarf, and a shield against wind or sand, a tourniquet, whatever the situation calls for. I drape the Assuit over one shoulder and float from my room enveloped in the scent of my new "Secret of the Desert" perfume oil. It's been a long time since I've felt so light and happy, even a bit giddy. I remove the sandals and walk down the carpeted hallway to the lift, putting them back on when almost to the lobby.

A quiet, formal dining room is not the best choice for a first date when trying to appear poised and nonchalant. I narrowly avoid knocking over my wine glass, an odd habit I've acquired just since first meeting Raphael on the plane. By the time the glass is empty, I'm relaxed enough to comment on his tie which has architectural instruments on it. Also, I can't stop myself from commenting on how nice he looks in his sports jacket. It's the wine talking, but I truly mean it and cannot take my eyes off him. He blushes right to his ears like a schoolboy. Not the reaction of a suave Romeo, I observe. His blushing response has the odd effect of easing my own nervousness. I'm beginning to see that his former swagger had more to do with shyness than ego and he has been trying his best to impress me. I'm reminded of old movies I used to watch with my mother; movies where Clark Gable courts his love in an endearing way, all the while fearing he'll be rejected by her. There's something sweet and old fashioned about him, and I have to admit he reminds me of my father in many ways.

That's not a bad thing, but I never thought I would have found it attractive after all my years with worldly non-American men.

I've long ago given up the notion of twin flames completing each other, but I do believe all of us have a number of possible soul mates; souls we agreed to meet up with for some sort of learning or sharing. No one is perfect, or exactly the match to our own energy. We all have our flaws and areas of unconsciousness. The challenge was to find someone with matching, or at least complementary, baggage to our own. I don't share these thoughts with my new soul mate, but observe that we do meet on many levels and in fact, we mirror one another. Both of us are misfits, artists, and sensitive souls.

After dinner, we walk in the scented garden of the hotel, reminiscing about the incredible two weeks we've spent in Egypt. It's a crisp night and there's a palpable sense of magic in the air. We talk about the interesting mix of people in the conference and the mystical experiences in the temples. He recalls the architectural details of each temple and remembers to which deity each temple was dedicated. I'm impressed with his memory for people and places and the way he says the names of the Goddesses with such reverence.

He turns to me and says, "I've been overwhelmed by the sacred architecture and the spiritual power of the land, the temples, and pyramids. Most of all, though, I'm touched by the openheartedness and humor of the Egyptian people. They're the nicest people I've ever met and not at all as I expected. Every movie I've seen has depicted them as terrorists, but it couldn't be further from the truth."

"I'm so glad you enjoyed your time here, you must come back again and stay longer."

I feel a sense of pride and happiness in hearing that my second home and the people I so love have affected him deeply. Here is a man who seems to get who I am, I think... Or, at least he knows where a part of my heart lives and why.

We walk arm-in-arm as we talk, and then we sit on a bench in the courtyard. The desert breeze is cool and I shiver. He removes his sports jacket, leans forward tentatively, as if approaching a feral cat he's about to pick up, and places the jacket around my shoulders.

Does he think of me as a cougar? Worse yet, a feral cougar? I think to myself with a smile. He pulls back as if I might hiss at him or bite. As if to compensate for the silence between us, he begins pointing out the various styles of architecture within the sections of the sprawling old building, or "structure" as he calls it.

"You can see in that corner where the structural member has been extended."

I choke back a naughty comment, noticing that he doesn't even smile while saying this. It's becoming clear to me that the man is not a big-city player, but a super-nerd with an often-submerged sense of humor. He obviously has been sitting at a computer for way too long. His earnestness and innocence, rather than being off-putting to me, is touching. I pretend to see the fine details of the hotel's architecture, although I'm really just fixating on his pouty lips as he speaks, and the smooth black chest hair that peeks out of his shirt.

The nomenclature of his profession is foreign to me, and in my wine-altered state, it's amusing to my childish self. Fenestrations, balustrades, overhangs, apertures, and members. My off-color quips go right past him and he continues on and on with more strange words and fine points of design, comparing the old and modern construction within the façade of the building. I feel as if I'm sitting in a college classroom and my mind is drifting.

It's not that I'm unappreciative of fine architecture. I've always admired old buildings; I just never had a desire for this much information about them. My eyes are growing heavy, the wine is beginning to wear off, and I feel myself becoming annoyed and impatient. Soon I'll be downright snarly if something doesn't happen.

I decide right then that the only solution is to seduce him. It's awkward, going back on my word after having told him I'm not interested in so many and varied ways for these past weeks. All my signals thus far have been stop signs, and I regret that I've been so obstinate with him. He's turning out to be such a sweet man. What's that saying about a woman having the right to change her mind? I changed my mind somewhere between dinner and the architectural history lecture. It's apparent that seduction is called for in this case, or a rare romantic opportunity will be lost forever.

Raphael senses my waning interest in the commentary, turns to me, and apologizes for going on for so long. "Sorry, I forget not everyone enjoys these details as much as I do. You must be bored."

I roll my eyes. "Not at all, who doesn't appreciate a fine balustrade?

"That's funny," he says, "You have a real talent for turning almost anything into a sexual innuendo. You've kept me surprised and laughing for weeks now."

" It's my Irish side, sorry."

"Oh, no. At first I was confused and I couldn't figure you out, but now I'm beginning to enjoy it."

The awkward tension between us dissolves into laughter as we get up to leave. He takes my hands, stands in front of me, and says in a sincere tone.

"I will never be the same after this. You and this country have changed me forever."

CHAPTER THIRTY EIGHT

SURRENDER

"The tender words we said to one another
Are stored in the secret heart of heaven
One day like the rain they will fall and spread
And our mystery will grow green over the world."
Rumi

I look up at his face in the starlight and I recall the stranger on the train, my 'dream lover,' for whom I've been searching and who has eluded me for years. All the dreams of the dark haired stranger come back to me. In that instant it becomes clear - Raphael is the man on the train, the man walking toward me on the street in Boston; the man I locked gazes with in an intimate 'mirror dance'. The dreams that have haunted my mind over the past years were all of him. That was the face, the smile, the square jawline, the gentle presence I had encountered so many times in my night journeys.

How could I have been so oblivious, so dense, and so stubborn?

I had been praying to meet someone with whom I could share my life, and the answer was being given to me in so many dreams. I was too caught up in my role of caretaker; manager, counselor, and I'd pushed aside all the signs. I had forgotten how to dream, how to have hopes and wishes for myself. I'd given up on the possibility of long-term love, if I had ever really believed in it, and yet some deeper part of me longed for it. I feel sad to have ignored the help of all the spirit guides that I know were with me through the search, and having been oblivious to my own inner guidance. How many years have I already lost in this isolation from real partnership? Master of the long-distance, exotic affair, I am clueless about real intimacy and love. The thought of committed partnership terrifies me, yet at the same time I long for it.

He puts his arm around me, "Why are you so quiet and serious all of a sudden? What are you thinking about?"

"Just thinking, it's nothing," I reply as we walk through the lobby holding hands. The front desk manager greets us with a knowing smile, catches my eye, and gives me a conspiratorial wink, which I do not appreciate. The thought of being viewed as a cougar is no longer appealing to me. I want to be just a woman in love, just a normal girl on a date with a man she's falling in love with.

We reach my room and begin to kiss. His lips are thrilling and enticing and his smooth caramel skin intoxicates me. He says something in Spanish. It might have been "Oh God, that dinner gave me gas," but to me it's exciting beyond all imagining. He then begins to take off my dress, unzipping it deliberately and slowly as if he isn't quite sure how these things work. We're lost in a flood of passion when we hear a key in the door and realize my roommate Molly has returned.

"Let's go up to my room," he whispers.

Not wanting to break the mood by turning on a light, I pull my black trench coat from the closet and grab my room key. We say a quick hello and goodnight to Molly as we rush out the door.

"Well it's about time." She laughs with delight that we're finally together after all her weeks of coaxing and matchmaking.

The lift is empty so we continue kissing. I wrap myself around him and my trench coat falls open as I pull him closer. I'm feeling feral and cougarish now that my prey is close at hand.

The lift silently stops and a group of tourists gets in and they giggle at seeing us in an embrace. We compose ourselves until they get out at their floor and then continue kissing all the way to the top floor.

Raphael's spacious penthouse suite, compliments of Marriott, his employer, has a spectacular view of the glittering city below. The Cairo Tower is illuminated and the Nile Pharaoh dinner-cruise boat floats along the dark water; a gold and jewel-colored replica of an ancient royal barge. Cairo at night is surreal, both ancient and modern and it's a city that's always awake.

Now that we were alone in his room, Raphael appears to be nervous and he moves closer to the window and peers out. "What's that structure on the water? That tower with the latticework design and the purple and gold lights. It looks like a lotus plant, doesn't it? Isn't that designed by the famous Egyptian architect named *Chebib?*"

Oh good God, I think, not again. There are far more important structures waiting to be addressed at this moment. My fenestration, for instance, is kicking. And then there's the issue of that extended structural member.

"The *Borg el Qahirra*," I answer, trying not to sound impatient. "That's the Cairo Tower." I pour us some wine. "You can visit it tomorrow when you go out with the ladies. You can even have lunch at the top."

"Really? I bet I can get some great shots of the city from there too. There's another building I saw earlier that I want to know about too."

I have to silence him before another architectural diatribe begins. I turn on the bedside radio to a soulful *Um Kalthoum* song, "*Alf Layla we Layl,*" A Thousand and One Nights. I turn the volume up loud and take off my ankle bracelet in a slow display in an attempt to distract him from the view of the city. It does nothing. Then I tie my Assuit shawl low on my hips and begin moving in slow outside infinities, allowing my shoulders and arms to roll and undulate slowly. Raphael turns and is transfixed in place beside the window, his eyes locked on my snakelike movements. It appears he's forgotten the Cairo tower for the moment.

Once I have his full attention, I layer a shimmy onto the movements to the intensifying sound of the kanoun, raise my arms overhead, and throw my head back in ecstasy. I then untie my shawl from my hips and turn with it overhead, slowly lowering it beneath my eyes and peering at him. When he reaches out to touch me, I spin away, avoiding his touch. He moves like a dark panther towards me and takes me in his arms and we fall onto the bed laughing.

Morning arrives too quickly and we've barely slept an hour. I send Raphael off on a city tour with my women friends who are only too willing to accept the assignment and fuss over him as they've done since they met him weeks ago. Guilt settles in on me as I remember the appointment I have with my former lover in Tahrir Square in just one hour.

I rush down to my own room, shower, and get ready for my date with Naim, hoping my sleepless night of passion isn't too noticeable in the glaring daylight. I feel as if I've done something wrong in taking the flirtation with Raphael to the next level, and yet it seemed so right. Subterfuge is not in my nature and never have I carried on a serious relationship with two men at the same time. Until now, my life has been balanced between long stretches of celibacy and serial monogamy. I dislike drama and am especially uneasy with the thought of hurting someone. My anxiety is building as I hail a taxi for Tahrir and rehearse the words I will say to him. It's time I ended it completely, for both our sakes. I want him to find a good woman who will be there in his life, beside him in his world.

☥

CHAPTER THIRTY NINE

LETTING GO

"Every true love and friendship is a story of unexpected transformation. If we are the same person before and after we loved, that means we haven't loved enough."
Rumi

Naim enters the Nile Hilton with the presence of a Pasha, the title often given him because of his gracious bearing and generosity. He wears a suit jacket that hugs his broad, muscular chest and then tapers at his slim waist. The gold watch against his tanned wrist brings flashes of memory - that same watch caught in my hair in moments of wild passion. That watch on the nightstand in countless hotel rooms in exotic locales. His subtle scent of exotic spices wafts toward me, an unidentifiable scent that carries me to far-off times and places, places I should not be going if I am to have a talk with him today. There are things that must be said, especially after last night.

He greets me with open arms and a broad smile. I think, "How could I let this man out of my life? What was I thinking in spending the night with that young man?" We sit at our usual table in the back of the cafe. Our hands touch and we look into each other's eyes for a long while. He speaks intoxicating words of love and I answer. I've become smoothly fluent in the Egyptian Arabic language of love - he has been a patient teacher. I feel myself falling under his spell again. I have to admit we have a great love; nothing will ever change that.

Naim clears his throat and then looks at me for a moment. I feel the passion from his eyes surrounding me in a warm embrace. He takes my hands to his lips, kisses them, and leans towards me.

"I've been waiting to tell you this." he begins. "Both my children are off to college now and I am finally free. This is our time at last, my love. Let's get married now, this week, and spend our lives together."

Stunned, I look at him and cannot speak.

"We can live here in Cairo, or at my house in Alexandria, as you like. Whatever you like, it is yours. I am yours. I won't smother you. I know you need your atmosphere as you tell me."

"Space, I need space."

"Yes, you can have your space, do whatever you want. Go to university and study what you like, open your own art studio. I am here to support you in whatever makes you happy. I will be your benefactor and your husband."

"I know you've always respected my 'atmosphere' as you

call it, but now I need more than anything to be near my own family, especially my son."

My heart is racing and I wish I could turn back time. However, life has changed. I have changed. I can no longer divide my life between two countries, always feeling homesick for one place or the other, for one family or the other.

"I wish things were different," I tell him, "I can't think of leaving my mother alone now that Dad has died. And Adam has made it clear he's staying in The States. He's already turned down the full scholarship to Cairo University and he's met a girl he wants to marry."

I'm not sure Naim is hearing me, so I wait and watch him.

"So you won't be staying this time?"

"No," I reply, "Adam's building a life of his own now, one he's not willing to leave, nor should he just for me."

Naim looks down. "I understand, I could never live so far from my family either. That's why we're still not married, after all these years."

"Finding each other has been a gift, a reward for something good we did in the past," I say, "We just didn't get the timing right."

"A past life, maybe... see, you've made me believe in past lives since I met you. But how else could we have loved each other so much the moment we met?"

I reach for his hand. "Let's plan to be together again next time. We can meet when we're both young and spend a whole lifetime together."

"I'm sure I will know your soul anywhere. I promise I will find you, he says. I'll never forget what we've had all these years."

It seems we've resolved the issue until he says, "Maybe we can still continue meeting here in this spot each time you return to Egypt,"

"I don't think that would be good, it would be too painful," I say as my voice fades. The thought of it really being over is unbearable.

We leave the cafe and hug goodbye at the fountain in front of the hotel, then we part and walk in separate directions. Tears blur my vision as I cross the square in hopes of finding my godfather still at work, although I know it's way past our agreed upon meeting time.

Noha, his assistant, meets me at the entrance and shakes her head. "He couldn't wait for you any longer. He just left, one minute ago for the airport and he'll be in meetings in Jordan for a week."

"And I'll be back home in the U.S. when he returns to Egypt."

She throws her arms in the air in frustration. "I've been relaying messages for days between the two of you. I did my best, but now it's happened again."

I feel sorry for the aggravation I cause her with my changing plans. "Sort of like herding cats, isn't it?" I reply.

It takes a few seconds before Noha gets the reference, and then she begin to laugh, "Yes, it certainly is."

Emotionally exhausted, I decide to walk the few miles back to the hotel and sort through the events of the past 24 hours. I regret having let the flirtation with Raphael go so far, and at the same time I can't stop thinking of how easily we had flowed together as friends and lovers. I cycle through feelings of elation and guilt with every step I take.

By the time I get to the other side of the El Tahrir Bridge, I've come to a decision. Even though it has been five years since we agreed to end our affair, I cannot deny I'm still in love with Naim. I know it could never work due to the distance between us. Today's conversation has brought an end to any possibility of another reunion. I need to tell Raphael and put an end to our fledgling romance. I just am not ready to begin a new relationship, and at this moment I'm not sure I ever will be. Raphael is young and far too trusting and sweet to be involved with me. I find myself again going over the reasons it could never work out with Raphael, the main one being that he was much too nice to be hurt by a woman like me.

I push thoughts of both men from my mind and focus on just getting to my room, drawing the shades and taking a hot bath, then collapsing into in bed for the rest of the day and into evening. After a good sleep, my mind will be clear enough to meet with Raphael and end it before someone gets hurt.

The phone rings as I'm in a deep sleep and I look at the clock. Three hours have passed as if a minute. "Come on down to the lobby," Raphael says. "I have to tell you about all the fun I had touring the city today with Molly, Suzie, and Hossam." He sounds so happy, so trusting and open to whatever might happen next between us. How could I have drawn him into what's sure to be a disappointment? The sound of his voice makes my heart beat faster as I recall our passion of the night before.

IT'S A CHILLY AFTERNOON AND I DRESS IN A SOFT SWEATER and tailored pants and go downstairs to the lobby, still sleepy and craving a cup of tea. In the lift, I apply some lipstick to bring some color to my pale face. There he is, seated in a deep red upholstered chair, his back to me, his hairline neatly shaven. He must have found a barber in the marketplace, and he looks so handsome wearing a suit jacket. I feel a rush of affection for him as I lean down and lightly nuzzle his neck, leaving a distinct, bright red lipstick kiss. At the same moment, I see Raphael across the room. The Gulf Arab man I have just kissed turns and glares at me as his wife approaches with an angry look, her black *niqab* flying behind her, and shrieks at me to get away from her husband. Everyone in the lobby turns to look toward the noisy altercation Mortified, I apologize profusely in Arabic, English, and then I add French to be sure I've covered all possibilities. I then slink over to where Raphael is sitting.

"Why didn't you warn me?" He can barely speak he's laughing so hard. "I thought that guy must be someone you know. I was surprised you kissed his neck, but why would I say anything? I'm just a visitor here," Gales shake his body as he puts his head down on the arm of the chair, hitting the cushion with his hand.

"You could have waved or something. You just sat there while I made a total fool of myself." I move to a chair a few feet away where I sit in my most dignified dancer posture and try to maintain composure while still in the public eye. I recall having heard once that the best way to learn humility was to be humiliated. I am more than humiliated, I am thoroughly mortified, and it will be a long while before I'll return to this hotel.

My embarrassment begins to fade as I look at him and we

both start to giggle again. I feel so happy to see him and to laugh so easily with someone. Together we walk out of the hotel and into the crisp night air. The evening is off to a good start, despite the incident of kissing a stranger's neck. I decide not to ruin it with news of my lunch meeting with an old flame. It would serve no purpose and I don't want to bring anyone else into this special magic Raphael and I share.

The *Khan el Khalili* souk beckons us for some night shopping where Raphael finds the perfect foot-tall blown glass blue shisha pipe for his apartment. At *El Fishawi* Coffeehouse, where Naguib Mahfouz often sits writing, we find a small table and order Turkish coffee. As we leave, a wedding party passes by and they implore us to join in their festivities a few blocks away. Attending an Egyptian wedding reception is always a thrill and we're so grateful for the serendipitous invitation. Hours later, we walk through the colorful section of tent makers, to the brass lamp section, and then stop at the *Miqla*, the nut shop, where every imaginable kind of delicious nut is being roasted. We buy a bag of pistachios and two Fanta sodas and sit on a bench in front of the el Hussein Mosque like two happy children. There's something so relaxed and natural about our being together.

"Oh, I almost forgot to tell you what else happened today," he says, "I went with Molly to pick up her gold cartouche at Mena House. When we were leaving, your uncle Mohammed called me back into his shop. Then he shut the door, stood in front of it with his arms folded, and asked me what my intentions are with you."

"Oh no, I'm so sorry. I knew nothing of this, but I should have expected it. Since the death of Uncle Zacharia,

Mohammed has assumed his brother's role of protector. He's taking this responsibility way too seriously."

"That's what he told me, that he has to watch out for you now. He called you a "little girl" and said you had no one to look after you now that both your dad and uncle Zacharia have died. It was weird, especially since you're a full-grown adult and mother of a college-age son. Your Uncle Mohammed's a big guy and I remember you said he's ex-military."

"Right, a lifer under Nasser's regime."

"Well, I didn't know what he expected me to say, so I told him I had good intentions and I hoped we would marry someday soon. I think that was the right answer, because he seemed pleased. He finally smiled, shook my hand, patted me on the back and stepped away from the door."

"You didn't tell him that! Now he'll be calling me to pursue this topic and the rest of the family will begin planning our wedding."

"Well, I say let's just wait and see. We just met and you haven't heard me snore. You can call him when we're both back home in the Boston. How's that?"

"Ok, and you should wait until you experience me in the throes of PMS for a few cycles."

Our flight home to Boston is on Valentine's Day. Raphael and I are wrapped in each other's arms beneath the saffron-colored Egypt Air blanket. I put my head on his shoulder and close my eyes as I recall the whirlwind of events of the past few weeks.

I hear the rattle of the beverage cart as the flight attendant reaches our row. "Would your wife like something to drink?" she asks in a whisper.

"Oh, she's not my wife," Raphael replies, then he quickly adds "not yet."

Oddly, I'm not annoyed by this arrogance and I secretly smile as I pretend to be asleep. Could I ever be someone's wife again? His wife? I'd not been involved with an American in a decade or more. He had never been married, or even lived with a woman. He doesn't seem at all put off by my beliefs or even my fierce independence.

I keep my eyes closed for a long while as I ponder the possibility, my face nuzzled against his chest. His heartbeat is strong and steady and he smells so good, like cumin and sandalwood...and is that a hint of Drakkar?

I ponder whether my son Adam will accept his mother being with someone this young. Adam is dating a woman six years older than himself, so he can't really object. He and I have had an agreement since he turned 16--- he can date someone up to ten years older and I can date someone as much as ten years younger. Raphael just makes it within those parameters. My list of impossibilities is growing shorter as I begin to make room for a small ray of hope of a romantic future. Then, the doubt steps in again. What if I get used to being with him and then it doesn't work out? What if he dies? Men don't stay in my life for long; they have a way of dying or disappearing on me. It could be another goodbye, another heartbreak...

Just live for the moment, I remind myself. Do what you counsel your clients to do all the time, let go, and trust in a higher plan. Maybe it's time to start taking my own advice.

CHAPTER FORTY

RETURN TO VENICE

"No one else, Love, will sleep in my dreams.
You will go, we will go together,
over the waters of time."
Pablo Neruda

I t didn't happen all at once. In fact, we waited five years
to be sure it was right. We both had issues of trust to
resolve and yet we were willing to walk through those
scary times together.

Our dear friend Meredith officiated at our marriage in
September 2001, just days before the tragedy of 9/11 that
changed the world. No flights were leaving the United States
and our honeymoon was postponed. We waited and grieved
with the rest of our country and much of the world.

The first Alitalia flight from Boston to Rome brought us to
the sparkling jewel that is Venice, where our Italian landlord

collected us at the dock in a speedboat. "I'm so sorry about what happened in your country," he said, a sentiment we heard from so many Italians.

We honeymooned in a sixteenth-century palace in the Piazza San Angelo that cost far less than even a three-star hotel. It was just two rooms of the palace, but all we needed. We stepped back in time to another era, one that was, for us anyway, free of terrorism and fear. We held each other for a long time, relieved to be away from the agonizing, non-stop coverage of 9/11.

From morning to evening, we walked to every museum and church in the guidebook, savoring the art, the food, and the full sensory feast that is Italy. The silence of Venice was blissful and we awoke each day to a serenade from the trash collector who sang love songs in a strong tenor like Pavarotti. It seemed everyone in the country had a magnificent singing voice and a gift for savoring the small things in life. There was so much love everywhere we went in Venice.

Raphael was in charge all of day-to-day negotiations and bargaining, Spanish being close enough to Italian that he was easily understood everywhere. It was a great thrill for me to relinquish control and not be in charge of anything. The burden of being on call for hundreds of passengers over so many years had been much heavier than I'd realized and the release of responsibility was exhilarating.

We celebrated my fall equinox birthday with a romantic dinner followed by a concert in the church of San Vidal where the "Red Priest," Vivaldi, had performed. Strolling home to our apartment, we stopped for gelato and then lingered at the Rialto Bridge. The full harvest moon shimmered on the canal.

We turned and held each other and it felt as if we were in a dream. I looked up at him and he brushed back a curl from my face and kissed my eyes, my cheeks, and my lips. He was so handsome in the moonlight, his dimpled smile so irresistible.

He looked at me with tears in his eyes. "I always dreamed of going to Venice, but only when I could share it with someone I love."

EPILOGUE

EGYPT RISES, 2010

"Obedience to Authority is the Worst Enemy of Truth."
Einstein

My tour work continues, although my schedule is much lighter since giving up the senior tours and just taking a few of my own tours each year. I'm back in Egypt leading another spiritual group and Raphael is home with the cat. I've sent my group back to Cairo with my land agent Rafiq in order to stay a few days in Luxor. I know he'll take good care of them, especially since they are all female and pleasing women is his area of expertise.

Out of nowhere, the old familiar feeling of foreboding sweeps over me as I await a return flight from Aswan to Cairo. I have not known this uncomfortable feeling in my solar plexus in quite some time, but it always signals a crisis. A *khamsin* is brewing, and the effect of the massive sandstorm is evident in the uncharacteristic moodiness of the people. In spite of the suffocating storm covering hundreds of miles, no flight cancellations are posted. I consider staying back and waiting another day in Aswan, but against my instincts, I get up and walk toward the gate, my boarding pass in hand.

I join the line and embark the 76-passenger plane for what is normally a 90-minute flight north. The crew does their best to present a cheerful demeanor as they welcome us and direct us to our seats. We lift off into a mud-colored haze that has enveloped the landscape and obscured visibility. Within moments of take off, the cabin air becomes oppressive and hot and people begin looking about in a panic. I feel my jaw clench with anxiety as I tighten my seatbelt and grip the arms of my chair. The man beside me unravels his prayer beads from his wrist and bows his head. A woman holds her infant child to her heart and murmurs prayers, rocking forward and back.

Fear has subdued even the most talkative passengers among us and the normally sociable and lighthearted locals have become morose. The small plane is struggling to make headway against a moaning, howling wind and zero visibility. We're gaining altitude in increments as if ascending a bumpy freight elevator. When it seems we have reached cruising altitude, there's a sudden drop, the plane seems to fall, and everyone gasps.

Then begins a sound, a chilling sound of fine sand entering the engines as the plane struggles to maintain altitude. The quiet whisper of hundreds of prayers in many languages can be heard above the scraping of sand against metal. For over two hours the plane bounces, then steadies, slowly levels, tilts sideways, storage bins open and their contents fall into the aisle.

Then at last the plane bumps and skids onto the runway in Cairo airport. There's a deafening silence as we register the fact that we've landed and it appears no one has been hurt.

It feels as if we've entered a thick, heavy swamp; nothing can be seen or heard around us and the color outside the window is a sickly greenish brown. My ears pop from the sudden change in altitude and my head begins to pound as if it will burst.

For a moment, I think perhaps we have all died and this is a between world, a terminal for the departed. If that's the case, this was no paradise, but a bleak holding area. I wonder if we'll be shuttled off to another level of heaven, or to purgatory, or even hell if such places exist.

The intercom crackles, the mumbling of prayers ceases, and everyone becomes still to listen to the pilot. A hushed conversation is heard from the cockpit and then at last there's an announcement.

"Ladies and gentlemen, we are safely on land now at Cairo Airport," comes the voice of the pilot. There's more silence and then coughing and throat clearing from the intercom as we strain to hear. The pilot then breathes in an audible deep breath as if trying to control his emotion.

"Unfortunately, the plane behind us, carrying Chairman Arafat, has crashed. There are casualties. Chairman Arafat's crewmembers and our Egypt Air colleagues, have been killed, but he is alive and unharmed. *El Hamdu l'Allah*, Praise be to Allah."

I wonder if any of the victims are friends I know from my years of travel on Egypt Air and I bow my head and say a prayer for them.

AT THE NILE BOOKSTORE, A FEW DAYS LATER, I PURCHASE a newspaper and a writing journal for the coming new year. Two male customers abruptly stop talking to the owner, stare at me, and exit the shop. The owner, always standoffish, is brusque towards me for the first time in all my years of visiting the shop. I hand him my purchases as I greet him, "Sabah el Kheer."

"Why do you always speak Arabic to me?" he demands in an angry voice.

"What? I speak to you in Arabic every time I come in here. You know I am studying all the time and buying Arabic books." I'm startled by his cold tone of voice.

"But how do you know Arabic? You're American aren't you?" He continues in a suspicious tone.

I stop and stare, startled by his odd questioning. "You know I study, I buy books from you, I practice everywhere I go. I love Arabic and as you know, I lived for a while in Zemalek."

"I think perhaps you're a spy." He looks me in the eye with outright hostility.

"A spy? For whom?" I think it must be a cruel joke and try to make light of the conversation, but he is dead serious. I pay him in Egyptian pounds and wish him a good day. He nods without speaking and watches me leave.

There's a silent and ominous presence as I walk across Tahrir Square, a presence I had not before sensed in my many years of walking this route across the square from the museum bookstore to the office of my godfather. I gaze around me, hoping to find the source of this odd feeling I have. My instinct tells me that something is about to happen, something monumental. The steely chill of apprehension that is so familiar from my past experiences of precognition races up my spine in spite of the calm all around me. I turn my collar up and adjust my scarf, feeling somehow I am being watched.

The suggestion that I might be a spy has made me paranoid. Not wanting to be too obvious, I stop and wipe my sunglasses on my scarf as I glance around me in all directions for anyone following me. I see nothing unusual and continue walking.

The Nile Hilton, with its blue-and-white mosaic façade and sparkling terraced fountains holds the center of the square, flanked by the salmon-colored Egyptian Museum. Tour busses are emptying as groups of school children line up outside. Even they seem unusually hushed as they stand with tickets in hand to enter. The oddity of quiet, solemn Egyptians makes me wonder if they also sense that something is about to happen.

The smell of grilled shrimp, shawerma, garlic, and cumin wafts past. I've always been on an 'as needed' basis with food and often forget to eat until I'm about to faint. Now, in spite of the delicious aromas and the fact that I am hungry, I'm not in the mood to eat. The gnawing in my gut would not be abated with food and I need to get someplace indoors and away from the crowds.

It's the same feeling I would get as a child, the presence of death in the air, of an unnamable but imminent threat. The strange foreboding is a lifelong companion, arriving uninvited and offering no reason for its arrival. Always, it portends something disruptive and ultimately inevitable and painful. What good is this gift of 'seeing' if there's nothing to be done but wait?

I search the faces of people passing by and they seem to be going about their day as any other day, except for their contemplative expressions. I wonder if perhaps I'm having post-anxiety or PTS. due to the terrifying plane ride of a few days ago. At the time, I was not thinking about my death nearly so much as not wanting to be there when it happened. I had tried to make light of the situation, which is how I deal with crisis. Given the choice, I'd prefer to die in a peaceful state of mind free of shrieking and fire burst, and with as little residual mess as possible. I'm a double Virgo after all, and I dislike messes. A tidy death would suit me better than a fiery one. I continue across the wide expanse of Tahrir while entertaining myself with various scenarios of death until I reach the office of my godfather.

As I sit waiting in the outer office, I reflect that the quality of life in Egypt is rapidly declining. A discontent, a sense of hopelessness, has crept into the consciousness of the people. Instead of the lighthearted playfulness and laughter, there's an ever-increasing cynicism and suspicion. Poverty and corruption are crippling the masses and it's clear that things have to change. It's well known that it will take a major upheaval to shake the old regime from its complacency and unite the people in their goal of freedom.

I pray that this needed change will come about with the least amount of suffering to the good people of Egypt. I wonder where I will be when this momentous upheaval takes place, here in Egypt, back home, or in any of the other places where I travel.

My godfather doesn't have time now to discuss the direction of the country. He has a more pressing crisis to deal with and is on his way to an emergency meeting concerning yet another act of terrorism, this one in a desert oasis that is a hotbed of fanaticism.

Returning across Tahrir Square to the museum bookstore, I pick up a print of the Goddess Sekhmet I requested. I reflect on Sekhmet's fierce compassion and the need at times for radical transformation in order to set the world right and bring about healing.

I do not yet know that the ground beneath my feet is simmering with discord, that millions, young and old, will live upon this bare earth for weeks in makeshift tents. They will march and die in this very location for the sake of a new life. I do not know that blood will stain the pavement and mothers will weep over their children amidst the torrent of angry voices calling for a new way. Drums, song and chanting would go on unabated for weeks, interrupted by the prayers of Muslims and Christians who would form circles to shield each other from danger at prayer times.

The gunfire, the bombs, the terrifying sound of tanks rolling through the city with machine guns firing would become the daily norm. Two presidents would be brought down by the sheer determination of a people, mostly youth, demanding freedom, an idea whose time had come. Revolution would roll through the countryside like a flashing ball of lightning, a revolution that would continue in waves for years to come. The so-called Arab Spring would reverberate throughout the region and the world and no one in it would be left unaffected.

Deeply shaken, I prepare to sleep that night and ask for guidance and insight into what is happening. I awaken from a long, tumultuous dream and between sleep and waking I hear the message: *"Like the phoenix who rises from its own ashes, Egypt will emerge again from the dust of conflict to reclaim its role as the keeper of the wisdom of the ancients, a spiritual light of the new world."*

BACK IN THE UNITED STATES A YEAR LATER, IT'S JANUARY, 2011. I turn on the news to watch another episode in the non-stop coverage of the ongoing revolution in Cairo. It's day 12 of the upheaval and things are looking very bad for the people. The brave young protesters are being fired upon from rolling armed tanks as they try to fight back with stones or anything they can pick up from the street. These are the sweet, funny children I know and love. I see their faces and recognize them. A small boy limps in an unmistakable gait and I recognize my little friend Sami. My heart is breaking and sobs shake my body.

Emotionally drained, I can't take any more and reach for the control to turn the TV off. Then, something tells me to wait. I look again, move closer to the TV, and there is my godfather, bent and frail, an aide at each arm assisting him. The dense crowd steps aside, forming a path for him as they smile and nod in greeting. He walks into the crowd; his head held high, an expression of triumph and childlike wonder lighting up his broad smile as the camera zooms in. It's been decades since I last saw that look on his face. It was back in Cambridge during the turmoil of the late 1960s when we had marched together for an end to the war in Vietnam, for women's rights, for civil rights.

A year passes and the unrest continues as a second revolution in Egypt takes down the elected interim president who has proven more corrupt than the last.

On a Saturday morning in September on Cape Cod, I bring my coffee upstairs to my home office and turn on my computer. The headlines make my heart jump. My beloved godfather has died and the news is on the front page of every paper in Egypt and the Middle East. Even Israel has posted a tribute to him for his tireless efforts to broker peace between Israel and Palestine.

By the ocean's edge, I walk for hours. My tears mix with the salty mist as I recall all our years together and thank him for saving me at a most vulnerable time in my life. A sudden burst of wind comes off the ocean and seems to be speaking to me.

"Ya habibti, binti! I'm right here!" I hear his laughter and feel his presence beside me. I know he lives on. I am certain that there are two things which remain eternal; energy or soul vibration, and love.

GLOSSARY

- **Abeya:** sleeveless gallaboya / vest
- **Abu, Baba:** father
- **Afrit (m) Afrita (f)** : devil
- **Ahlen wa sahlan**: welcome
- **Akhi:** my brother
- **Aiwa:** yes **La':** no
- **Ahwa:** coffee
- **Bahebik (ek):** I love you
- **Baksheesh:** money given as a bribe or reward
- **Beledi:** Of the countryside, my country, common
- **Binti:** my girl
- **Boab:** doorman
- **Caleche:** horse-drawn carriage
- **Corniche:** Street beside The Nile
- **Doumbek:** Egyptian drum made of steel with a plastic head

- **El Dunya:** the world
- **El-hamdu-l-Allah:** Thanks be to God.
- **Faiance:** bright blue ceramic glaze used since early times
- **Fellaheen**: farmers
- **Gallabeya:** loose fitting long garment
- **Habibi:** my darling, beloved (masc.) **Habibti** (fem)
- **Hadiyya:** gift
- **Hayyati:** my life
- **Helwe**: Sweet
- **Ibni:** my son
- **Imam:** spiritual leader of a mosque
- **Insha'Allah:** if God wills. Used as 'I hope', hopefully
- **Iskandriyya**: Alexandria
- **Izzayek?:** how are you?
- **Jinn**: Spirits, often mischievous, who inhabit the unseen world
- **Khallas**: finished
- **Khamaseen**: winds that blow fine sand into the city, a sandstorm
- **Khan el Khalili**: famous souk or marketplace in Cairo
- **Kull Sana w Enti Tayibba**: trans:Happy Birthday
- **Kwayyis** (a): fine
- **Ma'alesh**: never mind
- **Mafeesh**: there is none
- **Magnoon**: insane
- **Masha'Allah**: what God has willed or blessed one with

- **Mashrabeyya:** ornately carved wood screen used to protect privacy
- **Mawwal:** A plaintive song or cry, often preceding the song itself
- **Muezzin** :one who sings or chants the call to prayer
- **Minaret:** spire of a mosque from which the Muezzin chants the call to prayer
- **Miqla:** shop selling freshly roasted nuts
- **Mesah el Kheer**: good evening/resp: **Mesah el Noor**
- **'Oud:** lute
- **Hijab:** women's headscarf in Islamic tradition
- **Keffeya**: A checkered headdress/scarf of black and white or red and white, worn by men in parts of the Arab world.
- **Maalimah**: a woman skilled in folkloric music, story, and dance
- **Muezzin**-the person who makes the call to prayer.
- **Mushkellat**: problems
- **Niqab:** a black veil that completely covers the face and shoulders
- **Rais**: captain or boss
- **Raqs**: dance
- **Salamu 'aleikhum:** peace be upon you
- **W'aleikhim salam:** *resp*: and also with you
- **Shadouf**-water wheel still in use since ancient times
- **Wallahi-** I swear to God
- **Schura, sehura**: sorceress
- **Shisha:** molasses & fruit tobacco smoked in a shisha pipe

- **Sheikha:** female spiritual leader
- **Shukren**: thank-you
- **Shwayya:** a little bit
- **Sitt:** lady
- **Shai:** tea
- **Tayyib**: good, very well
- **Umi:** mother, my mother
- **Yalla:** let's go, hurry
- **Zagat**: zills or finger cymbals
- **Zaghareed**: ululations, high-pitched sound made by women.
- **Zar**: secret healing ceremonies run by older, wise women.
- **Zemalek:** residential district of Cairo encompassing the northern portion of Gezira Island

PHOTOS

Abd' Hakim Awyan, Khemetian Teacher

The Sphinx at Giza Plateau

Temple wall with Isis, Horus, and Pharoah

The Sacred Lake, Karnak Temple

Excavation at Luxor Temple, 1989

Stairway in Temple of Hathor, Dendara

Dendara, Temple of Hathor

Khan el Khalili Souk

Caleche ride on Corniche, Luxor

Katrina is honored to have taken part in the healing journeys of clients internationally since opening her practice, Transformations Center, in 1980. She is an adjunct professor of Middle Eastern Dance and Culture and Arabic language, a board member of Cape Cod Writer's Center, and a member of American Pen Women in categories of both writing and choreography. Katrina contributes articles to holistic publications in New England. This is her first full-length book. Katrina is available for book signing, readings and healing sessions in person or by phone.

E-Mail: katrinavalenzuelaauthor@gmail.com
Website: www.transformations-center.com

WITHDRAWN

Sanibel Public Library

3 5558 01018182 0

Made in the USA
Columbia, SC
18 August 2018